Embracing Wholeness

A Foundation for Life, Love, Leadership and Legacy

By
Dinean Lang

Contents

Contents Continued

Acknowledgments

To God, thank You for your steady guidance and unconditional love. You have been my anchor in the quiet moments and my strength in the hard ones. Your grace kept me grounded, and your presence gave me the courage to grow, heal, and keep moving forward.

To my husband, Tony, you are my rock and my safest place. Thank you for believing in me even when I was still finding my footing. Your patience, your steadiness, and the way you show up for me have shaped this journey more than you know. I'm grateful for the life we've built and for the ways we continue choosing each other as we grow.

To my children, Ayannah, Keonna, and Devin, you are among the greatest gifts God has given me. Each of you has brought so much love, joy, depth, and meaning to my life, and being your mother has shaped me in ways I will never fully be able to express. You inspire me with your strength, your hearts, your growth, and the unique purpose each of you carries. Thank you for the love you give so freely, for the laughter and light you bring into my life, and for the ways you continue to remind me what really matters. Watching you become who you are has been one of the deepest joys of my life. Being your mother is one of my greatest honors, and I am forever grateful for each of you.

To my special advisory board, my sisters Destinee, Dione, and Michelle, thank you for standing with me through every season and for supporting and holding me accountable throughout the writing of this book. Your honesty, wisdom, laughter, love, and steady encouragement kept me grounded and helped me keep going. You reminded me of who I am when life felt heavy, challenged me to stay focused when I needed to, and celebrated with me when life was good. I cherish our bond more than I can put into words.

To my family and friends, and to everyone who has walked with me on this journey, thank you. Your presence, your encouragement, and your love carried me in ways you may not even realize. I hold deep gratitude for the support you've given and the space you've made for me to keep becoming.

With heartfelt gratitude,
Dinean

Introduction

As you hold this book, something within you is already awake. Maybe you're tired of repeating the same painful cycles with different people across different chapters of your life. Maybe you've built an impressive life, but an ache remains that you can't fully name. Maybe you love deeply, lead well, and carry responsibility with grace, yet the version of you who shows up for everyone else hasn't always been the one who feels most held, most free, most whole.

I know that place.

For a long time, I thought wholeness was something you earned. You earned it by surviving what tried to break you. You earned it by achieving what you were told would validate you and by becoming so dependable that life could never catch you off guard again.

I didn't survive by backing away from life. I survived by stepping up. I became useful. I became productive. I became the one who could steady a room, a family, a mission, a moment. That strength served me, and I honor it. But I reached a point where survival was no longer the assignment, and a deeper question started rising in me:

Who am I when I no longer need to fight?

That question became a doorway. This book was born out of that doorway, and out of a truth I now hold with both clarity and tenderness.

People often say two halves make a whole. What I've learned across life, leadership, and love is that two whole people make a complete partnership. A relationship isn't meant to rescue your identity or repair what you refuse to face within yourself. It's meant to be a partnership between two people who have done the courageous work of becoming emotionally honest, grounded inside themselves, and steady enough to love without self-abandonment.

Embracing wholeness is not about perfect love or polished self-improvement. It's about becoming integrated again. It's about reclaiming the parts of you that had to go quiet just to get through life. It's about learning what peace feels like in your body, what clarity sounds like in your voice, and what safety looks like in your choices. It's about healing enough to receive love without fear, performance or disappearing inside it.

When I say "wholeness," I'm talking about living as one integrated person instead of being split between who you are and who you feel you have to be.

Wholeness doesn't mean perfection. It means integrity. It means you can tell the truth without abandoning yourself, respond instead of just reacting, and hold a boundary without drowning in guilt. It means you can receive love without turning it into an obligation. You can stay strong and stay soft at the same time because strength is no longer your hiding place.

This book moves through wholeness the way life actually does, through your inner life, your relationships, your leadership, and the legacy you're building, whether you've named it or not. You'll get my story because it shaped what I know, but this book isn't just about me. It's about helping you tell the truth about what you've normalized, what it has cost you, and what it looks like to heal in a real and practical way.

Some chapters will feel like confirmation. Others may press on what you've avoided. If discomfort shows up, don't rush to outrun it. Stay close long enough to learn what it's trying to reveal. That honesty is not a threat. It's a pathway.

And here's what I want you to hold as you begin: this book isn't asking you to be perfect. It's inviting you to be honest sooner, stop bargaining with your peace, and build a life and a partnership that can actually hold the real you.

This journey isn't about blaming your past or diminishing the strength that's carried you this far. It's about honoring that strength and letting it evolve into something even more powerful: peace, presence, and a sense of completeness that doesn't require a crisis to feel real.

If you've ever wondered whether you're allowed to fully be yourself without earning it first, let this be your answer: you are.

And if you've ever hoped love could feel like safety instead of strategy, like partnership instead of pressure, like peace with purpose instead of survival in disguise, you're in the right place.

Let's begin.

How To Use This Book

This is not the kind of book you need to rush through. Come back to it as often as you need to. You can read it straight through or start with the chapter that hits closest to home. If a chapter stirs something up or makes you want to avoid it, pay attention. That usually means there's something there worth listening to.

Some readers will want the full journey, start to finish, letting the progression build naturally from awareness to integration. Others will open to the chapter that makes them feel seen and begin there, because that's usually the right place.

As you move through the chapters, you'll notice a steady rhythm in how each one closes. That rhythm is intentional. It's there to help you move from insight into practice without pressure.

At the end of each chapter, I give you a few ways to stay with the work instead of just reading past it: a short reflection, one simple practice, journal prompts, a wholeness check-in, and a declaration to help you put language around what you're choosing now.

You don't need to answer every question. You don't need to complete it as if it's an assignment. Choose what stands out. Skip what doesn't. The goal is honesty, not volume.

There is no required pace. You are not behind. You do not need a crisis to earn this work. If you pause for a week, a month, or a year, you can return and pick up where you left off.

Wholeness is not a finish line. It's a way of living.

Part One
Becoming Whole

This first part is about the moment you realize you've been functioning but not fully living.

You've been showing up, carrying responsibility and keeping things moving. From the outside, it might look like you're doing fine, but inside, something has been running on fumes. This isn't because you're broken. It's because survival became normal, and somewhere along the way, "strong" started meaning "always braced."

In these chapters, you'll start naming patterns without shaming yourself. You'll notice what you reach for under pressure, what you avoid when things get tender, and what it has cost you to keep being the dependable one at the expense of being fully present with your own heart.

You won't be asked to reinvent your life overnight. You'll be invited to return to yourself in small, steady steps, building a foundation you can finally stand on without performing, pushing, or pretending you're okay when you're not.

If you've been carrying more than you've admitted, you're in the right place.

Chapter 1
The Awakening

People think awakening happens in daylight, but mine showed up in the dark. Not the darkness of night, but the kind that settles inside you slowly, layer by layer, until even sunlight feels far away. It wasn't one dramatic breaking point. It was a quiet reckoning. The kind you don't see coming because you've been functioning for so long that you stopped noticing the cost.

For as long as I can remember, survival was my language. It wasn't a choice. It was instinct. It was what I learned before I learned what safety felt like. I didn't grow up thinking in terms of trauma or nervous systems or inner child work. I grew up thinking in terms of what the mood in the room was, what the risk was, and what I needed to do to keep things from getting worse.

I was the oldest. The one who watched, listened, and learned what to do when things went wrong. And things went wrong often.

My mother loved us, but her love was complicated. Addiction blurred her promises. Some nights she'd laugh, full of warmth, and it almost felt like we were a normal family. Other nights, the air would tighten, and I knew to gather my siblings and get out of the way. We learned to read her moods like weather forecasts because we had to. You don't have the luxury of guessing when you're a kid in a house where stability can flip without warning.

Her addictions turned our world into a cycle of motion and instability. We lived in the projects, then in places people don't talk about. Shelters. Crack houses. Floors that weren't ours. I learned how to move through danger quietly. How to protect. How to make do. I hummed songs under my breath to help my brother fall asleep. I cut mold off cheese blocks when there wasn't much else to eat. I prayed that tomorrow would be better, not a well-crafted, masterful prayer, just a desperate whisper that felt like the only thread I could hold onto.

I became responsible before I was ready. I cooked, cleaned, soothed, and cared for siblings who looked to me as both big sister and mother. I didn't know how to say, "This is too much." I focused on what needed to be done.

When you grow up in instability, your body learns its rhythm. Back then, it wasn't a philosophy. It was an unwritten rule. Keep everyone alive. Keep everything moving. Don't fall apart. Don't make things harder. Don't take up too much space. And for the love of God, don't need too much.

Even then, somehow, I was never completely alone. I learned how to find God in the middle of it all. I didn't understand Him the way I do now, but I knew Presence. I talked to Him in the quiet moments when no one else could hear. Sometimes He met me through music that softened the edges of hard days. Sometimes through a sentence in a book that felt like it had my name on it.

Books were my escape, a way to breathe when the air around me felt heavy. Stories reminded me that there was another world beyond ours, and that maybe life didn't always have to hurt like this.

That hope mattered more than people realize, because when your life is unstable, imagination becomes your oxygen. It gives you a way to picture something you can't yet touch.

When "Safer" Still Isn't Safe

When my mom lost custody of us, after a few transitions, we were eventually sent to live with my grandparents. For a moment, I thought that would mean safety. I thought a quieter house would automatically mean a calmer heart. I thought stability on the outside would finally make everything inside me exhale.

But even in a quieter, supposedly more stable house, chaos can find its way in. My grandmother loved me fiercely, but she carried her own pain. Her words could comfort, and her words could cut. I learned to measure my steps, anticipate needs, and get quiet when tension rose. I learned that love can be real and still feel unsafe. I learned that being cared for isn't the same as being emotionally protected.

I kept my role as the oldest and the caretaker. I was the one who skipped school to give my grandmother her medicine and make sure she ate. The one who learned to make peace out of messes I didn't make. I learned to keep secrets. To hold everything together. To avoid asking for help. It wasn't that no one ever helped. It was that my nervous system didn't trust help to be consistent, so I became my own consistency.

By the time I hit my teens, I felt like I'd already lived several lifetimes. And still, I kept going. I graduated. I worked. I built. I loved. I led. I made something out of nothing.

From the outside, that looked like resilience. And in many ways, it was. But I didn't realize I was also building an identity that depended on never falling apart.

Competence As Comfort

From the outside, I looked like the picture of strength. Confident. Accomplished. Capable. The strong one. The dependable one. The one who could handle anything. And in many ways, I could.

When you grow up surviving, competence becomes your comfort. Achievement becomes your proof. Productivity becomes your safety. That's not just a personality trait. That's a

3

strategy. A survival strategy that can turn into a lifestyle so normalized that you don't even recognize it as survival anymore.

As I got older, the chaos around me didn't disappear. It evolved. I moved from one form of responsibility to another. From caretaker to overachiever. From protector to provider. From the little girl who cleaned up messes to the woman who held it together for everyone else. I wore my strength like a badge. I could handle anything. That's what I told myself, and that's what everyone believed.

And I was proud of that. It felt like redemption. Proof that the pain hadn't broken me. Proof that the past didn't get to win. Proof that I could build a life that didn't look like where I came from.

So I stayed busy. Always striving. Always contributing. Always being "the one."

What I didn't understand then was the cost of that identity. Supporting everyone else came so naturally that I didn't notice how much I had disappeared in the process. There's a danger in being the strong one if you forget how to be anything else. You forget what rest feels like. You forget that being capable and being whole aren't the same thing.

When you live too long in survival mode, peace can feel suspicious. Silence doesn't always comfort. Sometimes it echoes. And love can start to feel like another thing you might lose, so you stay prepared. You stay ahead. You keep yourself useful so you don't become disposable.

You keep producing so you don't have to feel what rises in the quiet.

4

When The Noise Stopped

For years, I functioned at a high level. I led teams. I raised a family. I did what needed to be done. It was a rhythm I didn't question because it was all I'd ever known. Take care of others. Push through. Keep moving.

Then, one morning, the noise stopped. There was no immediate crisis. No fire to put out. No one to save. Just stillness. And for the first time, I had to face a terrifying question I'd been outrunning my whole life: Who am I when there's nothing to survive?

The realization didn't hit like lightning. It came quietly. I sat on the edge of my bed one morning, sunlight spilling through the blinds, and I felt nothing. Not sadness. Not fear. Just emptiness. Like every piece of me had been poured into other people, other goals, other obligations, until there was nothing left to fill me.

I sat there, stunned by the weight of exhaustion I'd carried and tried to ignore for years. Not broken, just hollow. It was the strangest kind of grief, one without tears. Like I'd been running my whole life and suddenly realized no one was chasing me.

I didn't cry that day. I didn't pray for rescue. I just sat in the silence long enough to feel the truth rise in my chest.

I am tired.

Not body tired. Not work tired.

Soul tired.

That kind of tired is different. It's not solved by sleep. It's not fixed by a weekend off. It's the kind that comes from decades of bracing. From scanning for danger even when you're safe. From being everyone's anchor while quietly sinking yourself.

I whispered into the quiet, "God, I can't live like this anymore." It wasn't surrender as defeat. It was a surrender in honesty. A letting go of pretense. The kind of truth that doesn't come out until you've exhausted every other way of coping.

The Truth That Changed Everything

Awakening isn't always beautiful. Sometimes it's just the moment you finally tell yourself the truth.

For me, it wasn't light flooding into the room or an audible voice from heaven. It was space. Space to breathe. Space to be honest. Space to stop pretending I was okay.

I began to see something I'd missed for years. The same patterns that once protected me were now keeping me from feeling alive. The danger was no longer the same, but my body still reacted as if it were. Survival had carried me this far, but it couldn't carry me into peace.

That's when the questions started showing up. Not as a dramatic revelation, but as a steady pressure I couldn't ignore anymore.

Who am I without a crisis?

What do I want beyond achievement?

How do I live without needing to earn peace?

What does wholeness look like when you've never seen it modeled?

I didn't get all the answers at once. I got awareness. And awareness is powerful because it changes what you can tolerate. Once you see the pattern, you can't unsee it. Once you name the cost, you can't keep calling it normal with the same comfort.

This wasn't a moment of revelation. It was a moment of reckoning. And it began the day I finally admitted the truth.

I'm not okay.

That sentence can sound dramatic, but for me, it was grounding. It didn't mean my life was falling apart. It meant I was done pretending that functioning was the same as living. It meant I was ready to stop calling exhaustion a personality trait and start calling it what it was: a signal. A warning light. A holy invitation.

Learning To Live Safely

I'd been living on adrenaline and God's grace for so long that peace felt unfamiliar. I didn't know how to live in peace without waiting for chaos. I didn't know how to love without proving my value. I didn't know how to rest without guilt.

I wasn't tired from overwork. I was tired from decades of vigilance. From scanning my world for what could go wrong next. From being everyone's stabilizer while neglecting my own stability. From being the strong one so consistently that the world forgot I was a person who needed care too, and I forgot it sometimes as well.

When survival becomes your default, stillness can feel like danger. Healing can feel like standing unguarded in a room where you used to barricade the door. And if you've never had true safety, you can confuse peace with risk. You can confuse calm with vulnerability. You can confuse rest with irresponsibility.

It was humbling to realize that the strength that saved me earlier wasn't the same strength that would heal me. Survival had been a gift. It protected me. It made me capable. It made me resilient. I don't shame that girl. I honor her.

But wholeness required something different. It required surrender. Not surrender as weakness but surrender as trust. Trust that I could set things down and still be safe. Trust that I can slow down without losing my edge. Trust that I could be human without losing respect.

In the quiet days that followed, I began to notice small shifts. My urge to fix everything softened. The guilt of resting loosened its grip. The constant scanning for danger quieted just enough for me to feel something I hadn't felt in years.

Stillness.

And in that stillness, I began to hear God again, not as rescue but reminder. He didn't rush me out of survival. He stayed with me while I learned to walk out on my own.

I started seeing how much of my identity had been built on the idea of being needed. How much of my peace had depended on performance. How much of my faith had focused on endurance more than intimacy.

Then a sentence rose in me with startling clarity.

You're safe now, but you don't know how to live safe yet. It unraveled me because it was true.

I knew how to fight. I knew how to provide. I knew how to protect. But I didn't know how to rest. I didn't know how to receive. I didn't know how to experience joy without checking the fine print. I had mastered functioning but forgotten how to feel. I had built everything around strength but hadn't learned softness. And God was inviting me to do both.

I didn't know who I was without the fight, but I knew I wanted to find out.

The First Thing I Set Down

That day, I began setting things down. Expectations. Guilt. Responsibility for everyone's peace. The belief that rest had to be earned. The endless need to prove I was okay.

And beneath all of it, I found something holy.

Me.

It wasn't immediate healing. It was a slow remembering. A quiet, trembling rediscovery of what peace felt like in my own skin. There were no fireworks, just breath. Just presence. Just God whispering, "You don't have to hold everything anymore."

That was the beginning of my wholeness, not in triumph but in truth.

Awakening isn't about becoming someone new. It's about meeting yourself again after years of being who you had to be to survive.

Closing Reflection

Awakening doesn't always look like breaking. Sometimes it looks like finally admitting you're tired of surviving.

You didn't become the dependable one to perform. You became that person because it worked. It created structure. It reduced uncertainty. It helped you keep life from unraveling. And it may have earned your respect, opportunities, and a reputation for being strong. None of that is you being fake or wrong. But there comes a time when the fight ends and you're left with truth that you cannot outrun.

Peace is quiet enough to expose what noise used to cover. Healing is learning to live in that quiet without treating it like a threat.

Honor your survival instinct without letting it remain your default. Be proud of how far you've come without letting that pride block your softness. You can contribute powerfully without absorbing the entire burden of repair. You can be the strong one and still let yourself be cared for.

This is where wholeness begins.

The Practice

Choose one small act you can do next that tells your nervous system, "I don't have to brace right now." Make it simple enough to repeat and real enough to matter.

My next small practice:

Journal Prompts

Answer what stands out. Skip what doesn't. Stay honest.

1. What truth did this chapter put words to for me?
2. Where in my life am I still living like the stabilizer, even when I don't have to?
3. What do I assume will happen if I soften, slow down, or stop showing strength?
4. Where do I confuse peace with risk because peace feels unfamiliar?
5. What does my body do when I don't feel safe, and what is it trying to prevent?
6. What is one way I can receive love or support without having to explain my worth?
7. What is one "old rule" I'm ready to let go of because I don't need it anymore?
8. If I believed I was safe today, what would I change about how I move through this day?

Wholeness Check-In

Scan your pillars through the lens of awakening.

- Mentally and emotionally: Do I tell the truth about what I feel, or do I minimize it so I can keep functioning?
- Spiritually: Do I relate to God only as a crisis responder, or as a steady presence in calm times too?
- Physically: Does my body know how to rest, or does it stay on alert even when I'm "off"?
- Socially and relationally: Do my relationships make room for my humanity, or mostly my reliability?

One small shift that would bring me into greater wholeness:

____

____

____

____

Empowering Declaration

I don't have to brace to be responsible. I don't have to burn out to prove I'm strong. I can honor what I survived without living there forever. I'm learning how to live in safety, not just survive.

Chapter 2
Breaking Patterns

If awakening is the moment in which you finally admit the truth, then breaking patterns is the moment you start living like you mean it. This part isn't flashy, and it doesn't come with a clean "before and after" story. Most of the time, it looks ordinary from the outside, but on the inside, it's brave.

Because breaking patterns is when you stop calling everything "just how I am" and start telling the truth. Some things you have deemed your personality were really survival habits. Some of what looks like discipline may have started in fear. Even some of what you call strength may trace back to an old agreement you made with life when you didn't feel safe.

Patterns don't always show up in obvious ways. Sometimes they're quiet. Sometimes they hide inside the very habits people praise you for. That's what makes them hard to spot. When something has worked for a long time, you stop questioning it.

Familiarity starts to feel like safety, even when it's slowly wearing you down. So breaking patterns isn't about shaming yourself or trying to rebuild your entire life overnight. It's about noticing what's been running on autopilot and deciding you don't want your life led by old reflexes anymore.

Patterns Don't Start As Problems

Most patterns start as wisdom. They were adaptations. They were your way of staying steady in an environment that wasn't steady. You weren't broken. You were resourceful. If your early life taught you that people could be unpredictable, you learned to read rooms fast. If your home taught you that

15

emotions weren't safe, you learned to keep yours tucked
away. If you had to carry adult responsibilities too early,
you learned to be capable before you ever got to be
properly cared for. And even when your life becomes
calmer, your body doesn't automatically update. Your
nervous system keeps running what it learned because it
still believes those reflexes are the reason you made it.

Breaking patterns starts when you stop asking only,
"Does this work?" and you start asking, "Does this cost
me?" Because a pattern can work and still drain you. It can
produce results and still steal your peace. It can make you
look put together while keeping you emotionally braced
underneath the surface.

When Productivity Turns Into Protection

For a long time, I believed that if I stayed organized,
productive, and high performing, I could stay ahead of
pain. I didn't always say it that way, but that's what it was.
If I stayed busy, I didn't have to feel as much. If I stayed
ahead, I didn't have to worry as much. If I stayed useful, I
didn't have to risk disappointment.

And to be fair, that strategy made sense for who I had
to be early in life. Reliability wasn't just a trait. It was
survival. It was how I created stability in spaces where
stability didn't come automatically. As an adult, that same
survival strategy became competence that people praised. I
knew how to lead, anticipate needs, and execute. I knew
how to hold a family together, hold a team together, and
hold myself together when life demanded more than rest
could repair.

From the outside, that looks like drive and discipline.
Sometimes it is. But when productivity becomes
protection, you're not only working because you're

16

ambitious. You're working because your nervous system believes motion is safer than stillness. Quiet feels like exposure. Peace feels unfamiliar. Slowing down feels like you're letting something slip. So you keep moving, not because you're passionate every minute, but because movement gives you a sense of control, and control feels like relief.

My Strength Was Real, It Just Became Automatic

I need to say this plainly because it matters. I didn't learn survival by shrinking. I learned it by stepping up. I became competent, clear, and dependable. My strength was real. The issue wasn't that I was pretending to be capable. I was capable. The issue was that my strength became automatic.

Autopilot doesn't check in with your current season. It just keeps running the same script it learned years ago. It keeps you producing, fixing, handling, and carrying, even when your life has changed enough that you don't need the same armor anymore. Patterns aren't only about what you do. They're also about what your body expects. If you grew up staying alert, your nervous system could treat peace like a visitor instead of a home. Even when nothing is wrong, you're still scanning. Even when you're "off," your body doesn't fully believe you're safe enough to rest.

The Patterns Beneath The Patterns

What I started realizing was that a lot of my patterns weren't about preference. They were about protection. Overfunctioning can get mistaken for leadership when it's really fear driving the whole thing. Hyper-independence can look strong when it's actually self-protection. Even emotional steadiness isn't always maturity. Sometimes it's just how a person learned to stay composed when feeling the truth didn't feel safe. Being "low maintenance" can look like confidence, but sometimes it's self-abandonment that has learned to stay quiet to keep the peace.

I'm not saying that to shame anybody. I'm saying it because naming it is how you get free. If you're a high-capacity person, your patterns may show up in small, consistent ways that barely register because you've normalized them. You jump into problem-solving the second discomfort appears. You carry emotional weight that isn't yours. You notice everyone else's needs before you notice your own. You keep the temperature of the room stable so nobody else has to. Then one day you look up and realize you're valued for what you carry, not for who you are, and you don't know how you got there.

The Pause That Changes Everything

I started noticing my patterns not because I was failing, but because the life I'd built finally got quiet enough for me to hear what I'd been carrying under the surface. That's one of the strange parts about healing. Sometimes your biggest realizations don't come in crisis. They come in calm.

I began seeing certain responses as default settings. I noticed how quickly I went into "fix it" mode when uncertainty showed up. I noticed how fast I carried things that weren't mine. I noticed the pressure to keep everyone emotionally steady, even when I was the one quietly running out of room inside. Those patterns made me capable. They also kept me braced. My first sacred shift was naming that truth without shaming myself for it. There's a difference between acknowledging why a pattern formed and excusing why it remains. I could honor the

18

version of me who built those tools and still tell the woman I am now, "Those tools can't run the whole house anymore."

That's where the pause became powerful. Breaking patterns usually doesn't start with a huge change. It starts with a pause. A pause before you say yes out of reflex. A pause before you start overexplaining. A pause before you assume responsibility for someone else's emotions. A pause before you rush into fixing. That pause is small, but it matters because it gives you options. It creates space for a new response to exist. It gives your nervous system proof that you can slow down and still be safe.

What Breaking A Pattern Actually Looks Like

Here's the truth. The pause might feel uncomfortable at first. When you've lived in survival patterns for a long time, slowing down can feel like a risk. Your mind will try to justify, your body might tense up, and your emotions might rise because you've been managing them through motion. That doesn't mean you're doing it wrong. It usually means you're doing something new.

And awareness isn't the finish line. It's the doorway. You can name your patterns and still repeat them. That doesn't mean you failed. It means your nervous system is doing what it knows to do. Change takes repetition. It takes patience. It takes practicing your new response long enough for it to start feeling normal.

How These Patterns Show Up In Relationships

Patterns don't stay neatly inside your "personal" life. They show up in your relationships, in your leadership, and in your home. If you're trained to stabilize, you might carry the emotional load without even realizing it. You adjust, soften or fix first. You manage the temperature in the room so nobody else has to.

Then you wonder why you feel unseen, even when you're loved. A lot of times it's because you've unintentionally taught people you don't need anything. Not because you don't, but because needing feels unsafe. So people stop checking in. They stop offering softness. They stop noticing your fatigue. And you're left holding both the weight and the silence.

Breaking patterns isn't just about being "healthier." It's about being more honest. It's about letting your relationships adjust to the real you, not just the survival version.

Why Breaking Patterns Can Feel Like Grief

There's grief in this work because some patterns are tied to identity. Being the dependable one. Being the strong one. Being the one who needs little. Being the one who can handle it. Those patterns got you respect. They kept you safe. They gave you a role. So when you start breaking them, it can feel like you're betraying the version of you who protected you.

You're not betraying yourself. You're honoring yourself by evolving. The goal isn't to discard that version of you. The goal is to integrate that old self, letting them be part of your story without letting them run your life.

The Quiet Courage Of Choosing Something New

If you're reading this and recognizing yourself, let it land gently. These aren't character flaws. They're survival

20

strategies that have stayed active past their expiration dates. You're not weak because peace feels unfamiliar. You're learning how to live differently, and that kind of learning takes time.

Wholeness doesn't deny what you've survived. It just refuses to let survival define you forever. It's the choice to live from presence instead of performance, peace instead of pressure, integrity instead of autopilot. You don't have to fix everything at once. You have to start interrupting what no longer fits, one pause at a time, one honest choice at a time. That's how patterns break.

Closing Reflection

The patterns you carry are proof of how resourceful you've been, not proof that you're broken. Some of what you call "just how I am" was once a strategy. It kept you steady. It kept you safe. It helped you survive a season you didn't have the power to change. Healing now asks for a different kind of strength. It asks you to update what you rely on, pause before autopilot speaks, and let peace become a home instead of a visitor. Pattern breaking isn't punishment. It's maturity. It's the healed version of you stepping into leadership over the version of you who survived.

The Practice

Choose one small act you can do next that creates a pause. Make it simple, specific, and repeatable. Choose a pause before you fix, a pause before you overfunction, a pause before you assume responsibility for what isn't yours.

My next small practice:

____

____

____

Journal Prompts

Answer what stands out. Skip what doesn't. Keep it honest.

1. Where do I still live from survival reflexes instead of the present-day truth?
2. What pattern once protected me but now restricts me?
3. What do I tend to do immediately when I feel uncertain, and what might a calmer response look like?
4. Where do I use productivity to manage emotion, and what feeling might I be avoiding?
5. What does peace ask me to believe about my worth that survival never taught me?
6. When do I feel most tempted to overfunction, and what fear sits underneath that urge?
7. What's one boundary that would interrupt autopilot and protect my emotional energy?
8. What's one way I can receive support without having to explain my worth first?
9. What would it look like to let "good enough" be safe in one area of my life this week?
10. What belief do I want to practice that aligns with the healed version of me?

Wholeness Check-In

Scan your pillars through the lens of patterns.

- Mentally and emotionally: Do my thoughts assume the worst even when nothing is wrong yet, or do they make room for safety and trust?
- Spiritually: Do I relate to God mostly in crisis, or do I let intimacy exist in calm too?
- Physically: Does my body relax easily, or does it stay on alert even when I'm "off"?
- Socially and relationally: Do my relationships make room for my humanity, or do they mainly reward my reliability?

One small shift that would bring me into greater wholeness:

____

____

____

____

Empowering Declaration

I honor the patterns that have helped me survive and I release the ones that limit my freedom. I choose awareness over autopilot, and I'm letting my life be shaped by present-day truth instead of past fear. I'm learning that peace can be steady, that support can be safe, and that wholeness is a baseline I'm allowed to live from, not a moment I must earn.

Chapter 3
Returning to Self

By the time I reached this phase of my healing, I finally understood something that felt both freeing and disorienting. Awakening wasn't the finish line. It was the moment the fog lifted just enough for me to see how long I'd been living on instinct. Breaking patterns helped me interrupt autopilot. Returning to myself raised questions I couldn't answer on my own. If I'm not living from survival reflexes anymore, what am I living from?

That question sounds simple until you sit with it. Because if you've spent years being the strong one, the dependable one, the one who can handle anything, returning to yourself can feel like stepping into silence you don't know how to hold. Survival gives you structure. It gives you a job. It gives you a role. And when the urgency starts fading, you're left with space. Space can feel like relief. It can also feel like exposure.

When The Fight Ends And The Quiet Begins

Returning to myself didn't feel like a dramatic reinvention. It felt like recovery. It felt like finding and nurturing myself again after hearing everyone else's needs call louder than mine for years. It felt like breathing without bracing for impact. More than anything, it felt like meeting the woman I'd become and finally asking her what she wanted, what she needed, what she'd been tolerating, and what she was ready to stop carrying.

There's a strange kind of emptiness that can come when the fight ends, because the fight was familiar. It told you who you had to be. It gave you a rhythm, even if you were exhausted. It gave you purpose, even if it was built on pressure. If you grew up in uncertainty, you learn to stay ready. You learn to anticipate. You learn to prevent. You learn to solve. That's not a weakness. That's intelligence. But the problem with survival intelligence is that it doesn't automatically shut off just because your life gets better.

So when things calmed down, I noticed something that surprised me. I didn't feel instantly peaceful. I felt restless and slightly untethered. I had to admit that part of my identity had been built around holding things together. And if I wasn't holding everything together all the time, who was I?

From Fixing To Reclaiming

I returned to myself the moment I realized I'd become practiced at holding other people, but I hadn't practiced holding myself with the same tenderness. I gave patience away like it was endless. I offered grace as if it were natural. I listened, nurtured and guided well, but inwardly, I still treated my own needs like an inconvenience I should outgrow. I could coach about strength all day long, but I didn't always let myself be soft without guilt.

At first, returning to myself brought grief. Not the dramatic kind, but the slow kind. The kind that shows up when you finally see how long you've been living without checking in on yourself. It wasn't about blaming anyone. It was about telling the truth long enough to let it heal rather than harden.

I wasn't revisiting my past to relive pain. I was revisiting it to reclaim myself. To look at the parts of me who learned to survive before they learned to dream and say, "I see you. I know why you did what you did. And I'm here now."

The Difference Between Insight And Nurture

One of the biggest shifts for me was realizing that insight isn't the same thing as care. I'm good at insight. I can analyze patterns, connect dots, make sense of behavior, and build strategies that work. That's part of my wiring. It's also part of my leadership training. But healing asked me to go beyond understanding myself and learn how to nurture myself.

Nurture isn't a plan. It's a relationship. It's how you respond to what's true. It's how you treat yourself when you're tired, triggered, disappointed, or uncertain. It's the voice you use with yourself when no one else is listening.

For a long time, my internal voice sounded like pressure, even when it was disguised as motivation. It sounded like "You're fine, keep going." It sounded like "You can handle it." It sounded like "Don't be dramatic." It sounded like "You don't need that." Returning to myself meant I started practicing speaking in a different voice. One that felt like a partnership rather than a critique. One that sounded more like "What's going on with you right now?" and "What do you actually need?" and "What would it look like to care for yourself the way you care for everybody else?"

Presence Questions Instead Of Performance Questions

I started asking different questions in my quiet moments, and they weren't performance questions. They were presence questions.

What restores me when no one's grading my output?

When do I feel most like myself when I'm not proving anything?

What does my body need that I keep dismissing?

What would it look like to stop treating rest like something I earn and start treating it like something I steward?

The answers were humbling. Not because they were complicated, but because they were simple and I'd been overriding them for years. I didn't need a whole new life. I needed a new relationship with the life I already had. I needed rhythms that honored who I was becoming. I needed space that wasn't filled with guilt. I needed to stop acting like exhaustion was a normal cost of being me.

And I had to face this too. I wasn't always tired because I was doing too much. I was tired because I was doing too much without being emotionally present with myself while I did it. I was tired because I stayed responsible even when my soul was asking for rest.

Returning To Yourself Changes How You Receive

Returning to self isn't only about healing what hurt you. It's also about reclaiming what belongs to you. Your preferences. Your pace. Your joy. Your creativity. Your softness. Your ability to receive without explaining why you deserve it.

This part can be uncomfortable, especially if you've built your identity around being low maintenance. If you've been the one who never asks, never needs, and never takes up too much space, receiving can feel like a risk. It can feel like you're becoming a burden. It can feel like you owe people something.

But here's what I learned. If you never let yourself receive, you're not just independent. You're also keeping yourself at a distance, even from love. You're keeping your own tenderness locked behind competence. And you can't build wholeness while you're still living as though your needs are negotiable.

Returning To Self Is A Quiet Homecoming

Returning to self is a homecoming. It's the quiet decision to come back to the parts of you who have been on hold. It's letting your life reflect who you really are, not just who you've had to be. It's learning that you can be powerful without bracing, loving without disappearing, and dependable without being depleted.

Maybe the truest part is that returning to yourself isn't selfish. It's honest. It's what makes a healthy partnership possible for you. It's what makes leadership sustainable. It's what makes your life feel like yours again.

Closing Reflection

Returning to yourself isn't a dramatic reinvention. It's recovery. It's the moment you stop living by instinct and start living with intention. It's your choice to come back to the parts of you that learned to survive before they learned to dream. You can honor the version of you who held everything together without requiring them to carry everything forever. You're allowed to be known, not only needed. You're allowed to receive, not just produce. And you're allowed to live as if wholeness can be home, not a concept you visit when life finally slows down.

The Practice

Choose one small act you can do next that signals self-return.

My next small practice:

Journal Prompts

Answer what stands out. Skip what doesn't. Stay honest.

1. Where have I built an identity around being needed more than being known?
2. What part of me has been on hold because survival felt more urgent than softness?
3. What does my body do when life gets quiet, and what is it afraid quiet might reveal?
4. What restores me when no one is grading my output?
5. What do I keep controlling because I don't fully trust peace yet?
6. What would it look like to care for my body, mind, and spirit as sacred spaces to steward, not tasks to complete?
7. What boundary would protect my energy without hardening my heart?
8. What is one thing I want to reclaim in this season: a pace, a practice, a dream, a part of my personality?

Wholeness Check-In

Consider your pillars through the lens of self-return.

- Mentally and emotionally: Do my thoughts about myself sound like pressure or partnership?
- Spiritually: Do I believe God loves the whole of me, including the tired and still healing parts?
- Physically: Do I move, rest, and nourish my body as if it matters?
- Socially: Do I have at least one relationship in which my needs are safe to name?

One small shift that would bring me back to myself:

____

____

____

____

Empowering Declaration

I return to myself with honor, not shame. I thank the version of me who survived, and I welcome the version of me who's ready to live. I'm allowed to be known, not only needed. I'm allowed to rest without guilt, and I'm allowed to build a life that feels like mine again.

Chapter 4
Healing the Quiet Wounds

Some of the deepest pain in my life didn't come from one dramatic moment. It came from long stretches of responsibility that required me to be steady before I was old enough to understand what that steadiness was costing me. When a child carries adult weight, they learn to normalize what should've been protected. They learn to measure their value by how much they can hold, how much they can fix, and how little they ask for in return. Even when life becomes more stable, that kind of formation doesn't automatically disappear. It follows you into adulthood like muscle memory.

Quiet wounds are tricky because they don't always look like wounds. Sometimes they look like maturity. Sometimes they look like competence. Sometimes they look like they are "so strong." And when people praise what's been hurting you, you can start thinking that pain is just the price of being who you are.

What Quiet Wounds Look Like

The quiet wounds I carried weren't proof that I was weak. They were proof of my consistency. They revealed how long I'd stayed alert and played stabilizer. It also revealed how often I'd used discipline and productivity to keep life from unraveling. In my life, the threat wasn't always obvious. I wasn't always running from danger that had a name. I was running from uncertainty, emotional unpredictability, and the fear that peace might be temporary and love might be conditional, even when people promised otherwise.

Quiet wounds don't always shout. They whisper. They show up in the way you sleep lightly, even when you're exhausted, and in the way you reach for productivity when your soul is asking for softness. Quiet wounds show up in the way calm makes you uneasy, like you're waiting for the other shoe to drop, and in the way you feel most alive when you're needed and most unsure when you're allowed to be.

That's what makes them quiet. They hide inside normal. They hide inside responsibility. They hide inside "I'm fine." And because you can still function, you can convince yourself there's nothing to heal.

Emotional Fatigue Can Be Grief

I had to recognize that emotional fatigue can be grief. Grief for the childhood I didn't get to inhabit fully. Grief for the innocence I traded for responsibility. Grief for the version of me that became wise too early. This wasn't about blame. It was about truth. And truth is where healing starts.

A lot of people don't know what to do with quiet grief because it doesn't have a clean storyline. Nothing "big enough" happened to justify how heavy you feel. So you keep going. You outperform it. You stay productive. You stay composed. You stay useful. But your body doesn't forget. Your nervous system doesn't forget. And eventually, you start noticing you're tired in ways that sleep doesn't fix.

Healing Isn't Forcing Yourself To Hurry

Healing required compassion for the part of me that had only learned how to function under pressure. I stopped trying to force myself to heal faster than I safely could. I stopped judging my need for structure, and I stopped criticizing my instinct to stabilize what felt unsteady. Instead, I began treating that part of me like someone I was responsible for caring for, not someone I needed to correct.

I started mothering myself internally. I began speaking to myself with gentleness instead of urgency. I let it be okay that my body still braced sometimes, even when nothing was actually wrong. I also started noticing how often tension was present without me fully realizing it - tight shoulders, a clenched jaw, shallow breathing, a constant readiness humming like background noise.

That was when the work became less about what I understood mentally and more about what I needed to notice, honor, and release in my body.

Embodiment: Letting Safety Become Lived

Embodiment is the stage where healing becomes lived, not just understood. It's where you practice safety in your body through small, consistent choices until your nervous system starts believing what your mind already knows.

I practiced this in simple, everyday ways by paying attention to what was happening in my body and responding with more care. When I felt my chest tighten, I slowed my breathing. When I noticed myself bracing, I released my jaw, dropped my shoulders, and reminded myself that I did not have to stay in a state of readiness. I learned to pause before slipping into fix-it mode, and instead of pushing through emotional fatigue, I began to treat it as information my body was trying to give me. I started choosing rest before exhaustion forced it on me, and I let quiet moments be quiet without rushing to fill them with something productive.

At first, that kind of softness felt unfamiliar. In some ways, it even felt wrong. That is the part people do not always say out loud: when you have lived in vigilance for a long time, peace does not automatically feel peaceful. Sometimes it feels uncertain or undeserved. Sometimes your body meets it with suspicion because it has not learned to trust safety yet. So my practice became centering myself, again and again, to the small choices that reminded me I was safe. Not perfectly, but consistently. Over time, I began teaching myself that stillness was not something to fear. It was something to receive.

Quiet Wounds Show Up In Relationships

Quiet wounds affect our relationships too, especially the closest ones. When your nervous system is trained in vigilance, you can be loyal and capable and still struggle to be emotionally unguarded when a moment requires vulnerability without strategy. You can love deeply and still be slow to receive love and support. You can be present but still subtly guarded. This is not because you don't trust your partner. It's because your body learned long ago that neediness is risky.

That's why healing the quiet wounds isn't just about feeling better. It's about becoming more available. Healing is about receiving love without suspicion and being able to say "I need you" without feeling like you're failing.

The shift I needed wasn't to stop being strong. It was to stop letting strength be my only emotional language. I needed to allow softness to become a discipline, too,

40

because softness doesn't come naturally to someone who had to be steady early. Softness is learned. It's practiced. It's chosen.

Integration: Keeping Your Strength, Losing The Armor

Wholeness isn't the erasure of your survival self. It's integration. It's honoring the part of you that survived while letting the healed part lead.

That means you don't discard your competence. You stop using it as a shield. You can remain strong and dependable without being depleted and braced all the time.

Healing the quiet wounds is the work of learning that peace can be stable, not momentary. Love can be safe, not conditional. Rest can be allowed, not earned. That's what this chapter really comes down to. You're allowed to live as though safety is possible now.

Closing Reflection

Quiet wounds rarely announce themselves. They often live inside what people admire about you: your reliability, your competence, your steadiness. But what it costs you matters. Healing the quiet wounds isn't about rejecting your strength. It's about finally acknowledging what it required of you to stay braced for so long. It's learning that peace can be stable, love can be safe, and rest can be allowed. You can honor what you survived without letting survival be your lifelong default.

The Practice

Choose one small act you can do next that teaches your body something new: safety isn't something you have to prove.

My next small practice:

Journal Prompts

Answer what stands out. Skip what doesn't. Keep it honest.

1. What responsibilities did I carry too early, and how do they still shape how I show up today?
2. When do I feel uneasy in calm, and what might that unease be protecting me from?
3. When nothing is wrong, do I relax or brace?
4. What part of me still equates rest with risk?
5. Where do I default to productivity when my soul is asking for softness?
6. What would it look like to become the primary safe place for my own heart?
7. Where have quiet wounds affected my closest relationships, especially with my ability to receive love and support?
8. What does softness look like as matured strength, not weakness?

Wholeness Check-In

Scan your pillars through the lens of quiet wounds.

- Mentally and emotionally: Do I treat emotional fatigue as information or something to push through?
- Spiritually: Do I let God meet me in grief over what I carried too early, or do I rush past it?
- Physically: Does my body know how to rest without guilt?
- Socially and relationally: Do I have at least one relationship in which I'm allowed to be held, not just helpful?

One area I'm working on right now, and one small step I'm taking:

____

____

____

____

Empowering Declaration

I honor the version of me who carried what I had to carry. I release what is no longer mine to hold. I'm allowed to live in peace without suspicion. I'm allowed to be powerful without being emotionally braced. I'm learning how to live safely, not just survive.

Chapter 5
The Discipline of Becoming

There's a part of healing that people don't always talk about because it isn't glamorous. It's not the breakthrough moment or the tearful realization, and it's definitely not the big declaration that everything changes starting Monday. It's the daily part. The steady part. The part that looks simple from the outside but costs you something on the inside because it requires consistency.

That's what I mean when I say the discipline of becoming. Becoming whole isn't a mood, and it isn't something you wait to feel. It's something you practice. It's the willingness to keep choosing alignment even when nobody sees it, even when it isn't convenient, and even when you don't get instant feedback that it's working.

Discipline Isn't Punishment, It's Devotion

For a long time, the word discipline sounded like pressure to me. It sounded like striving and forcing myself to be better, like I had to earn peace by performing well enough. Healing taught me a different definition. Discipline, in this context, isn't punishment. It's devotion. It's what you do because you care about the life you're building, and it's the structure that protects your peace.

If you've lived in survival mode for a long time, you might confuse discipline with intensity. You might think you have to overhaul everything at once, or that it has to hurt to count. You might even believe that if you're not doing the most you can, you're doing nothing. But wholeness doesn't require intensity.

It requires honesty, repetition, and the kind of discipline that's quiet enough to be sustainable.

Becoming Happens In The Small Choices

Most of your life is shaped by small choices, often more than the big moments you tend to remember. We usually think transformation happens in some dramatic breakthrough, but more often it happens quietly, in the middle of ordinary life. It shows up in how you speak to yourself when you are tired, how you carry yourself after something has triggered you, and how often you say yes before you have even stopped to ask yourself what is actually true. Those moments may seem small, but they are not insignificant. Over time, they become patterns, and those patterns begin shaping the way you live.

Becoming starts when you notice those defaults and decide they do not get to lead unquestioned anymore. Sometimes that looks like catching yourself before you overexplain. Sometimes it is telling the truth without wrapping it in apology or choosing rest before you reach the point of emotional and physical exhaustion. Sometimes it is simply being honest enough to admit that a role, a rhythm, or a relationship dynamic is costing you more peace than it is worth. That is how change begins. Not all at once, but in real time, through choices that are small enough to practice and powerful enough to change the direction of your life.

You will not do that perfectly, and you do not need to. The point is not perfection. The point is that you begin living like you matter too. Like your needs are worth paying attention to. Like your voice, your peace, and your well-being deserve care.

48

The Discipline Of Boundaries

One of the clearest forms of becoming is the formation of boundaries. I'm not speaking about the harsh or defensive kind. I mean the honest kind that says, "I want to show up with love, but I'm not going to abandon myself to do it."

Boundary setting can be hard for high-capacity people because we're used to being the answer. We're used to being the ones who can handle it, and we've built an identity around being reliable. So sometimes setting a boundary feels like you're disappointing people. It can feel selfish. It can feel like you're changing the rules on everyone. But a boundary isn't a punishment for someone else. It's protection for what's sacred in you. It's you telling the truth about what you can carry without breaking, and it's you refusing to keep paying hidden costs to keep things smooth.

The clearer your boundaries become, the clearer your life starts to feel. Your yes becomes more trustworthy. Your no becomes less guilt, and your energy stops leaking into places that don't deserve your best.

The Discipline Of Emotional Presence

Another part of becoming is emotional presence. That means you stop treating your feelings like obstacles and start treating them like information. You begin noticing what you feel before you rush to manage it, and you stop using productivity to outrun discomfort.

This doesn't mean you become emotional in a way that derails your life. You become emotionally honest in a way that stabilizes your life. This shift enables you to stop forcing yourself to "be fine" when you're not, stop turning fatigue into a personality trait, and you stop pushing past warning signs and calling it strength. You learn to ask, "What's happening inside me right now?", "What do I actually need?" and "What would it look like to respond to myself with care instead of critique?"

That's discipline too. It's not dramatic. It's just mature.

The Discipline Of A New Pace

If your nervous system is trained to respond to urgency, slowing down can feel like failure. It can feel like you're losing momentum or becoming soft in a way that makes you less effective. Slowing down doesn't make you less powerful. It makes you more sustainable.

Becoming whole requires a pace you can live with, not just a pace you can survive. It requires rhythms that respect your body and your spirit, not just your responsibilities. For me, part of becoming was learning that rest is a decision I make because I'm worth caring for, not because I finally ran out of capacity. It was learning to stop waiting for my body to force the lesson and start treating my life as something sacred, not something to squeeze every ounce out of.

Becoming Whole Is Also Relational

Becoming whole also affects how you move in relationships. This fact connects to the book's premise. Two halves don't make a whole. Two whole people create something complete. That doesn't mean you show up perfect. It means you show up responsible.

The discipline of becoming shows up in a relationship when you stop expecting your partner to carry what you won't face. It gives you space to let tenderness be part of

50

your strength instead of hiding behind competence. You'll notice that you are no longer prioritizing passive communication and truth for peace. Instead, you'll tell the truth and hold your boundaries without punishing.

Wholeness isn't a solo project, but it is a personal responsibility. The more you commit to becoming, the safer your relationships become because you're not relying on other people to manage what you're unwilling to name in yourself.

Becoming Is Repetition, Not A Personality Shift

Here's the part that keeps people from getting discouraged. Becoming doesn't mean you wake up one day and never struggle again. It means you stop letting struggle lead. You choose to keep returning to the practices that support the person you're becoming, even when you don't feel motivated, strong, or clear.

You can still choose your next right step. You can keep practicing honesty, honoring your capacity. Choosing presence over performance, even in small moments, builds a life that feels more stable on the inside, not just impressive on the outside.

That's what discipline looks like when it's rooted in wholeness. It's steady, honest, and it's repeatable. It changes the way you live.

Closing Reflection

Becoming whole doesn't happen through one big moment. It happens through steady choices repeated over time. Discipline, in this season, isn't punishment or pressure. It's devotion. It's you choosing rhythms, boundaries, and emotional honesty that protect your peace and support the life you're building. You don't have to become a different person overnight. You have to keep choosing what aligns with the person you're becoming, even when old patterns try to pull you back into autopilot.

The Practice

Choose one small act you can do next that supports the person you're becoming. Make it simple enough to repeat and real enough to matter.

My next small practice:

____

____

____

____

Journal Prompts

Answer what stands out. Skip what doesn't.

1. What's one area where I keep relying on intensity instead of consistency?
2. When do I treat rest as a reward rather than a responsibility?
3. What boundary would protect my peace this week?
4. What emotion have I been managing through productivity instead of presence?
5. What does "becoming" look like in one ordinary moment of my day?
6. When do I still say yes out of reflex, and what would an honest no sound like?
7. What rhythm would make my life more sustainable, not just successful?
8. What would it look like to lead myself with partnership instead of pressure?

Wholeness Check-In

Scan your pillars through the lens of discipline and sustainability.

- Mentally and emotionally: Am I practicing self-talk that supports growth or pressures performance?
- Spiritually: Am I building steady intimacy or reaching for God only when I'm in crisis?
- Physically: Does my pace respect my body, or do I treat my body like it's expendable?
- Socially and relationally: Do my relationships reflect mutual care or do they mostly rely on my overperforming?

One small shift that would bring me into greater alignment:

Empowering Declaration

I'm not becoming through pressure. I'm becoming through devotion. I choose consistency over intensity, presence over performance, and rhythms that protect my peace. I'm allowed to grow steadily. I'm allowed to rest without guilt. And I'm committed to becoming the version of me who can build, love, and lead without abandoning myself.

Chapter 6
Learning Emotional Safety

For a long time, I thought emotional safety was something you found in the right people, the right environment, or the right season. I believed that if life became stable enough, my inner self would finally exhale. I told myself it would happen naturally; my body would notice the calm and follow suit. But that isn't what happened. My circumstances improved and my nervous system still lived as if it was bracing for impact.

That truth humbled me because it forced me to admit something I didn't want to admit. I wasn't just responding to what was happening in my life. I was responding to what had happened in my life. I could be in a quiet room with no real threat in sight and still feel my body on alert. I could be surrounded by people who loved me and still feel the old urge to stay one step ahead of disappointment. I was no longer in danger, but my body hadn't received the memo.

And that's the thing about survival. It doesn't always leave when the environment changes. Sometimes it stays because it has become a pattern, an identity. Sometimes it stays because your nervous system got trained in a language it never had the chance to unlearn. If you lived for long seasons in uncertainty, emotional safety can feel less like something you "get" and more like something you have to build.

I used to think the goal was to find safety. What I learned is that the deeper goal is to become safe inside yourself. That doesn't mean you don't need healthy relationships. It doesn't mean you don't want support. It just means you stop outsourcing your inner steadiness to external conditions. You learn how to sit with your own emotions without treating them like threats. You learn how to let your feelings be real without letting them run your life. You learn how to be honest without falling apart.

When Calm Still Feels Like A Setup

One of the most confusing parts about healing is realizing you could be living a "better" life and still feel like something's off. That's when you start questioning yourself. You start wondering if you're ungrateful or if you're broken. You start wondering why you can't just relax like everyone else.

A body that learned to stay ready doesn't instantly trust calm. It doesn't instantly trust joy either. When you've lived through enough unpredictability, peace can feel like the quiet right before the next shift because your system is trying to protect you from being caught off guard again.

For me, the signs weren't always obvious. It showed up in the way I couldn't fully soften my shoulders even when nothing was wrong. I listened for tone changes in conversations, like my mind was scanning for what I might've missed. Silence could feel personal, even when it wasn't. It showed up in the way I prepared for the worst, even in situations that didn't require it.

That kind of readiness can look like wisdom from the outside. People call it being disciplined, sharp, responsible, and emotionally mature. Sometimes it is those things. But sometimes it's also a nervous system that never learned it was allowed to stand down.

When I finally slowed down enough to notice this, it didn't make me feel weak. It made me feel honest. I didn't need another strategy. I needed safety. Not performative safety. Not "I'm fine" safety. Real safety. The kind that lets you breathe all the way down without having to monitor the room.

Emotional Safety Starts With You

This was one of the biggest turning points in my healing. Emotional safety didn't begin with different people. It began with a different relationship with myself.

I started learning that I could feel difficult emotions without drowning in them. I could hold sadness without turning it into a verdict on my worth. I didn't rebuild my identity from scratch just because I felt disappointed. I could feel anger and fear without trying to justify it as something more acceptable.

That's not something I used to believe. I used to think feelings were problems to solve. If I felt something uncomfortable, my instinct was to deal with it quickly. Translate it into action. Clean it up. Put it away. While that worked for survival, it also kept me emotionally braced.

I had to learn a new approach. I stopped treating emotions like interruptions I had to manage and started treating them as information I needed. That shift sounds small, but it changes everything. When you see emotions as information, you stop being at war with yourself. You stop acting like your heart is an enemy you have to control. You start listening instead of just overriding.

I began asking questions that felt simple and extreme at the same time. What am I feeling right now beneath my competence? Is this reaction rooted in what's happening in front of me or something that happened years ago? What part of me is trying to protect something old?

Those questions didn't magically make everything comfortable, but they did something more important. They separated my present from my past. They helped me see that not every surge of anxiety meant danger. Sometimes anxiety was a memory.

Memory Isn't The Same As Meaning

When you've lived a life where you had to stay ready, your body can interpret normal moments as threats. A delayed response can feel like rejection. A neutral facial expression can come across as disappointment. Feedback can feel like failure. A busy season can feel like a collapse. None of that is because you're irrational. It's because your body learned to attach meaning to things that once signaled risk.

That's why emotional safety isn't just a mindset. It's a practice. It's learning to slow down long enough to ask, "What's actually happening here?" instead of letting your body's first response become your truth.

I had to get honest about what my triggers were doing. They weren't evidence that I was broken. They were evidence that something in me was still trying to stay protected. And once I saw that, I stopped shaming myself for being triggered. I started understanding myself instead.

At this point, emotional safety begins to take shape. You stop shaming your triggers and start listening to them. You stop denying your patterns and start meeting them with maturity. You learn how to sit with your internal weather without turning every cloud into an emergency.

Instead of asking, "Why am I like this?" I learned to ask, "What is this part of me trying to keep me safe from?" That one question softened the way I spoke to myself, moving me out of condemnation and into curiosity.

Curiosity has a different energy than shame. Shame makes you hide. Curiosity makes you open. Shame makes you defensive. Curiosity makes you honest. Shame makes you push harder. Curiosity makes you slow down and see what's real.

The Difference Between Control And Safety

Many high-capacity people confuse control with safety. I did too. If I could anticipate outcomes, stay organized, stay prepared, and keep everything running smoothly, I told myself I was safe. But what I really had was control. And control can be useful, but it's not the same thing as safety.

Safety is internal steadiness. Safety is being able to experience emotion without abandoning yourself. Safety is being able to hear the truth without collapsing. Safety is being able to need something without judging yourself for it. Safety is being able to be imperfect without feeling exposed.

Control tries to prevent discomfort. Safety teaches you how to hold discomfort without losing yourself.

That distinction mattered to me because some of my "strength" was a response to fear. Not obvious fear, not panic, but quieter fear. The fear of being disappointed. The fear of being misunderstood. The fear of needing something and not getting it. The fear of being seen as too much or not enough. The fear of letting my guard down and paying for it later.

As my emotional safety grew, I didn't stop being capable. I just stopped needing capability to be my only emotional language. I could still lead, execute, and be dependable, but I didn't have to take on more than necessary to prove I deserved peace.

How Emotional Safety Changes Your Relationships

As my inner safety grew, I noticed it changed the way I moved through relationships, not in a dramatic way, but in a real way.

I needed less reassurance to feel anchored. I was less likely to read silence as rejection. I could hear feedback without spiraling into shame. I could name what I needed without believing need automatically equals burden. I could have hard conversations without turning them into a referendum on the relationship. I could let people be human without interpreting their humanity as danger.

That last one mattered more than I realized. Because when you've lived braced, you can start expecting people to disappoint you, even when you love them. You don't always say it out loud, but you live like it. You stay ready. You stay guarded. You stay slightly ahead.

Emotional safety doesn't make you naive. It makes you grounded. It helps you respond instead of react. It helps you stay present instead of scanning. It helps you give love without constantly worrying whether it will cost you.

It also changes what you attract and what you tolerate. When you're emotionally safe with yourself, you stop confusing intensity with intimacy. You stop confusing inconsistency with passion. You stop confusing emotional unpredictability with depth. You become more discerning; not colder, just clearer.

And here's what I had to learn the hard way. When you don't feel safe inside, you can accidentally build relationships that require you to stay armored. Not because the other person is evil, but because your system chooses what feels familiar. It selects dynamics that align with your internal baseline. Emotional safety raises your baseline. It makes certain patterns feel too expensive to keep paying for.

Learning To Stay Present With Your Feelings

One of the most practical things I did was staying present with my emotions for just a little longer than I wanted to. Not to wallow. Not to dramatize. I did this to stop abandoning myself the second something uncomfortable arose.

If I felt sadness, I let it exist without rushing to turn it into productivity. If I felt disappointment, I let myself name it without immediately trying to rationalize it away. If I felt fear, I acknowledged it without letting it run the moment.

I started treating my inner world like a place that deserved attention, not management. And I'll be honest: that took time. I had lived so long in "handle it" mode that "feel it" mode felt unfamiliar.

But emotional safety is built in those moments. It's built into the pause. It's built in the way you speak to yourself when you're triggered. It's built in how quickly you try to fix the feeling versus how willing you are to understand it.

Sometimes the most emotionally safe thing you can do is tell yourself the truth in a calm voice. Not a harsh voice. Not a dramatic voice. A steady voice.

"This is old."

"I'm safe right now."

"I don't have to rush."

"I can feel this without becoming it."

"I can take my time."

That kind of self-talk doesn't erase emotions. It gives them a safe place to land.

Faith And Internal Steadiness

Faith was woven into this process in a quiet way. Not as a performance, not as a set of perfect answers, but as a steady anchor that reminded me that I didn't have to keep bracing.

I began to believe God cared not only about what I could carry for everyone else, but about how safe I felt in my own life. I shifted from praying only for external solutions to praying for internal steadiness. I asked for grace to live without continual bracing and for courage to trust peace without assuming chaos was hiding behind it.

That shift mattered because sometimes we use faith as a coping tool rather than a relationship. We use it to push through. To override. To stay strong. To keep going. And there are seasons where "keep going" is necessary. But wholeness invites a deeper kind of faith; the kind that lets you be human in God's presence without needing to prove you're okay.

I started praying differently. I prayed for safety in my body, not just safety around my life. I prayed for clean discernment, not just a quick fix. I prayed to be guided, but also to be softened. I prayed to be strengthened, but also to be steadied. I asked God to help me stop confusing exhaustion with obedience.

And slowly, I began to trust that peace wasn't a trick. It was a gift: one that I could receive without suspicion.

Strength Without Armor

Wholeness is not the loss of your gifts. It is the healing of the fear that used to drive them.

That sentence became real to me as my sense of emotional safety grew. I didn't become less strong. I became less armored. And there's a difference. Armor is a strength that expects danger. It stays rigid. It stays ready. It stays guarded. Anchored strength is steady. It can move. It can soften. It can stay present without collapsing.

When you begin to feel more emotionally secure, you can still lead, execute, and be dependable. You don't need to overperform to prove that you deserve peace. You don't need to be perfect to be valuable. You don't need to be needed to be worthy. You don't need to stay braced to stay responsible.

64

You become trustworthy to yourself. And that's where emotional safety gets real, because the safest person you can become is the one who doesn't abandon themself when they feel something difficult.

It's not that you never get triggered again. It's that you know what to do when you do. You don't shame yourself. You don't spiral. You don't punish yourself for being human. You come back to yourself. You tell the truth. You choose presence. You choose partnership with your own heart.

That's how emotional safety becomes a home.

Closing Reflection

Emotional safety isn't a prize that other people hand you. It's a relationship you build with yourself. It grows when you stop shaming your triggers and start listening to them, when you stop treating emotions like interruptions and start treating them as information. You're not chasing a life without challenge. You're learning how to carry a challenge without turning your heart into hostile territory. And when you can be emotionally safe with yourself, you'll still value connection and support, but you won't need your relationships to manage your inner world for you.

The Practice

Choose one small act you can do next to build internal safety; make it simple enough to repeat.

My next small practice:

____

____

____

Journal Prompts

Answer what stands out. Skip what doesn't. Keep it honest.

1. Where do I still feel like peace is something I have to earn rather than something I'm allowed to experience?
2. How does my body respond when things are calm? Do I relax or brace?
3. What emotions do I tend to manage instead of feel?
4. What parts of my past may still be shaping how safe I feel, even when my present is stable?
5. What does my inner voice sound like when I'm triggered: punishment or partnership?
6. What would it look like to treat my feelings as information instead of interruptions?
7. When do I confuse uncertainty with danger?
8. What is one truth I can tell myself today that separates a memory from the present moment?

Wholeness Check-In

Notice where emotional safety is growing and where it still feels fragile.

- Mentally and emotionally: Do I name what I feel without judgment, or do I rush to fix it?
- Spiritually: Does my faith make me feel held or mostly just evaluated?
- Physically: Does my body get true rest, or am I half tense even when I'm sitting still?
- Socially and relationally: Do I have spaces where I can show up honestly, not only as the strong one?

One small shift that would strengthen my sense of safety:

____

____

____

____

Empowering Declaration

I'm safe enough to feel what I feel. I'm not in constant danger even when my body remembers old storms. I honor my emotions as information, not interruptions. I let peace be real in my life, not a reward I must earn. My strength doesn't require armor. It can live in safety.

Chapter 7
Faith in the Fire

Faith has never been decorative for me. It has been structural. When you grow up carrying more than you should, earlier than you should, you learn to build inner worlds that keep you alive.

For me, faith was one of the first places my spirit could breathe without needing anyone's permission. I did not have all the theology or language, but I knew Presence. I felt God in the music that softened the edges of hard days, and in books that let me imagine a life beyond my circumstances. I felt Him in the quiet comfort of being seen, even when everything around me felt unstable. Faith became my first safe room, and when my life shifted out of constant survival mode, faith had to evolve with me.

There is a version of faith that keeps you moving through hardship and a deeper one that teaches you how to live when hardship is no longer the center of your identity. The second version is less dramatic and less urgent, but it is more intimate. It requires you to trust that you are still guided when the path is quiet, still loved when you are not continually proving strength, and still called when you are learning about softness. If no one ever told you that this kind of shift is normal, it can feel like a spiritual crisis, even though it is the arrival of spiritual maturity.

Faith As A Survival Shelter

When I look back, I can see how faith held me before I knew how to hold myself. It wasn't always the kind of faith that looked polished or consistent. It was the kind that showed up as a whisper when the room felt too heavy, as a breath when

I couldn't find words, as a sense that I was not abandoned when circumstances suggested I was. In seasons when adults were unreliable, faith gave me a steady point that didn't shift with moods, threats, or unpredictability. That mattered because survival teaches you early that stability is fragile, and your body becomes trained to live as if safety is temporary.

This is why I say faith was structural: it didn't sit on top of my life like a decoration. It held parts of my internal world together when nothing else could. It gave me a way to keep going when I didn't have control, and it gave me comfort when I didn't have answers. It also gave me an anchor for dignity, because even when my environment didn't treat my tenderness like something to protect, my spirit still had a place where tenderness was allowed.

That kind of faith can carry you through a lot, and I will never diminish it. However, faith built primarily in survival can come with patterns you don't notice until you enter a calmer season. When your spiritual life is shaped in crisis, you can unconsciously come to expect crisis as the normal setting in which God feels most present. You can start associating closeness with urgency, and you can begin to feel spiritually disoriented when life gets quiet. The quiet can feel suspicious, not because you don't love God, but because your nervous system learned to relax only after the fire was contained.

When Peace Feels Like A Test

One of the most surprising parts of healing is realizing how much your body can resist the very thing your soul has been praying for. You can ask God for peace, then feel uneasy when it arrives. You can pray for stability and then wonder what you're missing once things finally stabilize.

You can be blessed with a calmer season and still feel the low hum of readiness underneath your day, as if something is about to fall apart any minute.

I had to confront a subtle pattern in my walk with God, and it wasn't the kind of pattern you catch easily because it looks like devotion. My faith had been shaped around endurance. I knew how to fight, carry, and hold everything together. I knew how to pray through a crisis. I knew how to ask for strength. I knew how to stand. What I had not yet learned was how to rest in God without feeling like rest meant I was falling behind. I had learned to trust Him in the fire of visible crisis, and I was still learning how to trust Him in the unfamiliar quiet of safety.

If you have lived most of your life with a braced nervous system, peace can feel like a setup. Your mind may interpret stillness as a gap in vigilance, and your body may interpret calm as the moment right before something happens. That doesn't mean you are ungrateful or faithless. It means you are human, and your system is still updating. It means you are learning how to inhabit what you used to only hope for.

Here, healing and faith meet in a deeply personal way, because wholeness doesn't ask you to abandon your calling. It asks you to stop sacrificing yourself to fulfill it. It asks you to trust that God never needed you to burn out as proof of your devotion. It asks you to believe that your humanity is not a threat to your spiritual life, and that your needs are not an inconvenience God tolerates. For someone who learned to survive by being strong, this can be one of the hardest spiritual upgrades.

When Prayer Becomes A Relationship Again

As this shift unfolded, I began letting prayer become less performative and more honest. I stopped showing up only with polished versions of my feelings. I stopped treating questions as spiritual weakness, and I stopped assuming that struggle was the only place in which God met me deeply. I began to believe that intimacy with God was not measured by how stoic I could be, but by how present I was willing to be with Him in whatever I was feeling.

Sometimes my prayer sounded like a plain sentence I didn't try to make pretty because I wasn't trying to impress God anymore. I would tell Him, "I know I'm safe, but my body is still bracing," and then I would sit long enough to notice what I was carrying under the words. Other times, the truth was even more tender: "I don't know who I am without the struggle" or "Teach me how to live as if peace is not suspicious." Even gratitude became more honest because I stopped forcing it to cover what I felt. I could say, "I'm grateful, and I'm still tired," or "I'm doing the right things, but I don't feel settled yet," and trust that intimacy with God could hold both the progress and the pain without requiring me to pick one.

I also learned to stop using spiritual language to override my emotional reality. I had done that without realizing it because high-capacity people are trained to keep it together, and we can turn faith into another place where we perform strength. We can confuse spiritual maturity with never needing support, never feeling weak, and never asking hard questions. That is not intimacy. That is spiritual perfectionism. That is a nervous system trying to stay in control while calling it faith.

Real intimacy is when faith and feelings can sit in the same room without either one needing to silence the other. It is when you can bring your emotional truth to God without apologizing for it. It is when you can admit you are unsure, tired, and still learning, and trust that God is not disappointed by your humanity. It is when you stop forcing yourself to be "grateful" before you are honest, and you allow gratitude to grow from a place that is real.

The Fire That No One Sees

When people hear "faith in the fire," they often imagine dramatic catastrophe, the kind that forces you to pray because you have no other option. That kind of fire is real, and many of us have known it. However, there is also internal fire, and it can be just as consuming.

Internal fire is what happens when the version of you who survived can no longer be the only version of you who lives. It is the burning away of identities built solely on resilience. It is the discomfort of learning that peace is not laziness. It is the grief of realizing how long you equated rest with risk. It is the deep rewiring required when you stop using urgency as the engine of your life.

In an external crisis, prayer often sounds like rescue language because your world visibly is on fire, so you ask for provision, a door, relief, and a clear way through. Internal fire is different, and it changes what you ask for. You begin praying for rewiring more than relief, because the threat is no longer outside you. It's the old bracing inside that refuses to stand down, even when the storm has passed.

Now, faith matures into a sense of wholeness. It becomes less about proving you are strong enough and more about believing you are safe to live differently on the other side of what you survived. There were days when I had to remind myself that God was not only with me when I was "handling it." God was with me when I was unsure, tired, quiet, or undone. That truth softened something in me because it meant I didn't have to keep earning closeness through competence. I could come as the daughter, not only the warrior.

Rest As Stewardship, Not Rebellion

One of the hardest shifts for a survival-trained person is realizing that rest is not rebellion. Rest is stewardship. Rest is not quitting. Rest is honoring. Rest is not a lack of discipline. Rest is a different kind of discipline, the kind that protects your ability to stay whole while you live with purpose.

I had to learn that God was not only the God who sustained me in survival. He was also the God who was teaching me to enjoy peaceful seasons without waiting for disaster. He was inviting me to know Him as provider, not only as protector; as restorer, not only as rescuer; as father and friend, not only as commander in a crisis. That shift mattered because my nervous system had made an identity out of being ready. I had equated being braced with being responsible, and I had equated being exhausted with being faithful. Faith was inviting me to stop confusing burnout with devotion.

When I began practicing rest as a form of stewardship, it did not feel comfortable immediately. It felt unfamiliar. It felt like letting go of a role I had mastered. It felt like trusting that I could slow down without losing my edge, and that I could be at peace without becoming passive. That fear is real for high-capacity people because competence has been one of our safest currencies. We have learned that we can count on ourselves. We have learned how to produce stability through output. We have learned how to prevent disappointment through preparedness. We have learned how to stay ahead of pain by staying useful.

Faith doesn't condemn the part of you that learned these strategies. Faith honors it and then invites it to mature. Faith says you are allowed to live as if peace is real. Faith says you are allowed to be strong and be held.

76

Faith says you are allowed to be called and be human. Faith says you are trusted and allowed to rest.

When Faith Stops Depending On Urgency

If your spiritual life has been built mostly around hardship, stepping into peace can make you feel like you've lost your spiritual edge. You might notice yourself looking for the next problem as proof that you still "need" God. You might confuse intimacy with desperation, and you might feel unsettled when the only thing in front of you is the quiet work of becoming.

I had to notice where my spiritual life still depended on urgency. I had to ask myself whether I allowed God to meet me in joy, rest, and ease with the same depth as He met me in desperation. I had to learn that intimacy was never designed to rely on disaster. Intimacy is designed to be steady. It is designed to be daily. It is designed to be honest, not just intense.

As I practiced this, my faith stopped being something I used to hold myself together and became something that held me while I learned to live differently. That is a subtle but powerful distinction. It meant I did not have to weaponize faith against my own emotions, and I did not have to silence my grief in the name of gratitude. I could tell the truth and still be faithful. I could be tired and still be loved. I could be in process and still be guided.

This is part of what wholeness means spiritually. It means you stop treating your humanity like a problem you need to solve before you can be close to God. You let your humanity become the place where God meets you. You stop treating your questions as disobedience and start treating them as conversation. You stop treating your needs as a weakness and start treating them as reality. You stop treating peace like a test and start treating it like a gift you're allowed to receive.

Faith That Can Hold Wholeness

Faith in the fire is not only about surviving what hurts. It is also about surrendering what no longer fits. It is the willingness to release old identities, old reflexes, and old definitions of strength that were built for danger, not for peace. It is the courage to believe that you do not have to keep suffering to stay spiritual, and you do not have to keep bracing to stay responsible.

In my life, this has meant learning to relate to God with less performance and more presence. It has meant learning to bring Him my real emotional weather, not just my best behavior. It has meant learning to accept that God is invested not only in what I made it through, but in how I live now that I've survived. It has meant trusting that peace does not make me less effective and softness does not make me less respected. It has meant letting my spiritual life become a home, not a battlefield.

If you recognize yourself in this, I want you to know that this shift is not a failure. It is formation. It is faith becoming whole. It is God who carried you in survival, teaching you how to live in restoration. It is intimacy expanding beyond emergency. It is the steady work of learning that you are allowed to build a life on the other side of the flames, and that you can still be deeply devoted without disappearing inside duty.

Closing Reflection

If your faith was formed in survival, stepping into peace can feel disorienting, and that disorientation does not mean your faith is weak. It often means your faith is growing into a new season in which God is not only the God of crisis but also the God of quiet. As you heal, you may have to practice letting rest be stewardship rather than guilt, letting honesty be intimacy rather than fear, and letting peace be real without waiting for punishment or interruption. You are not abandoning devotion when you stop burning out. You are honoring the truth that God never required you to sacrifice yourself to prove you love Him.

The Practice

Choose one small faith practice you can repeat in a calm season, not just in a crisis. Make it something that teaches your nervous system that peace is safe and that God meets you in quiet as much as in fire.

My next small practice:

Journal Prompts

Answer what stands out. Skip what doesn't. Keep it honest.

1. Where has my faith been shaped more by survival than by intimacy, and how does that show up in my daily life?
2. What part of me feels unsure about who I am when I am not managing a struggle?
3. Where do I still treat rest like I'm falling behind, spiritually or otherwise, and what fear sits below that reflex?
4. What does it look like for me to talk to God without performing strength or rushing to sound put together?
5. Where do I still depend on urgency to feel close to God, and what would steadier intimacy look like?
6. What is one emotion I tend to override with spiritual language, and what would it mean to bring it to God honestly?
7. What would change if I believed God cared as much about my wholeness as my obedience?
8. In this season, what does faith look like when there is no crisis to outrun?

Wholeness Check-In

Scan your pillars through the lens of faith and spiritual safety.

- Mentally and emotionally: Does my faith invite gentler self-talk, or do I silence emotions in the name of strength?
- Spiritually: Do I relate to God mostly as a crisis responder or as a steady daily presence?
- Physically: Do I treat rest as part of stewardship, or do I only rest when my body forces it?
- Socially and relationally: Do my spiritual circles support honesty and wholeness, or do they reward performance?

One small shift that would bring my faith into greater alignment with wholeness:

____

____

____

____

Empowering Declaration

I remind myself that my faith is not built only on crisis, and I do not need to manufacture urgency to feel close to God. God is with me in both the fire and the quiet, and I don't have to burn out to prove my devotion. I'm allowed to rest, heal, and live as if peace is real because peace is not a reward for collapse. It is part of the life I'm learning to steward with Him.

Chapter 8
Purpose Is a Decision

For a long time, I thought purpose would arrive like a lightning strike, loud and undeniable. I imagined one defining moment in which everything would lock into place, my calling would become obvious, and the path would unfold in one clear, dramatic revelation. That is how people talk about purpose when they want it to feel clean and cinematic. However, in my life, purpose has not felt thunderous. It has sounded like a quiet yes. Not a performance. Not an announcement. Just a steady agreement between who I was becoming and the life I was no longer willing to live on autopilot.

I have always been driven. I know how to set a goal, build a plan, and execute it. From the outside, that drive can look like clarity and intention. Sometimes it *is* clarity and intention. Sometimes it is conviction. Sometimes it is ambition in the healthiest sense, the kind that says I am willing to steward what I have been given and make something meaningful with it. But I had to face something honestly, because honesty is the only way to clarify purpose. Not all drives are born out of a calling. Some of them are born out of survival.

When Achievement Becomes Armor

When your early years teach you to anticipate instability, achievement can become a form of safety. Overfunctioning can become an identity. Competence becomes armor, so no one sees how tired your soul is. That kind of strength has built lives, sustained families, carried teams, and held up systems that would have otherwise collapsed. It opens doors. It creates opportunity. It allows you to serve in rooms you once only imagined.

For people like me, that strength can look like a gift, and in many ways it is. It is also often a strategy. I did not become driven in a vacuum. I became driven because drive gave me control, and control gave me relief. If I stayed one step ahead, I could keep the ground from shifting under my feet. If I anticipated needs, I could reduce uncertainty. If I remained capable, I could stay valuable. If I stayed valuable, I could stay safe. That may not have been my conscious thought, but it was an internal system that worked long enough to become normal.

This is why high-capacity people can have impressive lives and still feel the subtle strain of always being on. We can call it discipline and leadership. We can call it excellence and responsibility. We can call it being built for pressure. We can call it being dependable. Sometimes that is all true. But there can also be another truth underneath, a quieter one that says the reason I cannot slow down is that slowing down feels like losing my edge, and losing my edge feels like losing my protection.

Wholeness began asking me a question I couldn't avoid forever. What does this level of performance cost me? That question changed how I evaluated my success, what I celebrated, and what I chased. It changed what I was willing to tolerate and how I understood purpose. Purpose built on survival fuel can still produce results, but it often does so by draining the person doing the producing. That kind of purpose can look like impact and still cost you your internal peace.

Purpose Fueled By Survival Vs. Purpose Fueled By Clarity

There is a difference between purpose powered by fear of falling apart and purpose fueled by clarity on who you are. One is continually racing to stay ahead of collapse. The other is anchored in identity, rooted in alignment, and willing to move at the speed of peace. One says, "If I stop, it will all fall apart." The other says, "I can move faithfully without abandoning myself."

When survival is driving your purpose, you can feel the urgency in your body even when your life is stable. You can feel the pressure to keep proving yourself even when you are already respected. You can feel the pull to overdeliver even when what is being asked is reasonable. You can start treating your capacity as infinite because the truth feels too vulnerable. You can build a life in which your nervous system is constantly at a low simmer of readiness.

Survival-based purpose can also make you addicted to being needed. You can feel most alive when everything depends on you because the need for you feels like security. It feels like proof. It feels like a role you know how to win at. Then you can start equating importance with urgency and impact with sacrifice. You can tell yourself you're just committed, just responsible, just built differently, just devoted, just strong. You can even be right about your commitment and still miss what your body has been trying to tell you.

When clarity is driving your purpose, the pace changes. You still care. You still move, build and execute. The difference is the internal engine. You are no longer trying to outrun fear or trying to secure your worth through performance. You stop confusing pressure with purpose

86

and stop using exhaustion as proof that you are doing something meaningful. You're making decisions from an identity that is secure enough to choose what's aligned, not just what's possible.

Clarity-based purpose feels cleaner. It feels steadier. It feels honest. It is willing to say no when no protects the integrity of your life. It is willing to rest when rest protects your ability to show up whole. It is willing to choose long-term sustainability over short-term applause. It does not require you to be overdrawn to be effective.

Two Wholes Make It Complete

Two halves do not make a whole. Two whole people create something complete. That belief does not deny the beauty of growing together. It does not dismiss the sacredness of learning in a relationship. It simply refuses the lie that a relationship should be a substitute for identity.

A healthy partnership is not built on two people trying to fix each other's emptiness. It is built on two people committed to their own healing, aware of their patterns, and willing to bring wholeness into the space they create together. The work of becoming whole is not a detour from your life. It is the foundation of it. You are not pausing to focus on yourself as if wholeness is some side project you will eventually outgrow. You are preparing your life to be sustainable. You are choosing to build a foundation sturdy enough to hold the weight of your calling, relationships, and legacy without collapsing beneath them.

This is also where purpose takes a different shape in the context of love. If you have been survival driven, you may have unconsciously looked to partnership as the one place where you can finally exhale. You may have looked to love to rescue you from the pressures you never learned to release.

You may have looked to a partner to carry what you have carried alone for too long. Wanting support is not wrong. Wanting rest is not wrong. Wanting to be held is not wrong. But when your inner world is overdrawn, you can begin to expect your partnership to fix what your inner life has not yet stabilized.

Purpose becomes relationally healthier when it is powered by wholeness. When you are whole, you do not bring your partner an unspoken contract that says complete me, validate me, prove I am enough, rescue me from my exhaustion, or carry what I will not face. Instead, you bring honesty, self-awareness, and responsibility. You bring a willingness to grow. You bring a commitment to keep your inner work moving. You bring a capacity for love that is not a transaction.

That is what makes a partnership complete, not perfect, but complete in the sense that two whole people can create a strong and safe structure together. Love becomes multiplication, not rescue. Purpose becomes something you can sustain, not something you survive.

Purpose As A Daily Decision

Purpose is not discovering a secret assignment in the clouds. It is the decision to live awake. It is a commitment to stop measuring your worth by how much you can carry and to honor who you are while carrying what you are genuinely called to hold. That sounds simple until you realize how many of your decisions have been shaped by the need to stay safe.

There came a point when I had to grieve an old version of achievement because it came with hidden costs I could no longer afford. I had to notice how often I confused exhaustion with virtue, busyness with impact, and depletion with proof that I was doing something significant. I had to admit that parts of me felt important because I was always needed, not because I was aligned. I had to acknowledge that I had built a strong life and still had areas where my internal world was running on old fuel.

Wholeness did not ask me to abandon ambition. It asked me to examine the engine. It asked me to be honest about why I was moving the way I was moving. It asked me to distinguish between calling and compulsion. It asked me to ask whether my life was becoming more whole because of my choices or more fragmented despite my success.

Purpose becomes a daily decision when you stop waiting to feel perfectly ready and begin living as if your growth is already in motion. It becomes a daily decision when you commit to practices that honor your wholeness, even when no one is applauding. It becomes a daily decision when you stop treating rest like a reward for collapse and start treating it like part of how you protect your calling. It becomes a daily decision when you say no to what violates peace, even if you could manage it. It becomes a daily decision when you allow God to define your success, not just your metrics, culture, or past expectations.

Purpose gets honest when you accept that it is not only what you do. It is how you do it and who you are while you do it. Purpose is not just the visible outcome, title, achievement, or measurable success. It's internal alignment that allows you to move in your assignment without continually betraying yourself to meet expectations you never agreed to.

The Fear Within The Drive

I had to confront a core fear that many high-capacity people carry, even if we rarely say it out loud: What if I stop striving and lose my edge? What if peace makes me less effective? What if softness makes me less respected? What if rest slows me down and I miss something important? What if I am only valuable because I am available?

Those questions are not silly. They are honest. They are rooted in an old story. They are the kind of fears that sound like wisdom when you have lived a life where being prepared kept you safe. They are also the kind of fears that can quietly control you if you never put them in the light.

I had to learn that my edge was not created by exhaustion. My effectiveness was not dependent on panic. My respect was not earned through self-erasure. My impact did not require neglect. God did not design my gifts to destroy me. He designed them to move through me in a way that allows me to be present in my life, my heart, and with the people I love. Impact at the cost of wholeness is not sustainable. It is a slow leak.

I also had to learn that purpose can feel steady in the soul even when your life is full. Purpose does not require urgency. It does not require self-sacrifice as proof. It does not confuse burnout with faithfulness. It allows you to build a legacy without abandoning yourself. It allows you to be someone who can love from overflow rather than depletion, lead from alignment rather than panic, and give from a grounded place rather than a frantic need to be needed.

Purpose gets cleaner when you stop asking only what needs to be done and start asking who you are becoming as you do it. It gets cleaner when you stop asking only what your assignment is and start asking whether the way you are pursuing it is aligned with peace or quietly wounding you. It gets cleaner when you stop asking how to do more and start asking how to do what matters in a way that honors both your capacity and your calling.

Purpose That Makes Life Livable

As I healed, I began to understand that purpose is not separate from livability. It is not separate from emotional safety or from the rhythms that protect your body and the boundaries that protect your mind. If your purpose requires you to keep betraying yourself, it will eventually erode you. If your purpose requires you to keep running on adrenaline, it will eventually numb you. If your purpose requires you to keep being relevant through a crisis, it will eventually trap you. A purpose that honors wholeness is a purpose you can sustain.

This also matters for relationships, because you cannot build a complete relationship from a life that is continually overdrawn. You cannot create emotional safety for someone else when you feel chronically unsafe within yourself. You cannot expect your partnership to be the only place you rest, the only place you are poured into, the only place where you are allowed to exhale.

In the context of wholeness, purpose is the decision to live in a way that makes partnership possible, not as rescue but as multiplication. It is the decision to build a life that does not require you to be in crisis to feel relevant. It is the decision to be powerful and peaceful at the same time, and allowing your life to reflect what you believe, not just what you can accomplish.

I invite you to live a life in which responsibility does not cost you your self, and where purpose does not demand your depletion.

Closing Reflection

Purpose is not proven by pressure. It is revealed by alignment. Survival taught you how to push. Wholeness teaches you how to choose. You are allowed to build a life in which impact does not require depletion. Your purpose is not only what you accomplish. It is the integrity you carry while you do it. The goal is not to shrink your ambition. It is to upgrade the fuel behind it so your life becomes sustainable, steady, and true.

The Practice

Choose one small act you can do next that reflects purpose powered by clarity, not survival.

My next small practice:

Journal Prompts

Answer the questions that stand out. Skip what doesn't. Keep it honest.

1. Where do I confuse urgency with purpose, and what fear is underneath that urgency?
2. What goal in my life might be fueled more by fear than alignment, and what would it look like to pursue it differently?
3. What does purpose feel like in my body when it is rooted in peace instead of panic?
4. What boundary would protect my calling without hardening my heart?
5. What am I afraid will happen if I rest more, slow down, or say no?
6. Where do I equate being needed with being valuable, and what does value look like when I'm not performing?
7. What would it look like to lead, love, and build from an overflow state instead of depletion?
8. What is one decision I can make this week that reflects the whole version of me?

Wholeness Check-In

Scan your pillars through the lens of purpose and pace.

- Mentally and emotionally: Do my goals make me feel grounded or constantly pressured?
- Spiritually: Do I believe God defines success, or do I default to proving myself through output?
- Physically: Is my body included in my calling or sacrificed for it?
- Socially and relationally: Do my closest relationships receive my presence or mainly my productivity?

One small shift that would bring me into greater alignment:

____

____

____

____

____

Empowering Declaration

I choose a purpose that honors my wholeness, and I refuse to use exhaustion as proof of my value. My calling does not require burnout, and I can build, serve, and lead without abandoning myself. I am guided by alignment and peace, and I am allowed to move faithfully at a pace that keeps me whole.

Chapter 9
Align Your Life

I thought alignment was something you stumbled into once you had enough clarity: if I could name my values, define my priorities, and resolve the open loops of my past, my life would settle into a state of peace on its own. That belief sounds reasonable until you live long enough to realize that self-awareness does not automatically translate into a self-led life. Alignment does not happen by accident. It is not a reward for insight. It is a practice, and like any practice, it asks you to choose it repeatedly, especially in the quiet moments when no one is clapping, watching, or measuring your consistency.

For someone who spent decades in survival mode, alignment is a hard-won invitation. Survival trains you to do what works. Alignment asks you to do what is true. Survival helps you adapt quickly. Alignment asks you to stop adapting to environments that require you to betray yourself. Survival solves immediate problems. Alignment builds a life in which you do not have to dismantle yourself to keep everything running.

That distinction became one of the most sobering shifts of my wholeness journey because my life looked successful in all the ways people respect. I had built impressive systems and strong rhythms, and I had developed reliable leadership habits. I had earned a reputation for being the one who could carry what others could not. I earned that reputation honestly. I was not pretending to be capable. I *was* capable. The issue was not whether I could handle life. The issue was whether the way I was handling life reflected the person I was becoming.

When Success Is Real But Still Feels Heavy

When I slowed down enough to truly see myself, I noticed that I did not have a discipline problem. I had an alignment problem. I was living a high-performance life, but not always in high congruence with it. That tension is subtle until it becomes exhausting. You can do the right things and still feel unsettled. You can be faithful to responsibilities and still feel unfaithful to yourself. You can be surrounded by love and still feel the ache of being slightly misplaced in your own life.

That ache is hard to explain to people who have not lived it because on paper, you look like you should be grateful, and in your heart, you often are. You cannot ignore what your body is telling you. You cannot ignore the way certain commitments make your shoulders tighten before you even say yes. You cannot ignore how your mind races at night, not because you are chasing drama, but because something in you knows you are not living as cleanly as you could. You cannot ignore the quiet resentment that builds when your life requires you to keep overriding your needs to maintain the image of strength you have been praised for.

Misalignment is not always loud. Sometimes it looks like success but feels vaguely heavy. Sometimes it looks like being admired while feeling unseen or like being so capable that no one notices you are quietly yearning for more softness, more space, and more permission to live without bracing. Sometimes it looks like you're doing excellently, yet you still feel like you are always slightly behind yourself.

I had to admit that part of my exhaustion was not coming from the amount I was doing. It was coming from the internal split, the subtle distance between what I

98

believed and what I repeatedly practiced. It was coming from living in ways that were efficient, responsible, and respectable while still carrying an old, hidden definition of worth that linked peace to performance.

The Question That Changed Everything

Alignment gave me language for what I had been feeling. The question changed from "Can I handle this?" to "Does this reflect who I'm becoming?" That shift sounds simple, but it has weight because it requires you to stop evaluating your life only by outcomes and begin evaluating it by integrity.

When your life has been shaped by survival, "Can I handle this?" is a legitimate question. It is the question that kept you safe. It is the question that helped you navigate instability and pressure. It is the question that taught you how to stay ready. But when you are no longer in the same environment, and you are no longer the same person, that question becomes too small. It can keep you trapped in a life that you can manage but not fully inhabit.

"Does this reflect who I'm becoming?" forced me to acknowledge that I am not who I was when survival was my constant companion. I am not the girl who carried adult responsibilities before her nervous system learned what safety felt like. I can honor her without building my entire identity around the rules she had to live by.

That is where alignment became less of an idea and more of a form of spiritual housekeeping.

Spiritual Housekeeping And The Alignment Audit

I started reviewing my habits the way I would review a program plan, calmly and without drama, asking what still served me and what drained my peace. I looked at my schedule not only for efficiency but for truth. I examined my relationships not only for loyalty but for emotional health. I assessed my inner narratives, the ones that made me highly achieving and dependable, and asked whether they still matched the woman I wanted to be.

I felt uncomfortable with some of my answers, not because they were scandalous, but because they were honest. I was living with a hidden definition of worth that linked peace to performance. I was giving too much of my best energy to places that did not protect the wholeness I was trying to build, and I was normalizing emotional fatigue as part of leadership when I was meant to lead from a fuller well.

I had to be careful here because I wasn't interested in turning my life into a blame story. I didn't want to become the kind of person who resents her responsibilities. I respect responsibility. I believe in excellence. I value loyalty. I was not trying to become less dependable. I was trying to become more integrated.

Alignment creates integration. It reduces the internal split you feel when your life and values aren't matching. Your yes becomes more honest. Your no becomes less loaded with guilt. Over time, even when your nervous system starts to trust that you're safe enough to live with integrity, not just endure.

Survival Patterns That Masquerade As Maturity

The more honest I became, the more I saw how survival shaped my decision-making. Survival taught me to focus on what could go wrong. Alignment started teaching me to make room for what could go right. Survival had me moving fast, proving stability through achievement, treating rest like something I had to earn after everyone else was okay. Alignment challenged all of that. It taught me to move with intention, value consistency over image, and believe that rest was not a reward for overextending myself.

Survival taught me to treat pressure as a normal part of life. Alignment taught me to treat peace as possible.

That is a big retraining because survival has a way of making misalignment feel familiar. You can be misaligned and still be productive and praised. You can be misaligned and still look stable. You can also be misaligned and still be the one whom people count on. In fact, for some of us, misalignment is hidden inside what people admire. It is in our reliability, our composure, our capability, our ability to handle it.

When you grow beyond survival, you begin to see that being able to handle something is not the same as being called to carry it. You can do the right thing and still be doing it from the wrong place. You begin to see that some of your strength is reflexive, some of your discipline is a coping strategy, and some of your commitment is fear of disappointing people who benefited from the old version of you.

Alignment starts to require courage because it means disappointing people who were never aligned with your peace. It will drive you to adjust relationships built around your taking on more than your share. Alignment will compel you to change patterns that people have grown comfortable with, even if you are the one paying the cost.

Two Wholes Make It Complete, And Alignment Makes It Possible

Two halves do not make a whole. Two wholes make it complete. A whole person is not a perfect person. A whole person is committed to self-awareness, emotional responsibility, spiritual anchoring, physical stewardship, and relational maturity. A whole person is willing to look at their life honestly and make adjustments, not because they're failing but because they're growing beyond the version of themself they built to survive.

Alignment is about preparing for love without expecting your partner to rescue you. It's the way you enter partnership without expecting your partner to complete work that your soul has been asking you to do. Alignment is the way you lead without bleeding your internal peace to keep everyone else stable.

I had to face how easy it is to carry misalignment into relationships. If your life is built around endurance, you can unconsciously bring endurance into love and call it loyalty. You can bring self-abandonment into a partnership and call it sacrifice. You can bring emotional bracing into intimacy and call it being realistic. You can bring chronic overfunctioning into your home and call it being responsible.

None of that makes you a bad partner. It makes you a survival-trained partner, and survival training does not automatically turn off when you get into safe environments. Alignment is one of the ways you teach yourself to love from wholeness instead of from reflex.

Discomfort As Warning Or Expansion

One of the most practical changes I made was learning to interpret discomfort more accurately. Not all discomfort is a warning. Some discomfort is expansion. When you begin aligning your life with your values, you will feel resistance. Sometimes that resistance will come from people who benefited from the old version of you. Sometimes it will come from your nervous system, which is still adjusting to the reality that peace is not a trap and not a temporary break between storms.

When your body has been in a state of high readiness for a long time, calm can feel unfamiliar. It can even feel suspicious. You may catch yourself waiting for the other shoe to drop, even when things are objectively stable. You may feel anxious in moments that are supposed to feel restful, not because you are unappreciative, but because your body still thinks that stillness is the time when danger can sneak up on you.

Alignment requires patience because you're not only changing your schedule, you're changing your baseline. You are teaching your mind and body that calmness is allowed. You are teaching your spirit that joy is not suspicious and that you do not have to stay in motion to remain valuable.

This is why alignment can feel like both relief and grief. It is a relief because you begin experiencing coherence, the quiet exhale of not fighting yourself all the time. It is grief because you begin seeing how long you have lived in ways that were not fully true, even when they looked impressive.

Coherence And The Relief Of Living Clean

For me, alignment became the relief of living in coherence. I stopped explaining my needs as if they were inconveniences. I stopped apologizing for boundaries. I stopped shrinking my desires to match the comfort levels of people who have never had to rebuild themselves from the inside out.

I had to recognize how often I softened my truth to keep things smooth. I had to recognize how often I overdelivered to prevent conflict. I had to recognize how often I swallowed my needs because being low maintenance felt like safety. Those are not random personality traits. They are often survival patterns that appear to be maturity. Alignment helped me stop confusing the two.

Coherence also sharpened my discernment. I noticed that some commitments felt clean and life-giving, even when they were difficult, while others felt draining. That mattered because wholeness is not only emotional. It is logistical. It shows up in what your life repeatedly proves you value.

I became more intentional about protecting my yeses. I started saying yes to things that reflected my calling and long-term identity. I started saying no to things that required me to overextend for the sake of appearance. I stopped confusing urgency with importance. A survival-trained mind can mistake pressure for purpose. Alignment taught me to slow down long enough to choose what matched the person I was becoming.

Faith As A Quiet Filter

Faith remained present for me as a quiet filter. Not performance and not slogans, just a steady internal check. Is this how I am supposed to live? Is this pace sustainable? Does this choice serve the person I am called to become?

I began trusting that God was shaping my rhythms, not only guiding my outcomes. He was not interested only in what I could accomplish, but in the quality of peace I could sustain as I built. That belief helped me release an old version of strength that had to hold everything perfectly.

Alignment offered me a more mature type of strength, one that builds boundaries without guilt and chooses rest without apology. It offered strength that leads without sacrificing internal stability. It offered the ability to support others while remaining rooted in wholeness, which is the kind of leadership that lasts and the kind of love that can breathe.

When you live aligned, you become harder to derail, calmer in conflict, more emotionally consistent, and more trustworthy to yourself. That may be the deepest form of self-respect because self-respect is not only what you believe about yourself. It is what you repeatedly practice in your choices, your pace, your boundaries, and your willingness to live in truth.

Closing Reflection

Alignment is not a one-time decision. It is daily integrity. It is choosing what is true over what is familiar. It is releasing what no longer fits, even if you can still carry it. Survival taught you how to adapt. Alignment teaches you how to stop adapting to what costs you your self. You can honor who you were without living by old rules. You are allowed to build a life that feels like truth, not just one that looks like success.

The Practice

Choose one small act you can do next that moves your life into greater coherence. Make it realistic and repeatable.

My next small practice:

Journal Prompts

Answer what stands out. Skip what doesn't. Keep it honest.

1. Where do I feel successful but subtly disconnected from myself?
2. What commitment looks good on paper but feels heavy in my body?
3. What habit reflects survival more than wholeness?
4. What does a peaceful version of success look like for me now?
5. Where do I still see a link between worth and productivity?
6. What boundary-setting would make it easier for me to maintain my peace?
7. What relationship pattern needs a small adjustment to reflect who I'm becoming?
8. What is one thing I can remove, reduce, or reschedule this week to support alignment?

Wholeness Check-In

Scan your pillars through the lens of congruence.

- Mentally and emotionally: Do my thoughts and self-talk support the person I am becoming?
- Spiritually: Do my rhythms reflect closeness, not just endurance?
- Physically: Is my pace sustainable with dignity?
- Socially: Do my closest relationships make room for honesty and growth?

One small shift that would bring me into greater alignment:

____

____

____

____

Empowering Declaration

I choose alignment over autopilot, and I choose a sustainable peace. I honor the version of me who survived, and I commit to the version of me who is learning how to live whole. I do not need chaos to prove I am capable, and I am allowed to build a life that feels like truth.

Chapter 10
The Cost of Avoidance

When avoidance first came up in my wholeness work, I almost dismissed it. For most of my life, I thought avoidance belonged to people who were afraid of honesty, couldn't handle confrontation, or tiptoed around truth because they didn't have the spine for it. That was never how I saw myself. I have always been direct. I have always been the woman who names what needs to be named, addresses what feels misaligned, and chooses clarity even if it makes the room uncomfortable.

Then I learned something that changed the way I understood my emotional history. Avoidance is not always silence. Sometimes it is productivity or competence. Sometimes it is being the one who stays strong so that no one has to worry about you. Avoidance can also show up as excellence that looks like leadership but functions as self-protection on the inside.

My avoidance did not look like running away from life. It looked like mastering it. It looked like being so useful, dependable, and steady that no one ever thought to ask if I was okay. It looked like solution-first thinking with emotion as a second language. It looked like being the anchor in rooms that would have fallen apart without me. I learned early that steadiness made me safe, and I refined that lesson until it became instinct.

This chapter is not about shame. It is about clarity. Avoidance is adaptation, not moral failure, and it makes sense that our bodies learn whatever keeps us functioning when life does not feel safe. The issue is that what helps you function in one season can quietly keep you fragmented in another. You can build an impressive life and still live slightly outside yourself, and you may not even realize it until the quiet catches up with you.

Avoidance That Looks Like Strength

Avoidance has a reputation problem. People picture it as hiding, procrastinating, denying, or refusing to deal with hard truths. Those are real forms of avoidance, but they are not the only ones. There is also the kind of avoidance that is widely applauded. It gets awards. It gets promotions. It gets called leadership. It gets called maturity. It gets called "built for pressure."

If you grew up around instability, you learn to read risk faster than you read joy. You learn that being prepared is safer than being hopeful and that being needed can feel like the closest thing to security. I became valuable. I became effective. I became the one who could be trusted with what others could not carry.

In many ways, that strength is real and honorable. It built a life I am grateful for. It carried my family through hard seasons. It allowed me to thrive in careers that demanded composure under pressure. Wholeness did not shame that strength. It gently turned the light toward what my strength had been built to protect.

When you become known as the reliable one, you're not only demonstrating competence. Oftentimes, you're managing risk and controlling outcomes. You are staying ahead and limiting the chance that disappointment will catch you unprepared. That is why competence can become more than skill. It can become a shield.

A shield can look like strength, especially to those who benefit from it. They may not realize they are witnessing a coping strategy. You might not realize it either, because your life is working. You're handling things. You are

112

producing results, getting things done. The question is not whether you are capable. The question is: what are your capability costs internally?

The Quiet Truths I Was Avoiding

I was not avoiding the truth in obvious ways. I was avoiding slower, more intimate truths, the ones you meet only when the room is quiet, and no one needs anything from you. When urgency faded, I encountered a disorientation I didn't know how to name. My struggle wasn't simply that I said yes too often. My challenge was that I had never fully learned who I was when I didn't have to fight.

That is a specific kind of ache. Not a loud crisis. Not a dramatic collapse. A slow recognition that you have lived in high-functioning vigilance for so long that softness feels exposed, rest feels irresponsible, and receiving care feels like a debt you will owe forever. In that light, avoidance is not dodging life. It is dodging the vulnerability of calm.

I found it easier to keep solving problems than to admit that some problems were not meant to be solved quickly. They were meant to be witnessed, honored, and slowly rewired through safety.

There is a difference between problems that need a plan and pain that needs presence. Avoidance blurs that line. It keeps you reaching for the kind of control that feels familiar. It keeps you translating emotional realities into tasks you can complete. It keeps you moving because movement creates the illusion of relief.

If you are someone who knows how to execute, avoidance can hide inside your gifts. The mind learns, "If I can just handle this next thing, I won't have to feel what is underneath." Then you handle the thing, and you still feel what is underneath, so you handle another thing. It becomes a loop. A

clean-looking loop. A productive loop. A socially
acceptable loop. It just doesn't lead you home.

What Avoidance Costs

Avoidance is expensive, but not always in the ways
people assume. It doesn't always cost you relationships
immediately. Sometimes it costs you emotional range. It
costs you joy that can't penetrate because your body is still
waiting for the next storm. It costs you the ability to
recognize what you need before you're depleted. It costs
you intimacy with yourself. Eventually, it begins costing
you the intimacy you long to experience with others.

When you are not fully at home in yourself, you can
build relationships that let you remain half armored. You
may love deeply and still stay guarded. You may be loyal
and still be subtly unavailable in ways you don't intend.
You may say you want closeness while defaulting to habits
that keep closeness at a safe distance. That was sobering
for me because avoidance can live inside good intentions.
It can live inside faith. It can live inside service. It can live
inside leadership. It can live inside the very identity that
people celebrate.

Avoidance can also cost you clarity. When you do not
have access to your full emotional truth, older parts of you
can make decisions. You may choose what looks stable
instead of what is aligned, what feels familiar instead of
what feels true, or what keeps you needed instead of what
keeps you whole. You may even call those choices
"wisdom" because they seem responsible, but your body
keeps telling you something is off.

Avoidance can take a toll on your body, too. High-
functioning avoidance often runs on tension. Your
shoulders stay lifted. Your jaw stays tight. Your sleep

114

becomes shallow. Your digestion becomes sensitive. You carry a low-grade readiness that feels normal until it becomes the baseline. Then you start believing rest doesn't work for you, when the truth is that you haven't practiced safety long enough for rest to land.

Avoidance can also damage your spiritual life in subtle ways. You can use faith as another way to push through, another structure to hold you together, another place where you can exhibit strength. You can pray for peace and still refuse the stillness in which you could receive it. You can believe God is with you and still live as if you are alone because you have trained yourself to rely on your own output more than you rely on intimacy.

Avoidance is not one dramatic thing. It is often a quiet pattern that keeps you functional but not fully free. It keeps you stable but not fully alive. You look put together, but inside, parts of you are waiting for your attention.

How I Recognized It In Real Time

There was a season when I noticed how quickly my mind reached for the next task the moment my emotions got quiet. The second that space opened up, I would clean something, organize something, plan something, teach something, fix something. That rhythm isn't inherently wrong. It is one way I've built a meaningful life. But I started asking a new question in those moments: "What am I protecting myself from feeling right now?"

Sometimes the answer was simple fatigue. Sometimes it was grief. Sometimes it was the unresolved sadness of a younger version of me who learned to be mature too early. Sometimes it was the fear that if I slowed down, I would have to acknowledge how much I carried without being cared for in the same way. Not because people around me were cruel, but because I trained the world to see me as solid, and the world responded accordingly.

That was a hard truth because it meant I had been complicit in the pattern without realizing it. I taught people I was okay without needing what they needed, then wondered why they didn't offer me the softness I instinctively offered them. It wasn't that they refused to care. It was that I made care unnecessary by never letting myself need it.

High-capacity people can create this dynamic in their relationships without malice. We become so skilled at holding ourselves that we unintentionally teach people they don't have to hold us. Then we grow resentful when they don't because our heart still longs to be met. That longing is not weakness. It is humanity. The problem is that avoidance doesn't let that longing be honest. It keeps it hidden behind competence.

The Difference Between Confronting Others And Confronting Myself

For me, the shift wasn't learning to confront others. I know how to confront. The shift was learning to confront myself gently. That is a different kind of courage.

Confronting others can still keep you in control. You set the pace. You manage the dialogue. You maintain the posture that feels safe. Confronting yourself requires vulnerability. It requires you to listen to what you have been outrunning and finally admit that some of your strongest patterns were built to protect you from the tenderness you did not have space to feel.

It also requires you to redefine what you mean by "strength." Strength is not only composure. Strength is not only competence. Strength is not only about handling what

116

others can't. Strength is being present with yourself when there is nothing to manage, nothing to fix, and nothing to prove.

Avoidance is often a fear of internal complexity. It is not always fear of truth. It can be a fear of what truth will require. If I admit I'm tired, I may have to rest. If I admit I'm lonely, I may have to ask. If I admit I'm grieving, I may have to feel. If I admit I'm overwhelmed, I may have to change something. If I admit I'm hurt, I may have to stop pretending it doesn't matter.

Those are real costs, and that's why avoidance can feel safer than honesty. Not safer in a healthy way but in a familiar way. It lets you keep your systems running. It lets you keep your identity intact. It lets you keep your reputation. It lets you keep your role.

Wholeness asks for something deeper. It asks you to keep your integrity.

Avoidance And The Pillars Of Wholeness

Avoidance erodes mental and emotional health, spiritual grounding, physical stewardship, and relational maturity. It doesn't always shatter them in one moment. It softens your congruence bit by bit.

Mentally and emotionally, avoidance can make you overthink and underfeel. You become highly analytical about your life while remaining disconnected from your body's wisdom. You can be self-aware in theory and numb in practice. You can name your patterns while still living them.

Spiritually, avoidance can become a subtle form of distance. You still believe. You still pray. You still show up. But intimacy gets thin when you don't bring your real self. You can pray for transformation while staying busy enough to avoid the silence where transformation happens. You can use spiritual language to override emotional reality, not because you are fake, but because you are trying to stay stable.

117

Physically, avoidance often shows up as depletion. Your body becomes the place where unprocessed emotions land. Tension becomes normal. Sleep becomes inconsistent. Headaches become familiar. Your immune system becomes sensitive. You tell yourself it's just stress, just life, just being busy, but your body is still keeping score.

Relationally, avoidance can create a subtle inaccessibility. You may be present but not fully open. You may be engaged but still guarded. You may be loving but still braced. You may freely give care, but struggle to receive it. Over time, that limits depth. It limits softness. It limits the kind of intimacy that requires two people to be honest, not just reliable.

Avoidance keeps you functional. Wholeness makes you free.

Avoidance As Adaptation, Not Failure

One of the most healing perspectives I've learned is that avoidance is an adaptation, not a moral failure. Survival strategies are brilliant in unsafe environments, but costly when danger has passed, and your body never got the memo.

Avoidance helped me survive. It helped me lead. It helped me build. It helped me create stability. It helped me stay effective. I honor that. I do not demonize the part of me that learned those strategies. I refuse to let those strategies run my whole life now that I'm growing into a different season.

Wholeness required me to retrain my relationship with my needs. It required me to value internal truth as much as external excellence. It required me to accept that I am not

118

less powerful when I name what I need. I am more trustworthy in myself.

That is a major shift for high-capacity people because we are often praised for not needing. We are praised for being "low maintenance." We are praised for being strong. We are praised for keeping it together. Over time, that praise can become a trap. It can teach you that being lovable requires being unbothered, being valuable requires being useful, and being safe requires being in control.

Wholeness breaks that trap. It tells the truth. You are allowed to need. You are allowed to feel. You are allowed to be supported. You are allowed to be seen without being needed first.

Practicing Courageous Presence

I began practicing small acts of courageous presence. I sat a little longer in silence before filling it with activity. I named my feelings without trying to fix them right away. I said yes to support without apologizing for it. I let joy linger without scanning the horizon for what might ruin it. I honored the emotional truth only I could hear beneath my polished-looking life.

These practices were not dramatic. They were ordinary, which is why they worked. Avoidance often lives in ordinary moments, so healing has to live there, too. It has to meet you in the small gaps where you normally reach for a task. It has to meet you in the quiet moments you usually fill. It must meet you in the conversations where you normally say "I'm fine" without checking whether you're telling the truth.

Slowly, my inner world began to feel less like a system I had to manage and more like a home I was allowed to inhabit. Healing isn't only about making different decisions. It is

practicing safety in real time until your body comes to
believe what your spirit knows.

I am safe enough to be still.

I am safe enough to be soft.

I am safe enough to be seen without being needed first.

That shift doesn't happen overnight, but it does
happen. When it happens, your life reflects a new truth.
You are not just surviving. You are building a future in
which survival is no longer your identity.

Maturing Strength Instead Of Abandoning It

Avoidance loses its power when you stop treating it
like a character flaw and start treating it like a signal. A
signal that something in you is asking for care. A signal
that you are entering a new season. A signal that the
version of you who survived is ready to become the version
of you who lives.

I did not need to discard my strength to heal this. I
needed to mature it. I needed to let it become less armored
and more anchored. Less reactive and more integrated.
Less defined by crisis and more defined by clarity.

As that happened, the calling I carry didn't shrink. It
expanded. I was no longer empowering others from
constant strain. I was empowering others from a place that
felt steadier, quieter, more sustainable. I was not losing my
edge. I was gaining my wholeness.

That is the kind of leadership that lasts. That is the kind
of love that can breathe. That is the kind of wholeness that
becomes generational. Choosing to face what my old
patterns once helped me avoid did not dishonor my past. It
honored the future I am committed to building.

Closing Reflection

Avoidance is not always silence. Sometimes it is productivity, competence, and staying in motion so you never have to feel what rises in the quiet. It makes you effective, but it can quietly reduce your emotional freedom. It can keep you functional without making you fully present. Healing does not require you to abandon your strength. It asks you to mature it. It asks you to become safe enough to be still, to be honest, to be supported, and to be seen without first being needed. Avoidance loses power when you stop judging it and start listening to what it has been protecting.

The Practice

Choose one small act you can do next to interrupt avoidance and build courageous presence. Make it simple enough to repeat.

My next small practice:

Journal Prompts

Answer what stands out. Skip what doesn't. Keep it honest.

1. Where do I default to motion when my inner world is asking for rest?
2. What emotion do I tend to solve instead of feel?
3. What am I protecting myself from feeling when I immediately reach for a task?
4. Where have I been strong for so long that receiving feels uncomfortable?
5. What does my body do when things get quiet: relax or brace?
6. What would it look like to sit with truth without fixing it right away?
7. What has avoidance cost me emotionally, even if my life looks successful?
8. What is one way I can practice being fully here today?

Wholeness Check-In

Scan your pillars through the lens of presence.

- Mentally and emotionally: Am I processing my feelings or outperforming them?
- Spiritually: Does my faith feel intimate and grounding, or mostly built around pushing through?
- Physically: Is my body receiving real restoration, or is it only recovering between responsibilities?
- Socially: Do my relationships value who I am, not just what I carry?

One small shift that would bring me into greater alignment:

____

____

____

____

____

Empowering Declaration

I do not need a crisis to justify my existence. I am allowed to live in peace without apology. I am allowed to slow down without losing my value. I am allowed to be supported, not just relied on. I honor the strength that carried me, and I choose the wholeness that will keep me.

Part Two
Loving as a Whole Person

Love gets more honest when you stop pretending. You're no longer willing to call a surface-level connection "fine." You want emotional safety and honesty. You want peace that doesn't depend on everything going smoothly. That kind of love isn't built through intensity or chemistry alone. It's built through clarity, boundaries, communication, and repair.

This part is about what changes when you bring your whole self into a relationship. Not the polished or self-erasing version. The real one, the one who has needs, standards, tenderness, and a voice.

You'll explore what makes love feel safe, what quietly wears down connection over time, and how trust can be rebuilt without losing yourself in the process. And whether you're partnered or not, this section can help you adopt a healthier blueprint for intimacy, conflict, and commitment that keeps becoming better, not because it's easy, but because it's intentional.

Chapter 11
The Truth About Love and Wholeness

You may have grown up believing that romantic love would be your reward for finally becoming "enough" - someone with enough stability, enough success, enough self-control, enough strength. You may have felt that if you did life well, love would be easy, secure, and safe.

That belief isn't silly. That belief is often survival dressed up as hope. If love felt unpredictable for you early on, certainty became the goal. Competence became the shield. Being reliable started to feel like the only way to keep the ground from shifting again. Being capable reduced risk. Being steady kept you from needing too much, asking too loudly, or hoping too openly.

So you carried that posture into love. You showed up with effort and loyalty, and somewhere along the way, you made a quiet vow: "I won't be the reason someone else has to carry what I carried." That kind of devotion can look beautiful from the outside. But when it's powered by fear instead of freedom, you can start feeling lonely because you're still bracing as you love.

When Love Turns Into A Responsibility You Manage

If you're high functioning, you're used to getting results. You know how to solve problems, make plans, and keep moving, even when your heart is tired. That strength has probably blessed your life in a hundred ways. It's also the same strength that can quietly become your relationship strategy without your noticing.

You hold the standard. You carry the rhythm. You read the room. You notice what's off and try to correct it before it turns into a bigger issue. You keep the emotional climate stable because you can. And because you've been the capable one for so long, it almost feels normal to treat love like something you maintain.

But love can't live on management alone. You can be loyal and still feel unseen. You can be committed and still feel like you're bracing inside the relationship. You can be "doing the right things" and still carrying that ache you can't quite explain without feeling like you're being ungrateful. If that's ever been you, it doesn't mean you're difficult. It usually means you're waking up to what your heart has needed for a long time: more connection, more presence, and more being met.

Love Is A Mirror, Not A Rescue

Love doesn't complement your coping skills. It reflects them. It shows you what you do when you feel exposed, disappointed, uncertain, or misunderstood. It reveals how you interpret silence. It reveals whether you can receive care without having to calculate what it will cost or what you'll owe. It even reveals what your body believes about safety long before your lips have the words.

This is why strong people can feel confused in relationships. You can lead teams, manage pressure, hold responsibility, and still struggle to relax when someone offers steady love. You can be brilliant and grounded and still feel emotionally unsure of how to be held. That isn't a character flaw. It's often a story about your nervous system. Something you learned early. Something your body has been rehearsing for longer than your heart has had permission to name.

The Difference Between Carrying And Being Held

Many people know how to support someone through almost anything. Fewer people know how to let themselves be supported through ordinary heaviness.

You may know how to be the anchor, the planner, the stabilizer, but you may not know how to be the person who exhales. The person who doesn't rush to prove you're still fine or the person who lets someone stay close without turning closeness into a performance.

If you learned early that people can disappear emotionally, physically, or both, self-reliance can start to feel like the only guarantee. Over time, it becomes more than a habit. It becomes identity. It becomes that quiet inner rule you don't even realize you're living by: *If I'm strong, I'm safe.*

That rule protected you. It helped you build. It helped you survive. It might also be the reason love can start to feel like work you don't know how to put down.

Emotional Maturity Is Love In Motion

Love isn't a magical outcome that arrives once you find the right person. Love is maturity practiced in real time.

It's noticing what's true before it hardens into resentment. It's choosing connection in small moments, not just dramatic ones. It's staying kind when you're tired. It's learning how to return to each other faster without needing to win first.

Wholeness doesn't remove conflict. It changes what conflict means. It gives you space to stay anchored instead of spiraling. It helps you stay honest without making honesty feel like danger. That matters because many relationships don't fall apart because people don't love each other. They disintegrate because the emotional culture stops being tended to.

Truth Has Timing, Tone, And Tenderness

You might not struggle with honesty. You might not struggle with conviction. Your growth might revolve around refinement: learning how to carry truth with timing, tone, and tenderness. Not because you're trying to soften the truth, but because you're trying to protect the heart of the relationship while you hold your ground.

Tenderness isn't the dilution of conviction. It's the evolution of intimacy.

It's learning how to speak in a way that makes closeness possible instead of making your partner brace. It's learning how to name what's real without turning it into a courtroom. It's knowing when to slow down, when to pause, when to come back kinder, and when to say, "I'm still tender about that, and I don't want to leave it messy between us."

Those shifts sound small until you live them. Then you realize they change the whole climate.

The Story That Quietly Misled You

Many people were taught that partnership creates identity. That love gives completion, that a relationship makes you whole.

It sounds romantic. It also makes love heavier than it has to be.

130

When partnership becomes your completion, conflict starts feeling terrifying. When love becomes your proof of worth, distance feels like a verdict. When your stability rises and falls based on someone else's mood, your body never fully rests.

Here's the truth that can set you free: love isn't a missing piece. Love is a life shared between two complete people. Wholeness doesn't mean you don't need anyone. It means you stop outsourcing your stability.

Rooted, Not Emotionally Shut Down

Wholeness isn't emotional isolation. It's being emotionally rooted.

There's a difference between needing love in order to breathe and wanting love because you're building a good life with someone. When you're emotionally rooted, you stop using your partner as your emotional measuring stick. You stop treating their tiredness like rejection. You stop treating normal conflict as a sign that the relationship is unsafe.

You can still want closeness deeply. You can still long for tenderness, affection, and safety. You don't need those things to prove you matter. And that shift often feels like a deep exhale as you can finally love without gripping.

How Wholeness Changes What You Tolerate

When you become more whole, your standards get clearer. Not harsher. Clearer.

You stop confusing intensity with intimacy. You stop romanticizing emotional turbulence and calling unpredictability "passion." You stop normalizing inconsistency because you're used to being the one who adjusts. You start paying attention to character, consistency, and emotional responsibility. Not because you're picky, but because you're tired of environments that require you to keep bracing.

You also start to notice the difference between relationships that are difficult because life is hard and those that are difficult because the emotional culture remains unstable. Wholeness helps you name that difference without second-guessing yourself.

When Peace Feels Unfamiliar

If you were shaped by volatility, calm can feel suspicious. Not because you want drama, but because your body learned to stay ready.

So a delayed text can make your chest tighten. A quiet evening can make your mind start scanning for what's wrong. Even after a disagreement ends, you might still feel on alert, like your nervous system is waiting for the next wave.

Those aren't "crazy" reactions. They're learned reactions. Your growth comes from learning to notice them without obeying them, and from letting peace be peace without interrogating it as if it's a trap.

What Wholeness Actually Means

Wholeness doesn't mean you stop wanting love. It doesn't mean you become detached, guarded, or "too independent." It means you stop negotiating your identity to keep the connection. It means you stop shrinking your needs to make them more convenient. It means you stop carrying the relationship like a job you have to do perfectly so that you won't be abandoned.

132

Wholeness gives you options. You can pause before you react. You can ask instead of assuming. You can tell the truth early, before it becomes resentment. You can stay connected to yourself while staying connected to someone else. And that's the real flex: not being invulnerable but being honest without collapsing.

Love Is An Environment You Build Together

A healthy relationship becomes a place where two people practice empathy, honesty, accountability, and repair. A place where conflict doesn't become cruelty. A place where truth can be spoken without fear of punishment. A place where both people can be human and still be safe.

And when faith is present, it doesn't have to be loud or performative. It can be a quiet undercurrent reminding you that love is sacred work and peace is worth protecting. Not as a weapon. Not as pressure. Just as grounding.

You don't lose your power when you learn how to be held. You become the version of yourself who can lead without armor.

The Question That Reveals The Difference

Here's a question that clarifies everything: Are you asking love to complete you, or are you bringing your wholeness into love?

When love is asked to complete you, it gets heavy. You grip. You brace. You overdo. You panic when closeness shifts because closeness feels like a matter of survival.

When you bring wholeness into love, love gets lighter. Not shallow. Lighter. You can handle tension without losing yourself. You can ask for what you need without apologizing for being human. You can receive care without turning it into debt.

Two halves can cling. Two wounds can collide. Two whole people can build.

Closing Reflection

If you've been carrying love like a responsibility, you're not failing. You're noticing.

You're noticing the difference between relationship as survival and relationship as sanctuary. You're noticing what it costs to be the strong one all the time. And you're noticing that your heart wants something calmer, not because you've lowered your standards, but because you've raised them.

Wholeness doesn't make love effortless. It makes love sustainable. It gives you the ability to confront without cruelty, repair without humiliation, and stay connected without self-abandonment.

In the next chapter, we'll go deeper into what makes that kind of love possible, not as a vibe but as a real emotional culture you can build.

The Practice

Use this when you notice you're bracing in love, even if nothing dramatic is happening.

Name what your body is doing.

Notice your shoulders, jaw, chest, and stomach. Ask "Am I tense?" If you are tense, take three slow breaths and let your exhale be longer than your inhale.

Separate the moment from the memory.

Ask "Is this about what's happening now or what this reminds me of?" You don't need a perfect answer. You need honesty.

Choose one present-moment action.

Pick one small move that supports connection without performance:

"How are you, really?"

"I feel a little off today, but I'm still here."

"I'm making up a story. Can you tell me what's real?"

"Can we sit together for a few minutes?"

Let receiving be allowed.

When someone shows they care for you, notice the impulse to minimize it. Try saying "Thank you." Let that be enough.

If you're practicing this while single, it still works. You can name bracing, separate the moment from the memory, and choose one grounded action that protects your peace.

Journal Prompts

Write with honesty, not perfection.

1. Where did I learn that love is something I must earn?
2. In relationships, what do I work too hard at to prevent something from going wrong?
3. What does emotionally safe love look like in everyday moments, not in theory?
4. Where do I confuse intensity with intimacy, and what does intensity give me that feels like connection?
5. What would it look like to receive love without turning it into debt?
6. What is one standard I'm ready to raise without turning it into a demand?

Wholeness Check-In

Take an inventory across your pillars in the context of love.

- Mentally and emotionally: When my connection feels strained, do I stay anchored or spiral into proving, fixing, or bracing?
- Spiritually: Do my values ground me, or do I default to fear of loss?
- Physically: Does my body feel regulated in love, or does it stay on alert?
- Socially: Do my relationships reinforce wholeness or quietly reward overperforming?

One small shift that would strengthen my love in wholeness:

____

____

____

____

Empowering Declaration

I bring my whole self into love. I don't earn connections by exhibiting strength. I welcome peace without interrogating it. I tell the truth with tenderness, and I receive care without apology. Two wholes make it complete, and I am building that kind of love.

140

Chapter 12
Emotional Safety

Emotional safety is one of those phrases that sounds simple until you realize how much it changes everything. It isn't just "being nice." It isn't walking on eggshells. It isn't avoiding hard conversations.

Emotional safety is what your body feels when love is close. It's what your nervous system learns about what happens when you tell the truth. It's what your heart expects when you show a tender part of yourself and wait to see what comes next.

You can love someone deeply and still feel unsafe with them. You can be loyal and committed and still feel like you're bracing. You can share a home and a life and still feel like you have to manage the emotional weather.

If that's been your experience, you're not being "too sensitive." Your system is giving you data.

What Emotional Safety Actually Feels Like

Emotional safety feels like exhaling. It feels like you can approach your partner without rehearsing the conversation beforehand. It feels like you can be disappointed without being punished. It feels like you can say "That hurt" without the entire relationship turning into a courtroom.

You also feel like your feelings aren't treated as an inconvenience. You don't have to turn your needs into something "reasonable enough" to deserve attention. You don't have to earn softness by being perfect.

Safety doesn't mean there's never conflict. Safety means conflict doesn't become an emotional threat. You can disagree without being disrespectful. You can repair without humiliating. You can be honest without being afraid of retaliation.

This matters because your nervous system doesn't separate "relationship stress" from the rest of your life. If love is unpredictable, your body pays the price all day. If home feels tense, you don't truly rest. You might sleep, but you don't restore.

Why Strong People Miss This At First

If you've been strong for a long time, you've probably learned to adapt. You read tone quickly. You track energy. You sense what's coming before it fully arrives. You adjust to keep things stable.

That's not a weakness. That's intelligence. That's a system that learned how to survive.

In unstable environments, emotional vigilance becomes a skill. You learn how to become useful. You learn how to bring value. You learn how to stabilize the room. You become the reliable one, the capable one, the one who can "handle it."

The downside is subtle. If usefulness kept you safe, you may start believing that safety is something you create through effort. You may not even notice you're doing it. You just show up ready.

So when you enter relationships, you might default to performance without meaning to. You might carry the emotional labor because you're good at it. You might manage the climate because you can.

Then one day, you realize you're tired in a way that sleep can't fix. You're not tired because you don't love your partner. You're tired because your body has been bracing inside love.

142

That's the moment emotional safety becomes more than a concept. It becomes a need you can finally name.

Safety isn't something you demand. It's something you build.

A lot of people think safety is something you request, like you would a product. "Be safe." "Be kind." "Be gentle." Those requests matter, but they aren't the full picture.

Safety is built through repeated experiences. It's built in the small moments where someone proves you don't have to protect yourself from them.

It's built in tone. In timing. In the way a person responds when they're stressed and whether they can stay respectful when they're disappointed.

Safety is built into the moments that don't look dramatic. The text that says "I hear you." The pause before reacting. The apology without excuses. The willingness to come back and repair instead of staying cold.

It's also built into what doesn't happen. No mocking. No eye rolling. No sarcasm disguised as "jokes." No silent punishment. No emotional disappearing acts.

If you've lived with inconsistency, you know how loud those absences can feel. Safety starts showing up when your body stops scanning for what it needs to survive the interaction.

Emotional Safety Is Being Trustworthy With Someone's Nervous System

When you love someone, you're not just interacting with their personality; you're interacting with them. You're interacting with their nervous system patterns. Their past. Their triggers. Their stress thresholds. Their hope.

This doesn't mean you become responsible for their healing. It means you treat their tenderness with care. You

143

don't turn their vulnerability into ammunition. You don't punish them for having feelings. You don't disappear when things get uncomfortable.

You offer the same care to yourself, too. Emotional safety includes being trustworthy with your nervous system. Because here's the truth: you can't build safety with someone else if your internal world is constantly unsafe.

The Hidden Threats That Destroy Safety Quietly

People sometimes imagine "unsafe relationships" as only the extreme cases. However, emotional safety can also erode in ordinary households, not through cruelty but through establishing patterns.

Here are a few common ones:

- Defensiveness that turns everything into an argument.
- You bring up a concern, and suddenly you're explaining why you're allowed to feel what you feel.
- Tone that feels punishing.
- Words said might be "fine," but the energy feels sharp enough that your body pulls back.
- Silence used as power.
- Not "I need space," but "I'm going to make you suffer until you come back softer."
- Repair that never happens.
- The conflict ends because everyone gets tired, not because anyone truly returns.
- Dismissal disguised as logic.
- You're told you're "overreacting" when you're naming something important.

144

These patterns don't always mean someone is a bad person. They often mean they're unskilled, unhealed, or overwhelmed. But the impact still matters. If safety is inconsistent, intimacy becomes harder to maintain.

And if you're the one who keeps trying to hold everything together, your body will eventually start protesting.

When you're triggered, your body doesn't always care that you love each other. Your body cares whether you feel threatened. And if you feel threatened, your system goes into protection mode.

That can look like:

- Shutting down
- Escalating
- Getting sharp
- Being overly logical
- Walking away and not returning
- Trying to win the argument instead of protecting the connection

None of those responses automatically makes you "toxic." They make you human. The question is: What do you do after you notice?

You can build emotional safety when you and your partner start treating tension as a shared moment to handle rather than a battle to win. Safety grows when your default posture becomes "This is hard, but I'm still here." That posture changes everything.

Repair Is The Proof Of Safety

A lack of conflict doesn't define healthy relationships. They're defined by a reliable path back to each other.

Repair is what tells your nervous system, "You can be honest and still be safe." Repair is what prevents conflict from becoming residue. Repair is what keeps the relationship clean.

Without repair, even small disagreements accumulate. You start speaking less honestly because you don't want the consequences. You start withholding information because it's easier. You start managing the relationship instead of living in it.

Repair is not making a grand speech. It's often simple and clean:

"I didn't handle that well."
"I got sharp, and I'm sorry."
"I see how that landed."
"Can we reset?"
"I'm still committed. I want to come back."

Repair also includes changing behavior, not just saying words. Safety grows when someone adjusts, not when they apologize.

You don't need perfection to feel safe. You need consistency in responsibility. Safety requires work on yourself, not just relationship work. This part is personal. It might land.

If you struggle to sit with your own emotions, you may struggle to sit with someone else's emotions, too. If disappointment hijacks your body, you might become reactive. If fear lives beneath your anger, your tone might carry threat even when you "don't mean it that way."

This isn't about shame. It's about power. Self-awareness gives you options.

Emotional safety is built by people who can regulate themselves. Not perfectly. Just responsibly.

146

If you're used to being the stable one, you might not notice that your "stability" is sometimes shut down or your "clarity" sometimes comes out sharp when you're tired. Or that your "calmness" is sometimes avoidance.

Again, no shame. Just truth, which is what gives you a new choice.

The Difference Between Strong And Safe

You can be strong and still not feel safe. Strength is capacity. It's competence. It's conviction. It's being able to carry pressure, make decisions, and keep moving.

Safety is different. Safety is emotional trustworthiness. It's how your strength *lands* with the people closest to you. It's whether your partner can bring the tender parts of themself without bracing for impact or preparing for fallout. And if you've been praised for being strong your whole life, this can feel like a new lens at first. It's not an accusation. It's refinement. It's the upgrade that turns power into peace.

Safety isn't a weakness. It's strength with care. You don't have to become smaller to be safe. You can still be direct, firm, and clear, and be safe. The difference usually shows up in the way you carry yourself. Your tone. Your timing. Your posture. And your willingness to come back and repair when you miss each other.

How To Tell If Safety Is Missing

Most of the time, you can tell safety is missing by what your body starts doing before your mind even finishes a thought. Maybe you rehearse what you're going to say because you're trying to prevent a reaction. Maybe you edit your truth down to something softer so it won't "turn into a thing."

Maybe your chest tightens when your partner walks into the room, or you feel a little wave of relief when they leave, even though you love them. Maybe you keep the peace in the moment, then feel resentment later because your silence wasn't peace. It was self-protection.

Those signals don't automatically mean the relationship is over. They mean the emotional culture needs attention. And if reading this brings up tenderness, pause. This is deep work. It can stir grief. Grief for what you normalized. Grief for how long you told yourself you were "asking for too much" when you were asking for something basic. Safety isn't a luxury. Safety is the foundation that love sits on.

Why Emotional Safety Changes Intimacy

When safety is inconsistent, love can still exist. Affection can still exist. Loyalty can still exist. But intimacy often gets cautious. You start holding back without fully realizing it. You share less. You initiate less. You stop dreaming out loud. You stop asking for what you want because it feels like it might cost too much emotionally.

Over time, two people can become responsible roommates with a shared life, even while their hearts still care for each other.

Safety shifts that. Safety invites your full self back into the room. Tenderness becomes easier. Laughter comes back without effort. Conflict feels less like a threat and more like something you can work through. Safety doesn't remove tension, but it makes tension workable because you're no longer afraid of what honesty will trigger.

If You're The One Who Wants Safety More

Sometimes one person reads this and thinks, "Yes. This is exactly it." And the other person thinks, "This feels dramatic." That gap can feel discouraging. It can make you question yourself, like maybe you're too much, too deep, too sensitive, too intense. You aren't.

You may have a different threshold because of what your nervous system learned earlier in life or because you carry more emotional labor now. Or because you're ready for a healthier emotional culture than what you've settled for.

If you want more safety, you don't have to turn it into a diagnosis or a character critique. Name it as a desire. Clean. Clear. With care. Something like "I want our home to feel calmer emotionally." Or "I want to be able to tell you things without feeling scared of how it'll go." Or "I feel closest to you when repair happens quickly." Or "I want us to learn how to disagree without getting sharp."

That's not asking for perfection. That's asking for a better emotional culture. That's a mature request.

If You Realize You Haven't Been Safe

This can be hard to admit, especially if you love your partner and know you're not a bad person. But if you're noticing that your tone has gotten sharp, your silence has felt punishing, your defensiveness has been heavy, or your repair has been slow, you don't have to spiral into shame. Shame makes people hide. Responsibility makes people heal.

Responsibility sounds like owning the impact without arguing the intent. It sounds like: "I see it. I get why that felt unsafe. I want to do better. I'm going to practice pausing." The truth is, safety grows faster than people expect when responsibility becomes the norm, not the exception.

Emotional Safety And Wholeness Go Together

This is where the "two wholes" premise becomes practical. If you're using the relationship to stabilize your identity, achieving safety will be harder. Conflict will feel like a threat. Feedback will feel like rejection. Distance will feel like danger. You'll reach for control, reassurance, or defensiveness because your nervous system is trying to protect your worth.

But when you're emotionally rooted in yourself, you can stay steadier in the midst of tension. You can hear something difficult without collapsing. You can express disappointment without attacking. You can ask for reassurance without demanding it, like proof that you matter.

Wholeness doesn't remove your need for love; it removes your panic around love. And that's the ground that emotional safety is built on.

Closing Reflection

Emotional safety is the quiet difference between love you survive and love you can breathe inside. If you've been bracing in relationships, it doesn't mean you're broken. It means your system learned to protect you. You can honor that part of you without letting it stay in charge forever.

Safety is built when you and your partner practice emotional responsibility in the small moments. Tone matters. Repair matters. The ability to pause matters. The willingness to come back matters.

In the next chapter, you'll take that safety and put structure around it through boundaries. Not boundaries that harden you, but boundaries that protect what's tender so that your love doesn't have to keep recovering.

The Practice

Use this when a conversation is starting to feel tense, or you feel yourself bracing.

Step 1: Name what's happening without blame

Try one line:

"I'm feeling a little flooded."

"I'm starting to get defensive."

"I want to stay connected, and I can feel myself tensing."

Keep it simple. No speeches.

Step 2: Slow your body down

Take three breaths with a longer exhale. If you can, drop your shoulders. Relax your jaw. Unclench your hands.

Step 3: Choose one safety move

Pick one:

Clarify: "Can you tell me what you mean by that?"

Reflect: "What I'm hearing is…"

Repair quickly: "That came out more sharply than I meant. Let me try again."

Pause with a return: "I need ten minutes to regulate, then I'm coming back."

The key is that last part: if you pause, return.

Step 4: End with a connection line
This matters more than people think:
"I'm on your side."
"I care about us."
"I want this to feel safe for both of us."

If you're practicing this while single, you can do the same reset internally. Name what you're feeling, regulate, choose one grounding action, and remind yourself, "I'm safe with me."

Journal Prompts

Answer what stands out. Skip what doesn't. Stay honest.

1. Where do I feel emotionally safest, and what makes me feel that way?
2. What tones or behaviors make me brace even if the words are "fine"?
3. When I feel misunderstood, do I shut down, get sharp, overexplain, or go silent?
4. What does repair look like in my relationships right now?
5. What kind of repair culture do I want, and what would make it realistic?
6. If I could ask for emotional safety in one clean sentence, what would I say?

Wholeness Check-In

Look at emotional safety through the pillars.

- Mentally and emotionally: Do I regulate before I respond, or do I let my first impulse lead?
- Spiritually: Do my values shape my tone, or do stress and pride take over?
- Physically: What does my body do when tension rises, and what helps it settle?
- Socially: Do my closest relationships feel like refuge, or do they require constant bracing?

One small shift that would strengthen my love in wholeness:

____

____

____

____

____

Empowering Declaration

I am allowed to want emotional safety. I don't have to earn tenderness by being perfect. I choose regulation over reaction and repair over pride. I build relationships in which truth can be spoken, and I can feel safe to love.

156

Chapter 13
Boundaries That Protect the Heart

Boundaries can get a bad reputation. People hear the word and imagine conflict, distance, or coldness. They automatically picture a wall or a shutdown. They picture someone saying, "This is who I am, deal with it," and calling that maturity.

That's not the kind of boundary work this chapter is about. The boundaries that can change your life aren't usually dramatic. They're quiet and consistent. They're the simple choices that protect your peace before you feel desperate. They're the standards that keep love from turning into confusion, resentment, or continual emotional recovery.

If you've spent years being capable, reliable, and strong, boundaries may sound like something you "already do." You speak up. You're direct. You don't disappear. You don't pretend.

And still, you might feel overextended. You might feel emotionally drained. You might feel like life is always asking for more access than you have.

That's a boundary signal. Not because you're weak. Because you're human.

What Boundaries Really Are

A boundary is not a threat. It's a definition. It's how you name what protects your emotional health, your time, your body, and your relationships. It's how you decide what kind of energy you will participate in and what kind of energy you will step away from.

Boundaries don't exist only because people can harm each other. They exist because life is demanding, because love can get messy, and because your nervous system needs clarity.

A healthy boundary says, "This is what allows me to stay connected without losing myself." That matters in every relationship, but it matters even more when you love hard, lead hard, and carry a lot. If you're the type of person who can push through, people will gladly let you. If you're the type of person who can hold everything, life will happily pile it on.

So boundaries become a form of stewardship. Not pride. Not attitude. Stewardship.

Why Strong People Still Struggle With Boundaries

You can be confident and still struggle with boundaries. You can be direct and still overextend. You can be emotionally mature and still get pulled into patterns that drain you. Here's why.

If you learned early that stability came from you, boundaries can feel unnecessary until your body forces the issue. You might not feel "afraid" to say no. You might feel the responsibility to say yes.

Responsibility can be beautiful. It can also be a trap. It can quietly turn into a life where you're always available, always accommodating, always "fine," even when something inside you is begging for relief.

For high-functioning people, boundary failure doesn't always look like people pleasing. It can look like leadership mode that you never turn off. It can look like continual fixing. It can look like being the emotional adult in every room.

It can also look like subtle resentment you don't want to admit you have. Not because you dislike people, but because you're tired of being the one who holds everything together.

Boundaries aren't proof that you're hard to love. They're proof that you're learning to love yourself with the same consistency you offer everyone else.

The Difference Between Clarity And Protection

Clarity is telling the truth. Protection is building a life where the truth can be sustained. You might be great at clarity. You might name misalignment quickly. You might speak up when something feels off. You might not tolerate disrespect. And still, you might be living in a constant state of recovery. You might keep saying yes to things that don't fit. You might keep absorbing emotional weight because you're the "steady one." You might keep letting other people's urgency become your emergency.

That's where boundaries show up as a next level of wholeness. This isn't because you don't know what you believe, but because you're learning how to protect what you believe. Setting a boundary is the way to stop rebuilding yourself every week.

Boundaries Aren't The Opposite Of Love

Many people fear that boundaries will make them feel selfish, unkind, unavailable, or "too much." But boundaries don't kill love. They keep love clean.

They prevent resentment from taking over. They prevent exhaustion from becoming your baseline. They prevent you from living as a version of yourself that is always braced.

In healthy relationships, boundaries don't create distance. They create safety and predictability. They create respect. They create emotional room to breathe.

If you want closeness that lasts, boundaries are part of the structure. Without structure, even good love can collapse under confusion.

The Boundary You Need Most Is Usually The One You Avoid

Most people don't avoid boundaries because they're weak. They avoid boundaries because of what boundaries force them to face.

A boundary forces you to face the truth that you can't do everything. A boundary forces you to face the truth that some people benefit from your overextension. A boundary forces you to face the truth that your peace has a cost, and you're the one paying it.

Sometimes the hardest boundary to set is not with another person. It's with your own patterns.

- The pattern of overfunctioning.
- The pattern of saying yes too fast.
- The pattern of giving access before trust is earned.
- The pattern of staying in a conversation after it becomes unsafe.
- The pattern of carrying more than your share because you can.

That last one is big. Just because you can carry it does not mean you should.

Boundaries In Love Look Like Agreements, Not Ultimatums

In romantic relationships, boundaries can sound intimidating because they get confused with control. People picture one partner "laying down the law."

That's not the goal.

A healthy relationship boundary often sounds like a shared agreement. It sounds like two people protecting what they value.

It can look like agreeing to:

- Pause a conversation when the tone gets sharp
- Return and repair, not disappear
- Not bring private conflict into public spaces
- Value rest as part of the relationship's health
- Prioritize emotional safety more than winning

You're not trying to dominate your partner. You're trying to protect the emotional climate of your home. If you care about intimacy, boundaries belong in the relationship. They don't exist as punishment but as protection.

The Quiet Ways You Abandon Yourself

Self-abandonment doesn't always look like shrinking. Sometimes it looks like staying in "strong mode" even when you're breaking inside.

You might abandon yourself when you keep explaining after you've already been clear. You might abandon yourself when you keep trying to "earn" respect through overdelivering or when you keep tolerating small acts of disrespect because "it isn't that bad."

161

You might abandon yourself when you ignore your body and keep pushing through fatigue. When you keep postponing meeting your needs because other people "have it worse." That logic sounds noble. It's also how people get depleted. Your needs don't have to be dramatic to be real. Boundaries are the way to stop negotiating with your own humanity.

How To Set Boundaries Without Getting Cold

Some people set boundaries like they slam a door: They get the job done, but damage closeness. It creates fear. It creates defensiveness.

If you want boundaries that protect the heart, the tone matters. The timing matters. The words matter.

A clean boundary is usually:

- Clear
- Brief
- Calm
- Consistent

It doesn't come with a long apology. It doesn't come with a lecture. It doesn't come with a list of reasons that invite debate. It's a simple definition.

You're not asking for permission to protect your peace. You're naming what protects it.

Here are a few examples that keep warmth without your losing strength:

"I can't take this on right now."

"I'm available for twenty minutes."

"I'm not discussing this if the tone stays sharp."

"I need a reset. I'm coming back in an hour."

"I'm not comfortable with that."

162

"I'm open to talking about it when we're both calmer."

That's not harsh. That's leadership.

Why Boundaries Feel Uncomfortable At First

If your nervous system learned that love is earned through contribution, boundaries can feel like risk. You might feel guilt. You might feel anxiety. You might feel like you're disappointing people.

That discomfort doesn't mean the boundary is wrong. It often means the boundary is new. Your body is adjusting to a different rule: "I can be loved without being endlessly available." That's a big shift. It takes repetition.

Sometimes your first attempt at setting a boundary feels clumsy. Sometimes your words sound too sharp. Sometimes you overexplain. That's okay. You're learning a new language. The goal isn't to do it perfectly. The goal is to stop abandoning yourself.

The Boundary That Protects You From Resentment

Resentment often grows when you say yes while hoping someone notices the cost. It grows when you keep giving while quietly wishing someone would stop asking. It grows when you keep carrying while telling yourself you're "fine."

Resentment is usually a delayed boundary. If you want less resentment, practice attaining greater clarity earlier. Earlier clarity doesn't require a big talk. It requires a small pause.

A pause before you agree.

A pause before you volunteer.

A pause before you take on responsibility that isn't yours.

That pause is setting a boundary. It's you checking in with yourself before you hand over your precious time, energy, or emotional labor.

Boundaries That Protect Your Time And Attention

Time boundaries are often the most practical place to start. They're also the most revealing. If you constantly feel behind, distracted, and overstimulated, your time boundaries might be weak. Not because you're irresponsible, but because life is loud.

Time boundaries can look like:

- Deciding when you're finished working
- Ending phone calls that turn into emotional dumping
- Limiting social plans that drain you
- Creating protected time for rest, prayer, or reflection
- Choosing one priority instead of fifteen

Time boundaries aren't selfish. They're the way you remain yourself. If you're always rushed, you won't have the inner space to live whole. You'll live reactively.

Your life can be full without being frantic. Boundaries are part of the way you get there.

Boundaries That Protect Your Emotional Peace

Emotional boundaries are not about shutting people out. They're about staying grounded in yourself, even when someone else is expressing emotion.

They look like:

- Not absorbing someone else's panic

164

- Not taking responsibility for someone else's mood
- Not staying in conversations that become disrespectful
- Not trying to rescue people from consequences they need to face

Emotional boundaries also include what you allow yourself to keep revisiting. If you replay the same conflict in your head all day, you might need an internal boundary.

A boundary with rumination.

A boundary with self-criticism.

A boundary with "I should've said it differently" loops.

You can take responsibility without punishing yourself.

Relationship Boundaries That Protect Intimacy

In a relationship, boundaries can feel sensitive because closeness is the point. You don't want to create distance. Boundaries don't always create distance. Sometimes distance is created by the absence of boundaries.

When one partner is taking on too much, intimacy gets strained. When one partner carries everything, tenderness fades. When resentment builds, connection gets cautious.

Boundaries protect intimacy by preventing those patterns from becoming normal. Here are a few relationship boundaries that protect the heart:

"Tone matters here."

You can agree that truth is welcome, but disrespect isn't. You can decide that you will not speak to each other in ways you wouldn't speak to a coworker.

This isn't about being formal. It's about being safe.

"We pause before we punish."

If either of you needs a break, you take a break. But you don't disappear. You don't withdraw as a weapon. You pause and return.

"We repair before we move on."

You can go to bed without solving everything. But you don't normalize coldness. You don't let distance become comfort.

Repair can be small. It can be a touch. A calm apology. A simple reset.

"We protect the relationship from outside interference."

That means certain conflicts stay private. It means you don't build alliances against each other. It means you don't vent in ways that damage respect.

"Rest is part of our culture."

If you want a healthy relationship, you protect the people in it. Exhaustion changes tone. It changes patience. It changes desire.

Rest is not indulgence. It's maintenance.

When Boundaries Expose A Hard Truth

Sometimes you set a boundary, and the response tells you something important. A healthy person might not love your boundary, but they respect it. They adjust. They ask questions with curiosity. They don't punish you.

An unsafe person might mock it. Push it. Test it. Make you feel guilty. Call you selfish. Make it about their comfort. That moment can be clarifying because it shows you what kind of emotional culture exists right then.

If your boundaries consistently create backlash, you may be trying to build wholeness in an environment that benefits from your depletion. That's hard. It's also important information.

You can't do relationship work alone. Boundaries reveal whether respect is mutual. It's tempting to keep

166

explaining your boundary until someone agrees it's "reasonable." That rarely works. It often drains you more.

A boundary doesn't need agreement to be valid. It needs consistency. Consistency is what teaches people how to treat you. It also teaches your nervous system to trust yourself.

If you keep breaking your own boundaries, you teach your body that your needs aren't safe even with you. That's a painful pattern, but you can change it.

Start small. Keep it real. Keep it steady.

Closing Reflection

Boundaries aren't about becoming difficult. They're about becoming free.

When boundaries come from identity, they don't harden you. They protect what's tender so you don't have to keep rebuilding yourself every week. They help you stay openhearted without staying overextended.

If you've lived as the capable one for a long time, boundaries may feel like a shift in your definition of love. You may be used to proving your care through carrying. You may be used to staying available even when you're drained.

That version of you got a lot done. It also paid a price.

This chapter is an invitation to embrace a new kind of strength. Not strength that carries everything. Strength that protects what matters most. Your peace. Your body. Your emotional clarity. Your relationships.

In the next chapter, we'll talk about taking those boundaries and applying them to communication. Not scripts. Not techniques. A relational climate that makes your connections easier to build and easier to repair.

The Practice

Use this when you feel yourself about to say yes out of pressure, guilt, or habit.

Step 1: Pause long enough to check in
Before you answer, ask yourself:
"Do I have the capacity for this?"
"If I say yes, what am I saying no to?"
"Will I resent this later?"
If the pause feels awkward, that's okay. It's still progress.

Step 2: Choose your boundary type

Pick one.

- Time boundary
  - "I'm available for 20 minutes."
  - "I can do it but not today."
- Emotional boundary
  - "I'm not able to hold this right now."
  - "I can listen, but I'm not in a position to problem-solve."
- Respect boundary
  - "I'm open to this conversation but not with that tone."
  - "I'm going to step away if this becomes disrespectful."
- Responsibility boundary
  - "That's not mine to carry."
  - "I trust you to handle that."

Step 3: Deliver it in one or two sentences
Keep it short. Keep it calm. No long backstory.
Clarity is kindness.

Step 4: Follow through once
If you set the boundary and then break it immediately, your nervous system gets more confused. If possible, follow through one time.
One clean follow-through teaches your body "I mean it."

Step 5: Repair if you need to
If it came out too sharp, you can repair without undoing the boundary:
"My tone was tense. The boundary still stands."
"Let me say that again more clearly."
That's emotionally mature.

Journal Prompts

Answer what stands out. Skip what doesn't. Stay honest.

1. Where do I feel the most drained right now and what pattern is underneath it?
2. What do I consistently tolerate that costs me peace?
3. Where do I say yes too fast, then regret it later?
4. If I trusted that my peace was worth protecting, what would I change this month?
5. What boundary feels scary to set, and what am I afraid might happen if I set it?
6. Where do I need a boundary with myself (rumination, overworking, overexplaining, overgiving)?

Wholeness Check-In

Check the pillars through the lens of boundaries.

- Mentally and emotionally: Are you protecting your bandwidth or living in constant recovery?
- Spiritually: Are you creating space for grounding practices or treating them as optional?
- Physically: Are you respecting your limits or overriding them with duty?
- Socially: Do your relationships reinforce wholeness or quietly require self-abandonment?

Pick the pillar with the most need. Choose one boundary that supports it.

____

____

____

____

Empowering Declaration

My peace is worth protecting. I don't need burnout to justify a boundary. I choose clarity without coldness and strength without self-abandonment. I build relationships that respect my humanity. I protect what's tender so love can stay open and safe.

Chapter 14
Communication That Builds Connection

Communication is talked about as if it's a skill you either have or you don't. Some people are "just good at it" and the rest of us are stuck trying to learn scripts that feel awkward and fake. But communication isn't a personality trait. It's a relationship climate.

That relationship climate is highlighted by what your tone does to the room or what your timing does to your partner's nervous system. It's what your words invite or shut down. This reflects the difference between being heard and being handled.

If you've spent most of your life being competent, decisive, and emotionally steady for other people, your communication style probably works well in the world. At work, clarity gets rewarded. Being direct saves time and being composed earns trust.

But love isn't a project plan and your partner isn't a stakeholder in a meeting. Connection asks for something different. It requires a different posture, not less truth, clarity or strength.

This chapter is about how to keep your voice without losing your softness. How to tell the truth without creating fear. How to be direct without becoming sharp. How to speak in a way that protects emotional safety while still honoring what's real.

If you've ever walked away from a conversation thinking, "That wasn't what I meant" or "Why did that turn into a whole thing?" this is for you.

174

Communication Is Never Just Information

Most conflict isn't about the surface issue. It's about what the issue means.

Someone's late arrival can mean "I'm not important." A forgotten detail can mean "I'm not seen." A short tone can mean "I'm a burden." Silence can mean "I'm alone."

Even when those meanings aren't true, they can feel true in the body. And once the body feels threatened, communication stops being a calm exchange. It becomes a fight for safety.

That's why you can say something perfectly reasonable and still get a reaction that feels confusing. Your partner isn't only hearing your words. They're feeling your energy. They're hearing your tone. They're tracking whether you seem open or defensive, curious or closed, safe or unsafe. And you're doing the same.

So the goal isn't "perfect wording." The goal is a relationship culture in which you can both speak honestly without bracing for damage.

When Communication Turns Into Correction

Many strong people aren't afraid to communicate. You'll talk. You'll address it. You'll name what's off. The issue usually isn't avoidance. It's what happens in the seconds after you notice something's wrong.

When you process fast, you want the conversation to move fast. When you care deeply, your system ramps up fast. And when you're used to being the one who keeps things steady, you can slide into "fix-it" mode without realizing you've stopped connecting. You're making the point. You're trying to land the truth. You're trying to get it handled. But your partner isn't receiving "clarity." They're receiving pressure.

That's how communication turns into correction without you ever intending it. You bring up something that matters, and your partner feels evaluated. They get guarded. You feel dismissed. Then you both start defending, not because either of you is a bad person, but because the conversation stopped being about understanding and became a verdict.

The shift isn't about not being direct. It's about leading with your inner reality, not your conclusion. There's a huge difference between "Here's what you did wrong" and "Here's what happened inside me when that happened." You can still talk about behavior. You don't start with a label. You start with your experience. That's not soft in a weak way. That's strong in a connecting way. It's the kind of strength that doesn't demand a win to feel safe.

And if you've been high functioning for a long time, this may feel like an adjustment because being correct has worked for you. It's gotten you results. It's protected you. It's kept things from falling apart. But love doesn't need you to be right. Love needs you to be reachable.

Truth That Lands And Tenderness That Holds

Communication breakdowns live in one of two extremes. One side is truth with an edge, where you're saying the right thing, but it lands like a slap. The other side is tenderness without clarity, where you're being nice but leaving the real issue untouched. Both create distance. One makes your partner brace. The other makes them confused. And the longer either one becomes the default, the more honesty starts feeling risky.

Truth that lands is still truth, but it's delivered like you want connection more than control. Tenderness that holds is still tenderness, but it doesn't require you to shrink your

176

needs into something more convenient. The sweet spot is when your truth is clear enough to be useful and your tone is safe enough to be received.

This is where timing matters more than most of us want it to. You can be completely right and still lose the moment because your nervous system is ahead of your maturity. If either of you is depleted, distracted, hungry, rushing, or already flooded, the conversation will rarely go where you want it to go. If you're the kind of person who likes to address things immediately, that can feel frustrating because you don't want it lingering. You want it clean. You want it resolved. But immediate isn't always effective, and delaying a conversation isn't avoidance when the goal is to have it well.

What changes everything is when you can hold the relationship steady while you hold the truth steady. You can say in your own voice, "This matters to me, and I don't want to be messy." That one sentence protects both your point and your bond. That's skill. That's love that's being built, not just felt.

And tone is the door your truth walks through. You don't have to talk like a therapist. You don't have to exhibit gentleness. You have to make sure your delivery matches your goal. If your goal is connection, your tone has to feel like connection. Otherwise, your words can be right, but your partner will still hear danger.

Safety Is What Your Body Is Listening For

Under most conflict is a quieter question that rarely gets spoken out loud: Are we safe right now? Not physically. Relationally. Safe to be honest. Safe to be disappointed. Safe to say "that hurt" without it turning into a war. When people don't feel safe, they protect themselves. Some shut down. Some get loud. Some turn cold. Some get sarcastic. Some get overly logical. Those reactions aren't always character flaws. Most of the time, they're protection strategies.

And you have them, too.

This is why your body matters in communication. If your shoulders are tight, your jaw is clenched, your breath is shallow, and your voice is clipped, your partner feels it even if your words are technically perfect. Your nervous system is speaking before you do. And if your nervous system learned early that tension equals danger, you might not notice how quickly you escalate internally, even if you're not yelling.

One of the most mature communication moves is learning to regulate yourself in the conversation rather than trying to win it. That might look like pausing long enough to let your body soften before you respond. It might look like lowering your voice even when you feel justified. It might look like unclenching your hands and relaxing your posture so that your partner's body can stop preparing for impact. Small physical shifts change the emotional climate faster than long explanations ever will.

This is also where listening becomes a real skill. Listening isn't waiting for your turn to talk. It's staying open long enough to understand. If you grew up needing to protect yourself emotionally, listening can feel like vulnerability. It can feel like giving up power. So you interrupt. You correct. You explain. You defend. That makes sense. It's protection. But connection asks for a different move: respect first, perspective second.

When a person feels respected, they stop fighting. They start talking because the room got safer

The Reset That Keeps Love Becoming

The couples who stay close aren't the ones who never get tired or never miss each other. They're the ones who know how to return. They don't let tension sit for days to protect their pride. They don't treat repair like a special event that requires a perfect mood. They come back. They clean it up. They reset the atmosphere before it becomes the relationship's identity.

That's why "I miss you" can be one of the most powerful things you say in long-term love. Not as drama. Not as criticism. As intimacy. It tells the truth without blaming. It names need without making it a demand. It invites reconnection without starting a fight. And if you're the kind of person who prides yourself on being strong, it might feel more vulnerable than it should. That's the point. A relationship can't become a sanctuary if no one ever admits they want closeness.

If you keep having the same argument, it's rarely about the topic. It's about the meaning under the topic. It's about what the moment represents - being unseen and being unappreciated and feeling alone in responsibility and feeling disrespected in tone. Feeling like repair never happens. When you name that layer, the conversation stops looping because you're finally talking about what's actually hurting.

And I want to say this plainly, because it matters: communication doesn't require you to become a different person. If you're naturally direct, you don't have to become someone who talks in circles. If you're naturally logical, you don't have to become overly emotional. You need range. Range means you can be honest without being harsh, you can pause without avoiding, you can listen without collapsing, and you can repair without pride.

That range is maturity. It's not about losing your edge. It's about using your strength to build closeness rather than fear. And if your heart is quietly saying, "I just want it to feel easier," that's not weakness. That's wisdom. Easier doesn't mean no hard conversations. Easier means you can be honest and still feel close afterward. Easier means home feels like a place you can exhale, not a place you have to manage.

That kind of love isn't fantasy. It's built. And it's built by the people who keep choosing the reset.

Closing Reflection

Communication that builds connection isn't about saying the perfect thing. It's about building an emotional culture in which truth is safe.

You don't have to be less direct to be more loving. You don't have to dilute your standards. You don't have to become someone else. You get to become a more connected version of yourself.

This version of you can speak truth without turning it into a weapon. You can listen without treating understanding as surrender and stay calm enough to keep the conversation from becoming a contest.

When communication gets healthier, everything gets lighter. Conflict becomes less scary. Repair becomes more normal. Intimacy becomes easier to sustain.

In the next chapter, we'll take this skill and apply it to something deeper: alignment in a relationship. Not just loyalty or commitment. The shared direction and emotional agreements that make love feel like a team, not a tug-of-war.

The Practice

This is a simple way to talk about something real without triggering a full spiral.

Step 1: Set the tone in one sentence

Pick one:

"I want to talk about something small before it becomes something big."

"I'm not mad. I just want us to feel close."

"This matters to me, and I want to do it gently."

Step 2: Use the clarity formula (event, meaning, request)

Keep it short.

Event: "When _______ happened…"

Meaning: "I felt _______ / I started telling myself _______."

Request: "Could we ______ going forward?"

Step 3: Ask one question that invites your partner in
"How did you experience it?"
"Did you mean it that way?"
"What was going on for you?"

Step 4: Validate before you explain
Try:
"That makes sense."
"I can see how you got there."
"I understand why that hit you."
Then share your perspective.

Step 5: End with a small reconnection move
Pick one:
a hug
a hand squeeze
"I'm glad we talked."
"I'm on your side."
"Thank you for hearing me."

This practice isn't about being overly formal. It's about protecting the bond while telling the truth.

Journal Prompts

Answer what stands out. Skip what doesn't. Stay honest.

1. When I feel misunderstood, what do I usually do: explain more forcefully, get sharper, shut down, or avoid?
2. What tones or behaviors make me brace immediately?
3. Where do I confuse intensity with clarity?
4. What does "same team" sound like when I'm frustrated?
5. What's one topic I keep postponing because I'm afraid it will spiral?
6. What would it look like to repair faster in my closest relationships?

Wholeness Check-In

Before your next difficult conversation, check your pillars.

- Mentally and emotionally: Am I regulated enough to speak with care, or am I flooded?
- Spiritually: Am I grounded enough to value connection over ego?
- Physically: Am I tired, hungry, tense, or overstimulated right now?
- Socially: Do I have support and healthy outlets, or am I trying to carry everything alone?

One small shift that would strengthen my love in wholeness:

____

____

____

____

____

Empowering Declaration

I communicate with truth and tenderness. I don't need sharpness to be clear. I don't avoid hard conversations, and I don't turn them into battles. I choose regulation over reaction and connection over control. My voice builds safety and my love stays honest.

Chapter 15
The Alignment of Your Relationship

There's a version of a relationship that looks solid from the outside even though something inside you feels quietly off. Nothing is "wrong" in the dramatic sense. You're loyal. You're committed. You show up. Life keeps moving. The bills get paid. The calendar stays full. You still function as a team.

And yet, you may feel a low-grade ache that's hard to explain without sounding ungrateful. It isn't always a lack of love. Sometimes it's a lack of alignment.

Love is the reason you try. Alignment is what helps love last without costing you your peace.

If you've ever wondered why a relationship can feel stable and still feel heavy, this chapter will make sense. It's about the difference between doing life together and building a life together on purpose. It's about the shift from survival teamwork to intentional partnership. And it's about a truth many strong people don't name until they're exhausted: a relationship can be loyal and still be misaligned.

What Alignment Actually Feels Like

Alignment isn't sameness. It's not constant agreement, and it's not a relationship in which you never have tension. It's deeper than shared interests, shared routines, and even shared values on paper.

Alignment is when two people are headed in the same direction and share the same emotional standards for the ways they treat each other along the way. It's the quiet agreement that when life gets hard, you don't turn on each other. You turn toward each other. The relationship stays protected even when the mood isn't great and the day has been long.

At its simplest, alignment answers one question with consistent behavior, not just words: when pressure hits, do we still move like the same team?

Because lots of couples *say* they're a team. Alignment is when you can feel it in the ways you speak, repair, handle stress, and come back after hard moments. It's when your nervous system learns it doesn't have to brace inside love.

When A Relationship Runs On Management

A lot of relationships run on management. Not because people don't care, but because life is real. You manage logistics, schedules, kids, work, family, money, meals, appointments, and all the invisible decisions that keep a household functioning. You keep things moving. You solve problems quickly. You stay on top of what matters.

Management can keep a household stable. But management by itself can't keep a relationship nourished.

When a relationship becomes mostly management, conversations start sounding like coordination. You talk about tasks more than hearts. You solve problems more than you share inner worlds. You get efficient, and efficiency quietly starts replacing closeness.

What makes this tricky is that it doesn't always feel like a crisis. It can feel like adulthood. It can feel like maturity. It can even feel like success, especially if you've survived harder seasons and you're grateful things aren't falling apart.

But over time, management without alignment creates an emotional distance that's hard to name because everything is still "working." And if you're capable, you

188

can stay in that mode a long time. You can keep functioning. You can keep showing up. You can keep making it all look fine.

Alignment is what brings life back into the relationship. Not drama. Not chaos. Life. It creates a culture in which you aren't just partners in responsibility, you're partners in emotional safety, repair, and shared direction.

Why Misalignment Hides Inside "Fine"

Misalignment doesn't always show up as fighting. Sometimes it hides inside "fine."

You're not arguing. You're not leaving. You're not making threats. You're not blowing things up. You're just tired. Busy. Focused. Handling what needs handling. And because you're strong, you can function a long time without naming what you miss.

If you've lived in survival mode before, "fine" can feel familiar. It can feel safe. It can even feel like success.

But "fine" can also be a quiet form of disconnection. The kind that doesn't hurt all at once. It wears things down slowly, through postponed conversations, unspoken needs, and a shared assumption that closeness will return when life slows down.

Most of the time, life doesn't slow down. So alignment becomes a choice, not a phase you wait for.

And here's something else many couples don't realize until later: storms don't always reveal misalignment the way calm seasons do. In a storm, adrenaline bonds you. Pressure forces teamwork. You're cooperating because you have to. That can feel like closeness because you're constantly engaged.

But when things calm down, the deeper questions rise. Do we know how to connect when we're not managing a crisis? Do we know how to enjoy each other, not just depend on each other? Do we know how to be emotionally close without pressure forcing us into the same lane?

If calm makes you feel awkward, distant, or restless, it doesn't mean your relationship is broken. It may mean your relationship is ready for alignment at a deeper level.

Shared Ownership, Not One Person Carrying The Emotional Weight

One of the clearest signs of misalignment is when one partner becomes the emotional architect of the relationship. Not on purpose. Not because they're controlling. Usually because they care, and because they can feel what's shifting long before it becomes obvious.

That person initiates the hard conversations. They name the tension. They push for repair. They track the emotional climate. They keep the connection alive. The other partner may still be loyal, still loving, still present in many ways, but the emotional responsibility isn't shared.

Over time, that creates fatigue that sleep doesn't fix. The fatigue of feeling like you're the only one paying attention to what the relationship needs to stay alive.

Alignment doesn't mean both people contribute equally every day. It means both people own the responsibility. It means you don't have to "earn" emotional safety by doing all the work. It means the relationship isn't held together by one person's awareness, while the other benefits from the stability without helping build it.

And this is where strong people can get trapped without realizing it. When you're highly capable, you can turn love into a role. You stabilize. You organize. You plan. You carry. You lead. Those are real strengths, but roles can become cages if you live in them too long.

190

You can forget how to be fully human inside love. Presence gets replaced by performance. Tenderness gets postponed. Your body stays braced, your tone stays firm, and your heart stays guarded, not because you don't love your partner, but because you've learned how to keep things stable by staying armored.

Alignment invites you out of the role and back into partnership. Strong without being armored. Honest without being harsh. Loved without constantly proving you're worth the effort.

Alignment Is The Rhythm Of Reintroducing Yourselves

One reason relationships lose closeness is simple, and most people don't realize it's happening until it already feels like distance: people change, and then they stop reintroducing themselves.

Life keeps moving. You keep evolving. And somewhere in the middle of growth, stress, responsibility, and routine, you start assuming your partner still knows you the way they did before.

But you're not the same person.

You've learned things. You've healed in places that used to hurt. You've gotten tired in new ways. You're carrying different responsibilities. Your boundaries have shifted because your capacity has shifted. Your nervous system responds differently because you've lived through different seasons. Your needs have changed, not because you're "too much," but because you're human and you're paying attention.

The problem isn't that you're evolving. The problem is that a relationship keeps operating off of an older version of you, while the current version quietly waits to be seen again.

If you don't update each other, you start loving an older version of your spouse and expecting your spouse to keep loving an older version of you. Alignment includes a rhythm of reintroduction. Not a dramatic reinvention, just a steady update that keeps intimacy current.

It can sound like "I'm realizing I need more quiet than I used to." Or "I miss feeling emotionally close." Or "I want us to have more fun again." Or even, "I'm learning how to ask for what I need."

Those aren't criticisms. They're intimacy. They're what it sounds like when love stays alive instead of just functional.

And "same team" becomes a daily practice here, not a slogan. It shows up most when you're irritated, tired, misunderstood, or disappointed. It's choosing curiosity over assumption, catching your tone before it turns sharp, taking breaks to regulate rather than escalate, and repairing without needing pride to feel safe first. You don't have to become soft in personality. You have to become safe in posture.

The Quiet Truth: Alignment Protects Your Future

Some people hear "alignment" and assume it means heavy talks, deep therapy language, or a relationship that feels like constant work. That's not the point. Alignment often makes love feel lighter because you stop guessing all the time. You stop carrying silent tension. You stop hoping closeness will "just come back."

A relationship can be loving and still need structure. Not rigid structure, just a few reliable rhythms that protect the connection the way routines protect health. Without that, love gets squeezed into whatever is left over after life happens, and whatever is left over is usually fatigue.

It doesn't require a dramatic sit-down where you solve everything. It starts with one honest sentence delivered with care.

Something like "I want us to feel closer again." Or "I miss us." Or "I don't want just to run the household. I want to stay emotionally connected." Or "I want our relationship to feel like a safe place to exhale."

Those statements don't attack. They invite.

If your relationship matters to you, alignment isn't optional because your relationship is living. Living things need care. They need attention. They need protection. They need repair. They need honest updates.

Alignment is how you keep love from becoming something you only remember from earlier times in the relationship. It's the way you build a relationship that can hold pressure without hardening. It's the way you stay connected as you keep becoming.

Closing Reflection

Love can carry you through a lot. But love without alignment can also cost you more than it should. It can quietly turn into endurance instead of intimacy, cooperation instead of closeness, management instead of partnership.

You don't have to wait for a crisis to recalibrate. You don't have to wait until resentment forces the conversation. You don't have to pretend you're fine just because you're functioning.

You can choose alignment now. You can decide that your relationship will not only look strong but also feel safe. You can decide that your relationship will not only survive pressure but also stay tender within it. And you can build shared agreements that protect your "we" without requiring either of you to shrink.

In the next chapter, we'll go deeper into what makes an aligned relationship sustainable over time: emotional partnership. Not just loyalty. Not just commitment. The daily choice to meet each other's inner world with care, even on ordinary days.

The Practice

This simple practice can help you create alignment without turning your relationship into a continual analysis.

Set a timer for 15 minutes once a week. Pick a time you're both usually calm.

Step 1: Start with one thing you each appreciate about the other. Keep it specific.

"I felt cared about when you ______."

"Thank you for ______."

Step 2: Name one way in which you feel aligned. This builds confidence and reduces defensiveness.

"I love how we handled _______."
"I feel like we're strong in _______."

Step 3: Name something you want to strengthen. Use soft honesty. No blame.
"I miss _______."
"I'd love more _______."
"I've been feeling _______ and I want us to stay close."

Step 4: Make one small agreement for the week. Choose something doable.
"Let's eat dinner together twice this week without phones."
"Let's do a 10-minute check-in after work."
"Let's reset after conflict by talking within 24 hours."
"Let's protect bedtime as a calm zone."

Step 5: End with a reconnection move It can be a hug, a hand squeeze, or a short prayer, if that fits for you.
A simple "I'm with you."
Keep it light enough that you'll actually repeat it.
Alignment is built through repetition, not intensity.

Journal Prompts

Answer what stands out. Skip what doesn't. Stay honest.

1. Where does my relationship feel aligned right now, and what makes it feel that way?
2. Where does it feel like we're managing life more than meeting each other emotionally?
3. When I feel disconnected, what do I usually do: withdraw, overdo, get sharp, or go quiet?
4. What does "same team" look like for me during tension?
5. What's one conversation I've been postponing because I don't want to create discomfort?
6. If my relationship felt like a safe place to exhale, what would be different in the daily rhythm?

Wholeness Check-In

Look at your pillars through the lens of alignment.

- Mentally and emotionally: Do you feel safe telling the truth and being human or do you edit yourself to keep the peace?
- Spiritually: Do you feel grounded in shared meaning, or do you feel like you're walking separate emotional paths?
- Physically: Does your rhythm protect rest, affection, and health or does your body get sacrificed to duty?
- Socially: Do outside relationships strengthen your relationship, or do they quietly pull you into stress, resentment, or distraction?

One small shift that would strengthen my love in wholeness:

____

____

____

____

Empowering Declaration

I choose alignment, not just endurance. My relationship is not on autopilot. It's a living partnership I protect with honesty, tenderness, and shared ownership. I stay on the same team. I repair quickly. I tell the truth with care. We are building a "we" that feels safe enough to keep becoming.

Chapter 16
Emotional Partnership

Many relationships have loyalty. They have history. They have shared responsibilities. They have proof. They have the kind of commitment that can hold life together when pressure hits.

Still, emotional closeness can thin out when life gets loud, and the relationship can start to run on autopilot.

If you've ever felt lonely in a stable relationship, you're not imagining it. You're not being dramatic. You're not "too much." You're picking up on something real. What you're craving is emotional partnership.

Emotional partnership is the part of love that says, "You don't have to carry your inner world alone." It's the daily decision to stay connected to what's happening under the surface, even when the surface is busy, productive, and functioning. It's one of the biggest differences between a relationship held together by transactions and one that feels like home.

What Emotional Partnership Actually Is

Emotional partnership isn't the same as romance. It isn't the same as chemistry, shared humor, or fun, even though those things matter and keep a relationship light. It also isn't the same as being a good co-parent, a reliable teammate, or a dependable provider.

Emotional partnership is simpler than people make it out to be and deeper than they expect. It's when two people stay engaged with each other's inner experiences. You don't just coordinate your lives; you stay connected to each other in your joint life. It's the pause when you notice your partner's energy has shifted. It's the second question you ask after the first answer is given a little too quickly. It's the choice to turn toward each other emotionally instead of just passing by each other in the same house.

And it's not only about what you offer. It's also about what you allow. Emotional partnership requires a willingness to be known without turning that willingness into performance, and without needing to clean up your feelings before they're "acceptable."

How Strong Couples Slide Into Efficiency

If you're highly capable, you can build a beautiful life. You know how to keep things moving. You can handle stress. You can lead through difficult seasons. You can make a plan and execute it. You can solve problems quickly.

Those strengths can also become a quiet barrier to intimacy.

Efficiency is useful. It keeps a household functioning. But efficiency can start substituting for emotional presence if you're not paying attention. Conversations turn into quick updates. You start exchanging information instead of sharing yourselves. You start fixing instead of feeling. And because both of you are competent, neither of you may notice the shift at first.

The relationship is functioning. Your days are full. Nothing is "wrong." You assume closeness will return later.

Later isn't a strategy.

The hard part is that this kind of distance doesn't usually arrive with a warning sign. It arrives with routine. It shows up as a slow thinning: you talk plenty, but it's mostly logistics. You touch but it's mostly habit. You share space, but it's mostly parallel. And because you're strong, you can keep functioning right through it.

But your body knows the difference between being *around* someone and being *with* someone.

When "Nothing Is Wrong" Doesn't Feel Good

Some relationships don't have obvious problems. There's no betrayal. No explosive conflict. No constant tension. No dramatic break in trust.

Just that quiet sense that you're carrying your inner life alone more often than you want to admit.

When emotional partnership is missing, you can feel it in your nervous system. Irritation shows up faster. Withdrawing becomes easier. Even the idea of quiet, space, or being alone can start feeling more appealing, not because you don't love your partner, but because you're tired of being the emotional container for everything by yourself.

If that's you, take a breath. This isn't a verdict. It's a signal.

It's a signal that your heart wants something more than teamwork. It wants emotional partnership. It wants a relationship in which emotional safety is real, mutual respect is steady, and both partners feel responsible for the emotional climate, not just the logistics.

The Difference Between Fixing And Meeting

A lot of strong people love by fixing. If you're wired that way, you hear a problem and your brain starts building a solution before the other person finishes their sentence. You want to help. You want to reduce stress. You want to make it better. That instinct often comes from care, and sometimes it comes from an old belief that being useful is how you keep love safe.

But emotional partnership often requires a different move first. Not fixing. Meeting.

Meeting is what tells someone's nervous system "I'm not alone." It's what makes your body unclench. It's what creates tenderness without pressure. It's what allows honesty without shame. It's what gives room for differences in desire, needs, or timing without turning those differences into rejection.

A relationship can have love but still feel lonely if one person brings emotion and the other brings strategy. The intention might be good, but the impact still lands as distance. Because what most people want in their tender moments isn't a plan. It's presence.

Emotional Partnership Requires Real Access

You can't build an emotional partnership if you're not willing to be emotionally accessible, and accessibility isn't the same as being "nice."

Accessibility means you can be reached. It means your partner can come to you without bracing for dismissal, defensiveness, sarcasm, or shutdown. It means emotion is allowed to land in the relationship without instantly turning into conflict, correction, or debate.

If your default is to withdraw, emotional partnership asks you to stay a little longer than you normally would. If your default is to escalate, emotional partnership asks you to soften sooner than you normally would. If your default is to intellectualize, emotional partnership asks you to name what you feel, not just what you think.

None of this is about changing your personality. It's about building a safer bridge between the two of you.

And yes, consent still matters here, even in a committed relationship. Real emotional partnership keeps consent alive. It makes space for an honest yes, an honest no, a pause, a "not right now," without punishment or guilt. It treats closeness as something you build together, not something you take.

When One Person Carries The Emotional Load

Sometimes an emotional partnership is missing because one person is carrying most of the emotional labor.

When you're the one who keeps initiating the real conversations, naming the tension, pushing for repair, reading the room, or keeping track of what's unresolved, it can start to feel like the relationship depends on your effort to stay alive.

That's not partnership. That's pressure.

This isn't about who is "better" at emotions. It's about shared responsibility. Even if one of you is naturally more expressive, both of you can practice being emotionally present. Both of you can learn to notice, respond, repair, and stay engaged.

The Fear That Stops People From Building It

Some people avoid emotional partnership because they're afraid that if they open that door, it will never close.

Endless conversations. Endless feelings. Endless needs. Endless conflict.

If you grew up around emotional chaos or unpredictability, or in an environment in which it wasn't safe to express feelings, that fear makes sense. But emotional partnership isn't chaos. It's structure. It's a calm container for real life.

It usually reduces conflict by preventing the relationship from holding tension until it turns into resentment. When small things get named early, they don't harden. When disconnection gets noticed early, it doesn't turn into distance that feels impossible to bridge.

The Quiet Intimacy Of Being Known

People want to be known. Not admired, not tolerated, not managed. Known.

If you've been the strong one for a long time, being known can feel vulnerable in a way that surprises you. You may be great at sharing information. Great at leading. Great at showing up. But being emotionally known asks you to take off armor you didn't even realize you were wearing.

Sometimes emotional partnership begins with one unpolished, honest sentence. The kind that makes room for closeness instead of performance. The kind that says "This is where I am" without making it a fight.

That's not a weakness. That's courage. And it's also the doorway into the kind of intimacy that doesn't require pressure, shame, or pretending.

How It's Built Into Ordinary Days

Many couples assume emotional closeness requires a big talk. Sometimes it does. But most emotional partnerships are built in small moments.

It's built when you greet each other as if you're actually seeing each other. When you pause long enough for eye contact. When you ask "How are you, really?", and you don't rush the answer. When you offer affection that doesn't have to lead to anything. When appreciation is spoken out loud instead of assumed.

Ordinary days are when intimacy gets nourished or neglected. A relationship doesn't need a crisis to become emotionally thin. Routine can do it all by itself.

Emotional partnership is choosing to stay awake to each other, even when nothing dramatic is happening.

How It Holds Up In Hard Seasons

Hard seasons expose defaults. Stress can make you sharp. Fatigue can make you numb. Overwhelm can make you withdraw. Fear can make you controlling. Disappointment can make you cold.

Emotional partnership doesn't erase those tendencies. It helps you handle them with responsibility. It gives you a way to stay connected while the emotions move through, rather than letting them become your relationship's new climate.

This is where tenderness matters, not as softness for show but as care that keeps the relationship safe while you're both human.

The Simplest Sign That It's Growing

Here's one of the clearest signs that emotional partnership is growing. Honesty starts feeling safe again.

You can say what's real without fear of punishment. Needs can be named without mockery or minimization. Disappointment can be shared without it turning into a character attack. Repair becomes normal. Emotional safety becomes the culture, not the occasional good day.

And if you're thinking "I'm not emotional," let me say this plainly. Emotional partnership isn't about being dramatic or highly expressive. It's about being present. You don't need therapy language. You don't need a hundred words for feelings. You need willingness.

Because emotional partnership is the bridge from alignment to intimacy, it's what makes a relationship feel connected, not just committed. It's what makes a home feel like a refuge, not just a responsibility.

And it's what allows love to stay soft in a world that keeps asking you to be strong.

If you've been craving that softness, nothing is wrong with you. It means you're ready for a deeper kind of connection. The kind that doesn't require you to keep carrying alone.

Closing Reflection

Emotional partnership is not a luxury. It's part of what makes love sustainable.

It's what keeps loyalty from turning into loneliness. It's what keeps two capable people from becoming efficient roommates. It's what helps your relationship feel like a place where you can exhale, not just perform.

If you've been strong for a long time, an emotional partnership might feel like a new language. It might feel awkward at first. It might feel like you're stepping out of a role you've played well.

That's okay.

This isn't about losing strength. It's about letting strength stop being your armor.

You don't have to wait for a crisis to deepen an emotional partnership. You can build it on ordinary days, through small moments of presence, honesty, and repair.

In the next chapter, we'll go deeper into what often blocks emotional partnership without people realizing it: cycles. The patterns you inherited, the reflexes you learned, and the ways love can accidentally become a stage on which old survival scripts keep replaying. You're not stuck with those scripts. You can rewrite them.

The Practice

This is a simple practice that builds emotional partnership without making your evenings heavy.

Choose a time of day that works for both of you. Many couples do this after dinner or right before bed. Keep it short so you'll actually do it.

Step 1: Remove distractions

No phones. No multitasking. No scrolling. Just ten minutes.

Step 2: Ask two questions
Pick two from this list, and rotate them through the week:
"What felt heavy today?"
"What felt good today?"
"Where did you feel stressed?"
"Where did you feel supported?"
"What do you need from me this week?"
"Is there anything between us that needs a quick reset?"
"What's one thing you want me to understand about you right now?"

Step 3: Respond with presence first
Before you offer solutions, try one of these:
"I get that."
"That makes sense."
"Thank you for telling me."
"I'm here."
Then ask:
"Do you want advice or do you want me to listen?"

Step 4: End with one reconnection move
A hug. Holding hands. A kiss. A simple "I love you." Something small that says "I'm with you."

This practice works because it creates a rhythm of return. Emotional partnership grows through return.

Journal Prompts

Answer what stands out. Skip what doesn't. Stay honest.

1. Where do I feel emotionally close in my relationship right now, and what is creating that closeness?
2. Where do I feel emotionally alone even if I'm functioning well?
3. When my partner shares something difficult, do I usually fix it, minimize it, or meet it with presence?
4. What makes me feel emotionally accessible? What makes me shut down?
5. If I could ask for one form of emotional support without fear, what would I ask for?
6. What statement feels hard to say but would move us closer if I said it with care?

Wholeness Check-In

Check your pillars and notice how they shape the way you feel about your relationship.

- Mentally and emotionally: Are you regulated enough to stay present or running on stress and reacting quickly?
- Spiritually: Do you feel grounded in meaning and peace or are you moving from fear and control?
- Physically: Are you rested enough to be kind or is exhaustion making connection feel like work?
- Socially: Do you have support and healthy outlets, or are you expecting your partner to carry your entire emotional world?

One small shift that would strengthen my love in wholeness:

____

____

____

____

Empowering Declaration

I choose emotional partnership, not emotional distance. I stay present. I turn toward connection. I speak with honesty and care. I allow myself to be known without needing to perform. I share emotional responsibility instead of carrying it alone. Love feels safer when I show up whole, and I'm building that kind of love.

Chapter 17
Breaking Cycles in Love

Love can be real yet feel more challenging than it needs to be because old patterns are running in the background. A cycle is what happens when stress hits, and your nervous system goes into protection mode.

Most of the time, they look normal. They look like the same argument wearing a different outfit. They look like the same feeling of being disconnected showing up after the same kinds of days. They look like that familiar shutdown, that familiar sharp edge, that familiar need to prove a point, that familiar urge to withdraw and go quiet.

If you're honest, you may feel exhausted. Not because you're weak, but because your relationship keeps getting pulled into the same places even when both of you want something better.

Here's the good news: cycles are not destiny. They're learned. Which means they can be unlearned.

Breaking cycles in love isn't about blaming your childhood or psychoanalyzing your every moment. It's about noticing your patterns with clarity and compassion, then practicing a new response on purpose. And yes, it's practice. Not perfection.

The Pattern Isn't The Problem; It's The Protection

It's what you do when you feel unsafe, unseen, misunderstood, or emotionally stretched. It's how you protect yourself, even when protection isn't needed in the same way anymore. That's what makes cycles so

214

confusing. They can show up in a relationship in which you're committed, loving, and trying.

People think cycles are "behavior problems," but behavior is only the surface. Underneath is meaning. Underneath is a story your mind tells you in a split second.

"He doesn't care. I'm on my own again. Here we go. I have to handle this. I can't relax. If I don't win this, I'll be dismissed."

Those stories might not be spoken aloud, but your body responds as if they're true. Your tone changes. Your shoulders tighten. Your chest braces. Your love gets guarded. And then the relationship starts reacting to the fear beneath the moment rather than to the moment itself.

That's the cycle.

And once you can see that, you stop treating the cycle like proof that love is failing. You start treating it like information about what still needs healing and what still needs safety.

Why Cycles Feel So "Normal"

Most cycles start as survival strategies. At some point, your nervous system learns "This is how I stay safe in relationships."

Maybe you learned to shut down because expression wasn't safe. Maybe you learned to fight because being quiet meant you'd be ignored. Maybe you learned to over perform because no one else was reliable. Maybe you learned to stay "fine" because your needs weren't welcome. Maybe you learned to please people because tension felt dangerous.

Those strategies were smart at the time. They protected you.

The problem is your nervous system doesn't automatically update just because your life got better. So you can be loved and still brace. You can be safe and still scan. You can be committed and still act like you're about to be abandoned.

That isn't a weakness. It's wiring. The goal isn't to shame the wiring. The goal is to retrain it.

The Cycles That Show Up In Real Relationships

Even if your cycle doesn't match someone else's exactly, most couples recognize the shape of at least one. Sometimes the cycle looks like one person reaching harder when they feel distance, trying to close the gap quickly, pressing for resolution because the gap feels scary. The other person feels the pressure and pulls back because pressure makes them feel trapped.

Now both people feel unsafe. One feels abandoned. The other feels controlled. And the harder one of them reaches, the faster the other retreats. Nobody planned that. It's just the pattern.

Sometimes the cycle is less about distance and more about "being right." One person brings up an issue with heat or intensity, not because they're cruel, but because they care and they're tired. The other person hears an attack instead of an invitation and goes straight into defense, explanation, or counterattack. Then the original issue disappears under tone, ego, and escalation, and nobody leaves feeling heard.

And then there's the cycle so many strong couples get stuck in without naming it. One person becomes the emotional architect and stabilizer. They anticipate, manage, track the climate, keep the relationship moving, and carry the weight. The other person may love deeply, may show up, may contribute, but they don't carry the same ownership, especially emotionally. Over time, resentment

216

builds and the relationship starts to feel like something one person maintains instead of something two people steward.

Some couples hold everything in. They're polite, functional, capable, "fine." Until one day, the pressure breaks, and the blowup surprises everyone because the truth has been hiding behind composure for too long.

None of these cycles means you don't love each other. They mean your nervous system is following old instructions.

The Most Important Reframe: The Cycle Is Not Your Relationship

This is the shift that changes everything. The cycle is not your relationship. The cycle is something that happens within your relationship.

That means you can fight the cycle together instead of fighting each other.

Instead of "You always" and "You never," the focus becomes "This pattern keeps showing up. Let's name it and change it."

That one reframe lowers defensiveness fast because it moves you from personal attack to shared responsibility. It also protects the dignity of the relationship while you do the hard work of changing it.

If you've been carrying most of the emotional work, hear me clearly. The cycle is not your private assignment. It's a shared one. You don't have to be the only person studying the relationship to keep it alive.

Why Cycles Keep Repeating Even When You Know Better

Here's what people don't always want to admit. Even unhealthy cycles have a payoff. That's why they stick.

The payoff isn't always obvious, but it's usually related to protection. A cycle can help you feel less exposed. It can protect you from vulnerability. It can protect you from disappointment. It can give you a sense of control when uncertainty rises. It can help you feel powerful when fear is underneath. It can keep you from having to admit you're hurt.

So the question that reveals your cycle isn't "What did I do?" It's "What is my pattern trying to protect me from feeling?"

For many strong people, the feeling underneath isn't anger. It's fear. Hurt. Loneliness. Not being chosen, not being considered, not being safe. The cycle is the nervous system trying to avoid those softer emotions by reaching for a harder one.

But here's the cost. The pattern might protect you from a feeling in the moment while creating a new problem in the relationship over time. It might protect you from fear, but it creates distance. It might protect you from shame, but it creates defensiveness. It might protect you from uncertainty, but it creates control.

So breaking cycles means learning to tolerate the feeling without letting it hijack your behavior.

And that's why cycle breaking is not only communication. It's regulation. A calmer body keeps you in the part of your brain that can choose wisely. Sometimes your best relational move is not a better argument. It's a steadier nervous system.

218

The Moment A Cycle Breaks

Cycles don't break in the middle of an explosion. They break in the moment right before the familiar reaction.

That moment is small. It's a fraction of a second. It's the moment you feel the urge to snap, shut down, lecture, withdraw, prove, punish, or go silent. That moment is where wholeness lives.

Wholeness is noticing the trigger and choosing a different response. You might still feel the surge; you just don't obey it.

At first, that choice might look messy. It might sound like "Let me restate that." It might look like you're catching yourself mid-sentence and softening your tone. It might be you saying, "I'm triggered and I don't want to talk like this." It might be you choosing a pause instead of a weapon. That's not a weakness. That's leadership. That's how a new cycle gets built.

Accountability Without Blame

When you start naming cycles, you'll feel tempted to track who started it. That's normal, but it won't help.

Cycles don't break when someone finally "admits they're wrong." They break when both people take ownership of their part.

Ownership isn't global. It's specific. It's the willingness to say "When I feel pressured, I shut down, and I'm practicing staying present." Or "When I feel ignored, I get intense, and I'm practicing softening my delivery." Or "When I feel criticized, I defend, and I'm practicing listening first."

That's accountability. It's not self-condemnation. It's self-awareness with movement.

Blame says "You're the problem." Accountability says "Here's my part and here's what I'm practicing." That difference is everything because blame hardens people. Accountability softens the room.

Truth With Tenderness Changes The Climate

Many strong people already communicate in full truth. You know how to name what's real. You know how to speak up. You know how to address issues. The growth edge is tenderness, not because you need to become passive, but because tenderness protects your relationship while you stay honest.

Tenderness is what allows you to stop using intensity as proof that you mean it. It's what helps you say what's underneath your strength.

When truth is delivered without tenderness, the other person braces. When tenderness shows up without truth, resentment grows quietly. But when truth and tenderness are paired, the relationship becomes a safer place in which to be honest inside. That's when cycles start losing their grip.

Your Partner Is Not Your Past

This is one of the most freeing truths in relationships. If your cycle is rooted in an old imprint, you may be reacting to your partner through that imprint instead of through reality. You may not be responding to what they said. You may be responding to what it reminds you of. You may be reacting to an old fear instead of the current moment.

That doesn't make your feelings invalid. It just means you have a chance to separate the present from the familiar.

A simple question creates space: "Is this actually happening now, or is this familiar?"

Space is where new choices happen. Repair is what makes cycle breaking stick. If you want to break cycles in the long term, you need a repair culture. Repair teaches the nervous system that "We can come back." Without repair, the cycle becomes the story of the relationship. With repair, the cycle becomes a temporary detour.

Repair doesn't have to be dramatic. It just has to be real. It's the decision to reconnect instead of punish. It's the willingness to say "My tone wasn't it. I'm sorry." Or "I shut down. I'm here now." Or "I don't want to let this sit between us." Repair makes love feel safe again.

And when you can repair, cycles lose their power because your relationship no longer stores emotional debt.

A Note For The Strong, Capable Reader

If you're thinking "I do most of the work already," you may be right. You may be the one who notices patterns first. You may be the one who initiates the repair. You may be the one who brings language to what's happening. That is a gift.

It's also a responsibility you shouldn't have to carry alone. Breaking cycles doesn't mean you become quieter so that the relationship feels peaceful. It means you become clearer about what needs to change, and you invite shared ownership of that change. You can be gentle yet firm. You can be kind and still require accountability. You don't have to carry the relationship to prove your commitment. You're allowed to build something mutual.

Closing Reflection

The goal isn't to never get triggered. The goal is to stop letting the trigger decide who you become in that moment. Cycles don't end because you suddenly have perfect communication. They end because you get honest about what you do under stress, and you choose a new response often enough that your nervous system begins to trust it. That's the work. That's the power. And that's how love gets lighter without getting less real.

The Practice

Choose one small "interrupt" phrase you can use the next time your cycle starts to rise. Something simple that buys you a breath and gives your nervous system a new option.

My next small practice:

____

____

____

Journal Prompts

Answer what stands out. Skip what doesn't. Keep it honest.

1. Where do I see the same pattern repeating, even when the topic changes?
2. What feeling shows up right before my reaction and what do I usually do to avoid it?
3. What story does my mind tell me in conflict that instantly tightens my body?
4. What do I default to when I feel unsafe: intensity, silence, control, fixing, withdrawal, defensiveness?
5. If I could respond from wholeness in that same moment, what would I do differently?
6. What does repair look like for me, and what makes it hard for me to initiate?

Wholeness Check-In

Check your pillars and notice how they shape the way you handle conflict.

- Mentally and emotionally: When stress hits, do I stay present or go into protection mode?
- Spiritually: Do I believe love can be safe, or do I treat conflict as proof that something is wrong with us?
- Physically: What does my body do in conflict and what does that signal about my nervous system?
- Socially: Do we have a relationship culture in which repair is normal, or does pride run the room?

One small shift that would strengthen our cycle:

____

____

____

____

____

Empowering Declaration

I am not my old patterns. I am not my nervous system's first reflex. I can notice what rises in me and still choose what aligns with who I am becoming. I don't have to win to be safe. I don't have to shut down to be protected. I can tell the truth with tenderness, regulate before I react, and build a relationship in which repair is normal. Cycles are learned, and I can unlearn them.

226

Chapter 18
Love Without Self-Erasure

There's a kind of love that looks faithful on the outside but quietly costs you on the inside. Self-erasure rarely starts with something obvious. Most of the time, it starts with small adjustments that feel reasonable in the moment. You smooth something over because you don't want to make it bigger than it needs to be. You let something slide because you're tired and you don't have the bandwidth for a hard conversation. You keep it moving because you've always known how.

At first, self-erasure can feel like maturity. Like flexibility. Like being supportive. Like being the one who can handle things without making life heavier. If you've been strong for a long time, that posture can feel familiar. It can feel like love.

Over time, though, something inside starts sending a signal that's easy to overlook because it isn't loud or dramatic. It's steady, showing up as a low-grade ache that doesn't go away with a weekend off and a heaviness that's hard to explain without sounding ungrateful. You still care, you still show up, and you still function as a couple, yet some part of you remains braced, as if your heart has learned how to be loyal without ever fully relaxing.

Let's begin with a question that doesn't shame you but tells the truth: What if the version of love you learned to offer was shaped by survival, not wholeness?

Self-Erasure Rarely Looks Like Disappearing

When people hear "self-erasure," they often picture silence. Someone shrinking. Someone losing their voice.

But self-erasure doesn't always look like that, especially for high-capacity people. Sometimes it looks like competence.

You can stay present and start pulling back from the part of you that needs to be held. Withdrawal can come across as asking in a softer way than you really mean, like testing the water instead of telling the truth, like bringing something up once, then letting it go because repeating yourself feels exhausting. Like watching yourself decide, in real time, that it isn't worth the effort to explain again.

So you stay "in it," but you start editing yourself. You keep showing up as the capable version of you, the steady one, the one who can handle things. And slowly, the tender part of you goes quiet. The part that wants comfort. The part that wants care without having to ask perfectly. The part that wants to be met without making you feel like you're submitting a request.

You don't disappear from the relationship by leaving. You disappear by becoming the solution instead of the person. The tricky part is that this can happen while you're still deeply committed.

The "Strong One" Trap

Strength is not the problem. Strength is beautiful. Strength is often a gift. The trap is when strength becomes the only version of you that you allow in love.

That trap can show up quietly. You handle things before anyone else has to. You anticipate needs so no one can say you didn't. You keep your composure even when you're hurting. You downplay what you want so it won't become "a thing." You manage the emotional climate because you can feel tension fast. You keep your standards, but you soften your needs.

Most people don't realize they're doing it. It feels responsible. It feels mature. It feels like love. Over time, it can quietly teach the relationship something that needs updating: that you don't need much. That you're fine. That you can carry it. That you will adapt. And maybe you can, but being able to carry something isn't the same as being meant to carry it alone.

The Quiet Contracts That Form Without Permission

A lot of self-erasure doesn't happen through one big decision. It happens through quiet contracts that form without being signed.

They form because they keep things smooth. Because they reduce conflict. Because they protect you from disappointment. Because they make closeness feel less risky. The contracts sound like survival dressed up as maturity:

- If I stay easy to love, I'll be safe.
- If I stay low-maintenance, I won't be rejected.
- If I don't ask for too much, I won't be disappointed.
- If I handle it myself, I won't feel exposed.
- If I keep things calm, we'll be okay.
- If I stay useful, I'll stay valued.

These aren't character flaws. They're protective strategies. They make sense if your nervous system learned that needing could cost you something.

But there's a price. When love runs on contracts like these, you start living as a smaller version of yourself to keep the relationship stable. Even if no one tells you to shrink, your body can start shrinking automatically.

Peace That Depends On You Staying Small Isn't Safety

Some relationships feel "peaceful" mainly because one person keeps the peace. That kind of peace can look calm on the surface while still feeling tense inside. This isn't because you don't love each other, but because the emotional culture depends on one person staying quiet about what hurts or staying small about what matters.

Safety isn't just the absence of conflict. Safety is the presence of space. Space allows for truth that won't be punished, minimized, or treated like an inconvenience. It's where honesty doesn't cost you closeness. Safety creates a space where "not right now" doesn't get turned into rejection.

If you only feel accepted when you're easy, that isn't safety. That's performance. Performance might keep things stable for a while, but it will almost always leave you tired in a way that rest can't fix.

The Slow Way Self-Erasure Builds A Life

Self-erasure usually doesn't amount to one dramatic moment. It builds through small decisions that are easy to justify.

You agree to something because you're depleted and don't want the tension of saying no. You take on emotional labor because you know you'll do it better. You keep difficult topics in your head because conflict feels like more work than silence. You don't want to sound demanding, so you edit your needs. You excuse the inconsistency because you understand stress. You brush off loneliness because nothing feels "wrong enough" to bring up.

It becomes that phrase: "It's fine." Sometimes it is fine. And sometimes "fine" is self-abandonment with a polite tone. Here's a good question: When you tell yourself it's not worth bringing up, is it truly not worth it or does you feel scared to need something? That difference matters.

The Difference Between Sacrifice And Self-Erasure

Healthy relationships sometimes involve sacrifice. That's real. That's normal. That's love. But self-erasure feels different in the body.

Sacrifice can feel stretching but clean. It usually has a purpose and an end point. It exists inside mutual respect, even if the load isn't equal in that season.

Self-erasure is when you chronically trade your needs for stability. It's when you keep the relationship comfortable while becoming increasingly uncomfortable inside it. It's when you stay "fine" until resentment starts rising like heat under a floor.

Resentment isn't always a sign you're petty. Sometimes it's a sign you've been disappearing.

Why Receiving Can Feel Harder Than Giving

Giving can feel safe and controlled. It can feel like a strength you can rely on.

Receiving requires trust, and trust is different than love. Love can exist while your body still braces. Love can exist while your heart still calculates.

If you've carried for a long time, receiving can feel like exposure. Not because you don't want it, but because you're not used to being held without earning it.

So you stay impressive. You stay capable. You stay "fine." Love becomes a place where your competence shows up more easily than your tenderness. Keep in mind that mutual love isn't only about what you contribute. It's also about what you allow.

It's not just "Can I love well?" It's also "Can I let myself be loved in a way that reaches the real me?"

The Fear Beneath Self-Erasure

Under self-erasure, there's almost always a fear, and it doesn't always speak in full sentences. Sometimes it's just the hesitation in your chest before you ask for what you need or the way you rehearse the conversation in your head. Sometimes it's the way you soften your truth before you say it, or even the way you decide that it's easier to handle something alone.

The fear often sounds like this: "If I ask, I might be disappointed. If I need, I might be rejected. If I'm fully honest, I might create distance. If I stop carrying, things might fall apart."

That fear isn't silly. It's information. It shows you what your nervous system has learned. And the point isn't to judge it. The point is to see it clearly enough that it doesn't get to run the relationship in secret.

Wholeness Brings You Back To Yourself Inside Love

Wholeness doesn't make you less devoted. It makes you less willing to abandon yourself to prove devotion. Wholeness is the ability to stay connected and stay aligned at the same time. It's being honest without becoming harsh and tender without becoming invisible. Wholeness

232

empowers you to name what you need without apologizing for being human.

It's the shift in which your needs stop being treated as an inconvenience and become valid information about what love requires to stay healthy.

Wholeness makes room for love to include you. The real you, not the polished version. Not the "fine" version. The real version. The tired version. The tender version. The one who wants to be met without perfect delivery.

Closing Reflection

If something in you feels exposed while reading this,
let it be honest without turning it into shame. Self-erasure
is not always proof that love is wrong. Sometimes it's
proof that an old strategy is still running. Sometimes it's
proof that you learned how to be strong before you learned
how to be held. Sometimes it's proof that you've been
loyal in ways that required you to quietly disappear.

The shift isn't becoming someone else. The shift is
letting your full self stay in the relationship. Love shouldn't
require you to become smaller to keep it. Love should be a
place where you can exhale.

The Practice

One small act of self-honoring. Not a speech. Not a
confrontation. Just a moment when you choose presence over
editing.

My next small act of self-honoring is:

____

____

____

234

Journal Prompts

Answer what stands out. Skip what doesn't. Stay honest.

1. Where have I been calling self-erasure "maturity" because it felt safer than being fully known?
2. What do I keep editing before I say, and what am I afraid might happen if I said it plainly?
3. When do I feel myself pulling back from emotionally, and what usually triggers that moment?
4. What part of me wants to be held, not managed, and what has kept me quiet?
5. If my relationship stayed exactly as it is, what part of me would keep getting smaller over time?

Wholeness Check-in

Through a lens of being fully transparent reflect on your pillars.

- Mentally and emotionally: do I tell the truth early, or store it until it hardens?
- Spiritually: Do I believe I'm worthy of tenderness without earning it through performance?
- Physically: what does my body do when I consider asking for support?
- Socially: Do I feel safe to be fully human in my closest relationships?

One small shift that would protect my wholeness in love is:

Empowering Declaration

I don't have to disappear to be loved. I'm allowed to be honest without apologizing for being human. I'm allowed to need. I'm allowed to receive. My self-erasure will not sustain love. I bring my whole self into love, and I choose relationships that can hold me with respect, care, and truth.

Chapter 19
Conflict Without Destruction

Conflict doesn't scare you because you're fragile. It scares you because you know what it can cost when it's handled poorly.

You've seen words do damage that doesn't go away just because someone apologizes later. You've seen tone change the atmosphere in seconds. You've watched silence stretch into cold distance, not because anyone meant to be cruel, but because no one knew how to come back without pride in the way. You've lived long enough to know that a simple disagreement can turn into something that lingers for days. When something lingers long enough, it starts rewriting the emotional safety of a relationship.

So it makes sense if part of you wants to avoid conflict altogether. Or solve it fast. Or control it. Or come in prepared, like you're walking into a meeting where the stakes are high and the margin for error is small. That's not you being dramatic. That's you being experienced.

But here's the truth: most people don't learn early enough. The goal isn't a relationship with no conflict. The goal is a relationship in which conflict doesn't destroy safety, and hard moments don't turn into harm. A relationship that doesn't become a place you brace yourself for. That kind of relationship doesn't just happen. It's built.

Why Conflict Feels Bigger Than It Is

A lot of conflict isn't really about the surface issue. The surface issue is just the delivery vehicle. What's happening underneath is meaning.

Small things can set you off. A late text can make you feel like you don't matter. A short response can come across as rejection. A forgotten detail can make you feel invisible. A disagreement can make you feel misunderstood in a way you've been misunderstood before. That's why some arguments feel "too big" for what happened. Your mind knows the topic is insignificant, but your body is responding to what the moment represents.

If your nervous system learned that tension led to danger, conflict will feel urgent even when your relationship is safe. Your body reacts before your mind can sort it out. You might feel your chest tighten. Your words speed up. Your tone sharpens. Your brain starts collecting evidence. Or you go the other direction and start disappearing in the room, not because you don't care, but because your system is trying to protect you from escalation.

This is where so many people misread themselves. They think they're "too sensitive," "too intense," or "bad at conflict." Most of the time, it's simpler than that. Your system remembers. And when you understand that you can stop judging yourself and start getting curious. Curiosity can bring your power back.

Conflict Is A Body Event, Not Just A Conversation

People love to talk about conflict as if it's mostly about communication skills. Sometimes it is. But often, it's about regulation.

When you're grounded, you can listen. You can be fair and hold your truth without overpowering. You can stay connected as you disagree. You can even say difficult things in a way that still protects your love.

240

When you're overwhelmed, you lose that access because your body shifts into protection mode. And protection mode doesn't care about closeness. It cares about safety.

That's why two good people can argue in ways that feel damaging. It's not that they're bad. It's that they're dysregulated. If you want conflict without destruction, you don't start with the perfect words. You start with the ability to come back to yourself while the truth is being spoken.

The Two Protection Styles That Keep Conflict Toxic

Most destructive conflict patterns come from protection. They protect differently.

Sometimes protection looks like control. The conversation turns into a courtroom. You come in with evidence. You list examples. You tighten your tone. You work to prove the point so you can feel safe in your reality. You might call it clarity or leadership, and some of it might even be accurate, but it lands as pressure. The other person stops feeling like your partner and starts feeling like your opponent. You might win the point and still lose the connection.

Other times, protection looks like withdrawal. You shut down. You go quiet. You become "fine." You leave the room. You stop responding. Sometimes you tell yourself you're staying calm or you don't want to escalate. But the other person experiences it as abandonment or punishment, even if you didn't mean it that way. The silence becomes loud, and the distance starts to feel like a statement.

Both patterns come from the same place: the body trying to stay safe. One protects by pushing. The other protects by pulling away. Neither builds safety.

The Difference Between Clarity And Intensity

If you're naturally direct, this part matters. There's a difference between being clear and being intense.

Clarity is steady. It's focused. It doesn't need to overpower to be heard.

Intensity is urgency. It's sharpness. It's the nervous system trying to force resolution because it doesn't feel safe to wait. You can be right about the content and still harm the relationship with the delivery. That doesn't mean you need to soften your truth into silence. It means you need to deliver your truth in a way that keeps the connection possible.

The goal of conflict isn't victory. It's alignment. It's the ability to say "Something is off" without turning each other into the enemy.

The Posture That Changes Everything

This is the shift that makes conflict safer: moving from me versus you to us versus the issue, not just saying it, but actually treating each other that way when things get hard.

That shift is the difference between proving your point and protecting your partnership. It's the difference between making your partner the problem and making the problem the problem. It's the decision to keep dignity intact even when you're hurt.

Relationships don't break because people have hard conversations. They break because hard conversations turn into harm. They break because dignity gets attacked. They break because the relationship becomes unsafe during tension.

What Makes Conflict Destructive

Conflict becomes destructive when it turns into disrespect. Sometimes that disrespect is obvious and sometimes it's subtle, but your nervous system hears it either way.

You feel it when sarcasm replaces honesty, when contempt slips into the tone, when someone refuses responsibility and turns everything into defensiveness, when silence becomes punishment, when history gets weaponized, when a conversation becomes less about the moment and more about winning.

If you've been on the receiving end of that, your body learns to brace before you even speak. And if you've used any of those moves under stress, it doesn't make you a bad person. It means you're human and you have a pattern that needs refining. You can change patterns.

The Decision That Protects Love

Here's the decision that changes conflict: "I won't treat my partner like the enemy when I feel triggered."

That doesn't mean you won't feel angry. It doesn't mean you won't be disappointed. It doesn't mean you won't need to name something difficult.

It means you'll refuse to turn pain into punishment. It means you'll remember, even in tension, that the person across from you is someone you love, not someone you need to defeat.

That one decision can shift your pace. Your tone. Your willingness to ask instead of assuming. Your ability to take a breath before the moment escalates. It creates room for safety to stay intact even when the topic is tender.

What "Same Team" Looks Like In Real Moments

Staying on the same team doesn't mean you skip the truth. It means you lead with what you actually want, not what your fear is trying to protect you from.

It's the difference between "You don't care" and "I want to feel considered." It's the difference between "You never listen" and "I want to feel heard." It's the difference between "Here's everything you've done wrong" and "Here's what happened inside me when you said that."

When the conversation starts to get messy, the most mature move isn't always to push harder. Sometimes it's protecting the moment long enough to respond well. A pause can be love when it has a return plan. A pause becomes harmful when it turns into disappearance.

This is why repair matters so much. Not as a bonus feature. As the whole point.

Repair Is What Keeps Conflict From Turning Into Erosion

A tense moment doesn't break a relationship. An unrepaired tense moment does.

Repair is what tells your nervous system "We're safe again." It's what tells your partner "You still matter to me even when I'm upset." It's what keeps conflict from becoming identity.

Repair doesn't have to be poetic. It just has to be real. It can sound like "My tone was sharp. I'm sorry." Or "I got defensive. I see it." Or "I don't want this to sit between us." Or even "Can I try that again?" That last one is underrated. It's humility without humiliation. It's maturity in motion.

If you want love that lasts, you don't need to avoid conflict. You need to normalize repair.

If Your Partner Doesn't Repair Well

Your partner's ability to repair is important because sometimes you can do everything with care and still feel like you're carrying the emotional work alone.

If repair doesn't come naturally to your partner, you can still invite growth without becoming their therapist or their emotional manager. You can be clear about what you need after tension. You can tell them you don't want days of distance. You can ask for a simple agreement about circling back. You can hold the line on disrespect without escalating into cruelty yourself.

Healthy conflict isn't about who communicates perfectly. It's about whether the relationship has a reliable way back to safety.

Conflict Can Be A Doorway, Not A Threat

When conflict is handled well, it doesn't just prevent damage. It can deepen intimacy. It teaches you where you're still tender, what you need, what your partner values, and how both of your nervous systems respond under stress.

Conflict becomes refinement instead of rupture. It becomes the place where the relationship gets more honest, more mature, and more emotionally safe because you both know how to come back.

That's what "conflict without destruction" means. Not calm voices every time. Not perfect conversations. Not never getting triggered.

It means love stays dignified even in hard moments. It means you fight for connection more than you fight to win. It means safety remains the standard, not the casualty.

Closing Reflection

If you've avoided conflict because you didn't want to damage love, that instinct makes sense. It means you respect the weight of words. It means you understand the power of tone and distance, and how they can affect a relationship over time.

But you don't have to choose between honesty and safety. You can build a relationship in which the truth can be spoken without fear, tension doesn't turn into harm, and both of you know how to come back to each other without pride standing in the way.

That's not a fantasy. That's a culture. And you can build it.

The Practice

Think of one conflict pattern you default to when you feel stretched. Don't shame yourself. Just notice it.

My first small shift in conflict will be:

____

____

____

Journal Prompts

Answer what stands out. Skip what doesn't. Stay honest.

1. What did conflict look like around me growing up, and how did it shape my instincts?
2. What happens in my body when tension starts?
3. Do I tend to fight for control, shut down for safety, or rush for closure?
4. What does "same team" look like in real time for me?
5. What makes repair hard for me: pride, fear, shame, exhaustion?
6. What is one change that would make conflict feel safer in my relationship?

Wholeness Check-In

Reflect on your pillars and how they affect how you show up.

- Mentally and emotionally: Can I stay honest without becoming sharp or shutting down?
- Spiritually: Can I choose humility and truth without turning conflict into a power struggle?
- Physically: What does my body do right before I escalate or withdraw?
- Socially: Do we have a safe culture for repair or do we avoid and store tension?

One small shift that would protect safety in conflict is:

____

____

____

____

____

Empowering Declaration

I can be honest without being harmful. I can be firm without becoming unsafe. I can pause without disappearing. I can repair without losing dignity. Conflict doesn't have to destroy love. My relationship can hold truth and stay safe.

250

Chapter 20
Creating Unbreakable Unity

"Unity" sounds beautiful. This word also gets misused.

Sometimes "unity" becomes code for keeping the peace at any cost. Don't bring it up. Don't push. Don't rock the boat. Don't make it awkward. Just move on. That isn't unity. That's pressure wearing a nicer name. It's the kind of "togetherness" that depends on one person staying quiet and the other staying comfortable, and over time, it teaches the relationship something dangerous: truth is a threat.

Real unity doesn't require you to shrink. It doesn't ask you to swallow what matters. It doesn't depend on everyone being in a good mood and it certainly doesn't disappear the moment you disagree. If anything, unity proves itself in the moments when disagreement arises, and the relationship remains protected.

Unity is a culture. It's the climate you build on purpose over time through a hundred small decisions that keep the two of you on the same side, even when the moment is tense. And the best part is that you don't have to become a different kind of person to build it. If you're naturally direct, strong, and clear, those qualities can absolutely serve unity. They need to be paired with a kind of emotional leadership that knows when to slow down, soften the edge, and choose connection without sacrificing truth.

Not perfection. Leadership.

The Difference Between A Mood And A Culture

One of the biggest reasons unity feels fragile in some relationships is that it's being held together by mood.

251

Mood is real, but it isn't reliable. It changes with sleep, stress, hormones, hunger, workload, an awkward text, a misunderstood tone, a long day, a short fuse. Mood is the weather.

Culture is what you return to when the weather changes. Culture is what keeps you connected when you're tired. It's the way you speak when you're stretched. It's what you do with tension before it becomes distance. It's the way you repair, the way you reset, the way you remember you're building something bigger than the moment you're in.

If your relationship depends on mood, unity will always feel like something you're trying to preserve. If your relationship builds culture, unity becomes durable. It starts to feel unbreakable, not because you never get irritated, but because irritation doesn't have the power to turn into disrespect and distance.

How Unity Quietly Erodes

Unity rarely breaks in one dramatic moment. Most of the time, it erodes in ordinary patterns that feel normal until you notice what they cost.

It can look like co-managing life so efficiently that you forget how to actually be with each other. It can feel like conversations that get stuck in logistics while your heart slowly grows quiet. It can look like "fine," becoming the default atmosphere, not because anything is exploding, but because the connection keeps getting postponed. Not intentionally. Just repeatedly.

If you're strong and capable, you can live in that kind of "fine" for a long time. You know how to function and keep life moving. You know how to carry responsibility

252

without falling apart. From the outside, it can look like maturity.

But functioning can quietly replace intimacy if you don't notice the slow shift. The relationship stays intact, but tenderness thins. The laughter still happens, but it feels more like relief than closeness. You're still a team, but the "we" feels more operational than emotional.

That's not a reason to panic. It's a reason to pay attention. Good intentions don't protect unity. Repeated choices protect it.

Unity Is Shared Ownership, Not Shared Personality

Some couples treat unity as if it means "We think the same way." or "We respond the same way." or "We feel the same way at the same time." That's not unity. That's sameness, and it's not realistic or necessary.

Unity isn't built on having the same temperament, communication style, or emotional needs. Unity is built by shared ownership.

It's two people deciding that the relationship is something they both protect. That repair matters to both of them. That tone matters to both of them. That respect stays intact even when the day is long. That "same team" isn't something you say when things are easy; it's the way you move when things are tense.

Life won't always be 50/50 in capacity, and it doesn't have to be. But ownership does need to be shared in responsibility. If one person becomes the emotional architect while the other coasts, unity will start to feel heavy. It might look stable from the outside, but it will feel lonely on the inside. Unbreakable unity is two people carrying the culture together.

The Simplest Unity Question

Here is one of the most grounding questions you can ask in the middle of tension: "Are we acting like we're on the same team right now?"

Not "Who's right?" Not "Who started it?" Not "Do you get me?" Not "Are you listening the way I want you to listen?"

Same team.

Stress makes people turn inward. It makes you self-protect. It makes you interpret a hostile tone as a threat. It makes you want to win the moment because winning can feel like safety. The "same team" question interrupts that spiral. It brings you back to what matters: the issue is not the person. The issue is the issue. If you're building unity, the relationship is never collateral damage.

What Makes Unity Feel Safe

Unity isn't just closeness. It's closeness that your nervous system can trust.

That kind of unity isn't built through big speeches about commitment. It's built through consistency in a few non-negotiable behaviors, especially when you're irritated, tired, disappointed, or misunderstood. It's built when respect stays intact under stress, when repair becomes normal rather than rare, when truth is delivered in a way that protects dignity, when boundaries protect the relationship from outside interference, and when both people keep choosing "we," even when their egos want to pull them into their corners.

This is where unity becomes more than a romantic idea. It becomes a structure. A shared agreement that says,

254

"This relationship is not where we take our stress out on each other. This is where we handle stress with each other."

The Hidden Ways Unity Gets Weakened

Sometimes unity doesn't fall apart because of big problems. Sometimes it gets worn down by habits that seem small but repeat often.

It can happen when love turns into a scoreboard, when the relationship starts feeling like quiet math. Who did more, who carried more, who initiated more, who sacrificed more. Some fairness conversations are real and necessary, but when everything becomes a tally, unity starts to feel like negotiation rather than devotion.

Unity can weaken when emotional responsibility is delegated without anyone naming it. One person becomes the one who first notices the distance, initiates the hard conversations, pushes for repair, tracks the emotional climate, and keeps the relationship from going cold. The other person may still love deeply, but over time, the pattern sends a message: connection depends on one person's effort. That isn't unity. That's pressure.

It can also happen through parallel living. Life is shared on paper but not in the heart. You talk about schedules more than feelings, plans more than presence, responsibilities more than realities. You're together but not really with each other.

And then there's one assumption that quietly misleads a lot of couples: the belief that love automatically equals closeness. Love can be real, and closeness can still require practice. Unity is love plus stewardship.

A More Intimate Truth, Especially For The Strong One

If you've been the strong one for a long time, unity can start to feel like something you personally have to hold together. You notice the shifts first. You feel the distance sooner. You want to reset faster. You don't like an emotional mess lingering in the air. You value alignment. You want the relationship to feel intentional, not accidental.

That sensitivity can be a gift. It can also become a burden if you start believing it's your job to maintain the relationship's emotional temperature.

Unbreakable unity doesn't mean you carry unity alone. It means you stop doing silent emotional labor and start building shared agreements. It means you can say, calmly and clearly, "I want us. I want us to feel connected. I want us to be a team on purpose." That isn't neediness. That's leadership in love.

If your heart has ever whispered "Why am I always the one bringing us back?", that's important information. It's pointing you toward a healthier structure.

Unity Is Built Through Agreements You Live By

Unity rarely becomes unbreakable by accident. It's created through agreements that both people understand and honor.

Not formal contracts. Not therapy language. Just clear expectations that remove guessing. Agreements that make the relationship feel emotionally predictable. Predictability builds safety. Safety strengthens unity.

It's the kind of clarity that says "We don't threaten the relationship during conflict." We don't use contempt. We can take breaks, but we always return. We repair within a day. We protect each other's dignity in public and private. We talk to each other before we vent outside the relationship. We name disconnection early instead of pretending we're fine."

When those agreements are lived, unity stops being fragile. You don't have to wonder what happens when tension rises. You know the culture you're committed to.

Unity Gets Stronger When The Relationship Has Meaning

Unity becomes stronger when the relationship has meaning beyond the moment. Not just goals like schedules and finances, although those matter. Meaning is the deeper "why" that helps you stay connected when you're tired. It helps you remember what you're building when your ego wants you to pull away. It keeps you from treating the relationship like a convenience that exists only when things are smooth.

Meaning might look like building a peaceful home, raising emotionally healthy children, healing family patterns, becoming emotionally safe for each other, protecting rest and health together, living with integrity, and creating a legacy of love that feels steady and real.

When you share meaning, unity becomes less fragile because the relationship isn't only about how you feel today. It's about what you're building over time.

Closing Reflection

Unbreakable unity isn't the absence of irritation. It's the refusal to let irritation become disrespect.

It's not pretending everything is fine. It's staying honest without turning honesty into harm.

It's not one person continually adjusting to keep the peace. It's two people choosing shared ownership of the culture, especially when life is loud.

If you've ever thought "I don't need perfection, I just want us to feel like we're on the same side again," that's not a small desire. That's the heart of unity. That's your nervous system asking for a relationship it can trust.

Unity becomes unbreakable when "same team" is not a slogan but a practice.

The Practice

What is one thing you can say this week that strengthens "same team" without starting a fight:

____

____

____

Journal Prompts

Answer what stands out. Skip what doesn't. Stay honest.

1. In my relationship, when does "unity" feel like pressure instead of safety?
2. Where have we become efficient but emotionally distant without meaning to?
3. What does my nervous system need in order to feel like we're on the same side during tension?
4. What agreement would reduce guessing and increase safety for both of us?
5. What does "protecting the relationship" look like on ordinary days, not just challenging ones?

Wholeness Check-In

Reflect on your pillars through the lens of unity.

- Mentally and emotionally: Do I stay connected in tension or go into control/withdrawal?
- Spiritually: Do we return to humility and shared meaning or to ego and power?
- Physically: How does my body signal "same team" versus "self-protect"?
- Socially: Do we protect our bond from outside interference and inside disrespect?

One small shift that could strengthen our unity is:

____

____

____

____

Empowering Declaration

We are building a culture, not chasing a mood. We protect our dignity even when we disagree. We return, we repair, we reset. We stay on the same team when life gets loud. Unity does not require shrinking. Unity is love with structure, safety, and shared ownership.

Chapter 21
Intimacy That Honors Your Whole Self

Intimacy can look fine on the outside and still feel lonely on the inside. You can share a home, a bed, a calendar, responsibilities, even laughter, and still notice that something in you stays slightly guarded. Not because you don't love each other, and not because you're doing something "wrong," but because real intimacy asks for more than proximity. It asks for presence. The kind you can feel.

And if you've spent years being the strong one, the capable one, the one who holds it together, intimacy can feel like stepping out of a role that once kept you safe. You may know how to lead, manage, solve, stabilize, and keep life moving. You may even know how to be loving. But being *known* requires a different kind of courage. It requires you to stop exhibiting wellness and start practicing honesty.

This chapter is about intimacy that doesn't require you to fragment yourself. Intimacy that makes room for your mind, your emotions, your body, and your spirit in the same relationship. Not perfectly. Not every day. But consistently and enough that you feel like you can exhale and be fully here.

Intimacy Isn't One Thing, It's A Whole-Body Experience

Some people talk about intimacy as if it's a single category that's usually tied to physical closeness. But intimacy is layered. It's the way you feel emotionally safe with someone. It's the way your body relaxes or braces when they reach for you. It's the meaning you share, the values you live, the ways you repair when life gets messy, and the quiet choices that say "I'm here" in a way your nervous system can actually believe.

When intimacy is strong, you don't just feel loved. You feel *met*. And when intimacy starts to thin out, it doesn't always show up as a dramatic crisis. Sometimes it shows up as a quiet emptiness you can't quite explain without sounding ungrateful. You start noticing that you're together a lot but not always connected. You can still function as a team while quietly missing being held.

That's usually the sign that intimacy needs your attention, not your shame.

Emotional Intimacy: Being Known Without Performing

Emotional intimacy is the ability to be real without bracing for backlash. It's not oversharing to force closeness. It's not emotional dumping. It's not turning every conversation into a deep dive. It's simpler than that. Emotional intimacy is being able to say what's true in you, in real time, and trust that your truth won't be punished.

For strong people, this can be the hardest kind of intimacy because strength often comes with a reflex to manage yourself. You've learned how to stay composed. You've learned how to keep moving. You've learned how to take care of what needs to be done. And without realizing it, you may have also learned how to keep your softer needs quiet.

So you share plans before feelings. You explain what happened without saying how it landed. You give the facts because facts feel safer than vulnerability. And it's not that you're cold. It's that you're practiced.

But love doesn't only want your competence. Love wants your presence.

Emotional intimacy grows when you practice small honesty as it happens. Not the kind that turns into a speech. The kind that sounds like "That hurt more than I expected," or "I'm feeling tender today," or "I miss you," or "I need reassurance right now," or "I don't need solutions, I need you close." Those aren't weak sentences. They're emotionally clean sentences. And when your partner can hold them with care, something in you starts to unclench.

Physical Intimacy: Connection, Not Performance

Physical intimacy is often treated as the main definition of intimacy. That's part of why so many people feel confused. Sex can be present while safety is missing. A body can cooperate while a heart is closed. And if you've lived in survival mode, physical intimacy can quietly become a shortcut to reassurance. It can become proof that everything is okay. It can become the way tension gets smoothed over without being named.

But physical intimacy that honors your whole self doesn't ask you to use your body as a peace offering. It doesn't pressure you to be available when you feel emotionally distant. It doesn't treat consent like a technicality. It doesn't make you feel like you have to "keep up" to keep the relationship stable.

This is one of the clearest places trust shows up in real life. Because physical closeness is vulnerable, it's not just skin. It's exposure. It's surrender. It's your nervous system asking "Am I safe here?" It's your heart asking "Do I matter even when I'm not performing?"

Healthy physical intimacy has room for differences. Two people can love each other deeply and still have different rhythms, different levels of desire, different needs for connection before they're ready. Healthy intimacy doesn't punish that. It talks about it. It makes space for it. It stays curious instead of keeping score.

And consent matters here too, even inside a committed relationship. Not the technical version. The real version. The kind where your yes stays yours. The kind where "not right now" doesn't get treated like rejection. The kind where you can pause, adjust, change your mind, and still feel safe and wanted.

For a lot of people, especially strong people, physical intimacy gets better when they stop performing and start being present. Not because they learned a trick, but because they finally felt safe enough to stay in their body without bracing. They can say what they need without shame. They can say "Slow down," or "I want more closeness before we go there," or "This feels good," or "That doesn't feel good," or "I want you, but I need us emotionally first."

And here's the truth that ties it all together: healthy physical intimacy is not something you give to keep love stable. It's something you share when love feels safe. It's the meeting place of emotional safety and mutual respect. It's tenderness without pressure. Honesty without shame. Consent that stays real, not assumed. It's when your body is not a tool, a transaction, or a performance. It's a language. And when it's healthy, it leaves you feeling connected, not used. Seen, not managed and chosen, not obligated.

Spiritual Intimacy: Meaning, Values, And Your Inner World

Spiritual intimacy isn't reserved for couples who share the same beliefs. It's deeper than shared routines. It's the space where your values, your sense of meaning, your inner world, and your faith or life philosophy can be seen and respected.

It's being able to ask and answer questions like what matters most to you right now? What are you carrying that you haven't said out loud? What are you growing through? What do you want your life to stand for? What kind of love do you want to build?

For some couples, this includes prayer, worship, and shared faith practices. For others, it looks like shared values around family, integrity, legacy, service, and healing generational patterns. Either way, the point is the same. You get to bring your whole self, not just the presentable parts.

And there's a quiet caution here. Spiritual language can be used to avoid emotional work. It can become a way to bypass conflict, excuse imbalance, or normalize suffering. Intimacy that honors your whole self doesn't ask you to spiritualize your loneliness. It invites you to name it honestly and ask for what you need.

The Real Intimacy Question

If intimacy has been hard for you, it might not be because love is missing. It might be because you learned to survive by staying in control. Intimacy asks you to loosen control safely. Not recklessly. Just enough to be known.

So here is the question beneath intimacy: Can you stay connected to yourself while you let someone else get close?

Because that's what makes intimacy feel safe. Not chemistry. Not shared interests. Not even loyalty. Safety. The kind built through a relationship culture in which truth isn't punished, tone stays respectful, repair happens consistently, curiosity replaces assumptions, and presence matters more than performance.

When Intimacy Starts Thinning Out

Most couples don't lose intimacy all at once. It usually fades in small, quiet ways. Life gets busy. The relationship starts running on autopilot. You talk, but it's mostly coordination. You touch less without realizing it. You assume closeness will return on its own, and you keep postponing the conversation because nothing is "wrong enough" to bring up.

That's why naming it early matters. Not with blame, but with care.

Sometimes one honest request shifts everything. "I miss us. I want more closeness. Can we reconnect this week?" That kind of honesty isn't a complaint. It's devotion.

If You've Always Been The Strong One

If you're the one who's always been strong, you may not be used to asking for intimacy directly. You might hope your partner notices. You might try to create closeness through doing, managing, giving, or being impressive. And you might feel awkward naming what you want because a part of you learned that needing is risky.

So let me say this plainly. Wanting intimacy doesn't make you needy. It makes you human. You don't have to

268

earn closeness by being exceptional. You don't have to deserve tenderness by carrying more. You don't have to prove your worth before asking for a connection. You're allowed to want, and you're allowed to be met.

When you permit yourself to want intimacy, you stop settling for the version of it that looks fine but feels empty. And you start building the kind that feels like home.

Closing Reflection

Intimacy that honors your whole self is not just physical closeness. It's emotional safety you can feel. It's mutual respect that doesn't disappear in vulnerability. There's room for differences without punishment. It's tenderness without pressure. Honesty without shame. Consent that stays real even within a commitment. It's being fully present in the relationship without fragmenting yourself to keep it peaceful. And when intimacy is healthy, it doesn't just connect bodies. It connects people.

The Practice

Choose one small thing you can do this week to enhance intimacy that signals presence, not performance.

My next small practice:

Journal Prompts

Answer what stands out. Skip what doesn't. Stay honest.

1. What part of me still overthinks or performs in intimate moments instead of being present, and why?
2. Where do I feel safest with my partner, and where do I still brace?
3. What do I need emotionally in order to feel open physically?
4. What have I been hoping my partner would "just notice" instead of me having to name it directly?
5. If I believed my needs were cared about, what would I ask for more often?

Wholeness Check-In

Reflect on your pillars and how they affect intimacy in your relationship.

- Mentally and emotionally: Do I feel safe to name truth in real time, or do I edit myself until I'm resentful?
- Spiritually and values-based: Do we talk about what matters, or do we only manage what's urgent?
- Physically: Do I feel pressure, obligation, or freedom in physical closeness?
- Socially: Is our relationship protected from outside stress, or do we bring the noise from the whole world into our intimate moments?

One small shift that would strengthen our intimacy this week:

____

____

____

____

Empowering Declaration

I do not have to perform to be loved. I'm allowed to be present, honest, and fully myself. Intimacy is not pressure. It's connection I can actually feel in my body. It's respect that doesn't disappear when life gets hard. It is tenderness that makes room for me to be fully human. I am worthy of intimacy that feels like home.

Chapter 22
Love as Legacy

"Legacy" can sound like a big word. The kind of word that makes you picture wealth, awards, headlines, and people who seem larger than life. But most legacy isn't loud, and most of it never makes it into public view. It lives in ordinary places: the way your home feels after a hard day, the tone you use when you're irritated, the way you come back after tension, the way you handle stress without turning on each other.

Legacy isn't a highlight reel. It's the environment your relationship creates over time. It's what becomes normal between you. Whatever becomes normal in your relationship will shape your future. Whether you realize it or not, you're already building a legacy in small moments.

Legacy Starts With The Culture You Repeat

Love isn't only a feeling. It also shows up in what the two of you keep creating day after day. That's why legacy doesn't begin with grand gestures. It begins with daily culture.

Culture is what your relationship returns to under pressure. It's the default way you speak when you're tired. It's the posture you take when you feel tender, inconvenienced, or misunderstood. It's how quickly you repair, how gently you tell the truth, how often you protect each other's dignity when it would be easier to take a shot and feel justified.

Over time, those small patterns don't stay small. They become the shape of your relationship. They become the version of love your nervous system expects and the home you live inside, emotionally, long after the moment passes.

When Love Starts Carrying Weight It Was Never Designed To Hold

Some relationships look romantic on the surface but feel heavy underneath, and it isn't always because anyone is doing something "wrong." Sometimes it's because the relationship is carrying weight it was never designed to hold.

When wholeness is missing, love can quietly become an identity project. The relationship starts doing jobs it can't do well. It becomes the place where worth is measured and safety is tested. When old wounds try to negotiate for reassurance, you may not say it out loud, but the undercurrent starts sounding like: Prove I'm safe. Prove I'm chosen. Prove I'm enough. Fix what life bruised. Carry what I don't want to face.

At first, those expectations can feel intense and meaningful. They can even look like devotion. But over time, they create pressure. They make normal conflict feel like a threat. They make connections feel fragile because love becomes the place where everything is on trial.

Two whole people build something different. They don't outsource identity to love. They bring identity into love so that the relationship can be a place of shared growth rather than emotional rescue. That one shift changes the feel of everything. Love becomes lighter without becoming shallow. It becomes steadier without becoming dull. It becomes safe enough to last.

Legacy Love Is Steady, Not Performative

Legacy love isn't a highlight reel. It isn't built on perfect chemistry or always getting it right. It isn't built on looking good in public. It isn't built on never struggling.

It's built on consistency. Consistency in tone, even when you're stressed. Consistency in respect, even when you disagree. Consistency in repair, even when pride wants you to hold distance. Consistency in choosing the "we," even when the moment is tense. It's the kind of love that doesn't require an audience to be real. It's love you can live when nobody's clapping, when nobody's watching, when life is just life.

That's why legacy love matters. It isn't impressive. It's trustworthy.

The Legacy You're Actually Leaving

If you have children, they are learning what love means by watching what you normalize. Not what you tell them. What you rehearse. They're absorbing whether an apology exists in your home. Whether repair happens, tension sits, or respect stays intact when people are tired, whether truth can be spoken without punishment. Whether emotional warmth feels normal or rare.

Even if you don't have children, your legacy still matters. Your friends can feel the difference between a peaceful relationship and one that is quiet but tense. Your community can sense when a couple is safe together. Your future self will live in the patterns you practice today. Legacy love is the emotional blueprint you repeat until it becomes your life.

The Strong-Person Trap That Quietly Shapes Legacy

Strength is a gift. It builds. It protects. It stabilizes. But strength becomes a trap when it turns into the only way you know how to love. If you're the one who carries the emotional climate, keeps the rhythm, tracks what's off, smooths things over, and makes it work, it's easy for a relationship to quietly benefit from your strength more than it honors your humanity.

That doesn't always happen because a partner is selfish. Sometimes it happens because you're so capable that nobody sees what it costs you. Sometimes it happens because you make it look easy, even when it isn't.

Legacy love asks different questions. Not "Can I carry this?" but "Is this shared?" Not "Can I handle it?" but "Is this healthy?" Not "Can I keep the peace?" but "Is this emotionally safe for my whole self?" A relationship shouldn't run best when one person is doing most or all of the heavy lifting. It should feel strongest when both people are participating fully.

Love That Lasts Is Love You Steward

Legacy love is stewardship. Stewardship is care with intention. It's protecting the relationship without making it a cage. It's leadership without domination. It's attention without anxiety.

Stewardship means noticing disconnection early and naming it with kindness and making repair normal instead of a rarity. It looks like telling the truth before resentment builds, protecting each other's dignity in private and in public, and building small rituals that keep the connection alive. It looks like boundaries that guard the relationship's

278

peace, rather than exposing it to everyone's opinions and noise.

Stewardship is the long view. It's the way love becomes legacy.

The Love Your Nervous System Can Trust

One of the clearest markers of a legacy relationship is this: Over time, the relationship becomes a place where your nervous system can exhale because you've learned to be honest without destroying each other. That safety gets built in the ways people don't always celebrate: choosing tone, practicing humility, returning after tension instead of distancing, refusing to normalize contempt, caring as much about impact as intent.

Legacy love is love that feels steady enough to be real. It's love that creates a home inside the relationship. Not a performance space, a courtroom, or a battleground. A home.

If you've ever wanted that kind of love, the kind that feels both honest and safe, you're not asking for something unrealistic. You're asking for a culture. The good news is that you can build one.

Closing Reflection

Legacy can sound like a big word until you realize you're already creating one in your home, your tone, your repairs, and your defaults. You're building it every time you choose respect instead of contempt, every time you come back after a hard moment instead of letting distance become normal, every time you tell the truth early instead of waiting for resentment to do it for you. Legacy love is not a highlight reel. It's the emotional climate you keep creating on ordinary days, especially when nobody is applauding. And the freedom in that is simple: You don't have to be perfect to build a legacy. You have to be intentional. You have to care about the culture you're rehearsing because what you repeat becomes the "normal" your relationship lives inside.

The Practice

Pick one day this week and keep your check-in short. No speeches. No courtroom energy. Just a clean reset. Ask each other:

What has our relationship felt like lately, in my body?
What have we been protecting well, and what have we been neglecting without realizing it?
What is one small thing we can do this week that would make our love feel steadier, not just functional?

Then choose one action you can actually do, not a promise you'll forget next week.

Journal Prompts

Answer what stands out. Skip what doesn't. Stay honest.

1. Where do I feel most proud of the culture we're building, and where do I feel the quiet cost?
2. What do I normalize when I'm tired that I wouldn't choose if I were fully present?
3. What do I want our home to feel like a year from now, emotionally, not just logistically?
4. Where have I been carrying more than I've admitted, and what would shared ownership look like?
5. What is one legacy pattern from my past that I refuse to repeat, even though it's familiar?

Wholeness Check-In

Before you label something a relationship problem, check the condition of your inner life. Sometimes the "issue" is depletion wearing the mask of distance.

- Mentally and emotionally, am I present or overloaded?
- Spiritually, am I grounded or controlling?
- Physically, am I rested enough to be kind?
- Socially, are outside demands draining the best of us and leaving leftovers for the relationship?

One small shift that would strengthen my love in wholeness:

____

____

____

____

Empowering Declaration

I build love with a long view. I choose tone that protects, truth that stays clean, and repairs that return us to safety. My relationship is not a stage. It is a home for wholeness. I am building a legacy I can live inside.

Chapter 23
The Kind of Love That Keeps Becoming

There's a point in love where the question changes. It stops being "Do we love each other?" and becomes "Can we keep building while life keeps changing?" Because life doesn't stay still.

Pressure reshapes you. Growth stretches you. Healing softens some edges and exposes others. Responsibility adds weight in places you didn't expect. Even good seasons can change you, not because anything is wrong, but because you're human and you're evolving. And if a relationship is going to last, it has to be able to hold that evolution without turning it into quiet distance.

Love that keeps becoming isn't loud. It isn't dramatic. It doesn't require constant excitement to feel real. It's built on maturity. It stays alive because you keep choosing it on purpose, even when the season changes the way you show up.

When Love Shifts From Chemistry To Craftsmanship

Early love can feel like momentum. You're learning each other. Everything feels fresh. You feel pulled in, curious, energized by the discovery.

Later, love becomes craftsmanship. Not because the magic disappears, but because you're no longer just feeling love, you're building the culture of it. You start noticing what protects the connection and what quietly wears it down. You learn how to stay tender without losing honesty, and how to stay honest without losing tenderness. You stop relying on momentum and start practicing intention.

This is where many good relationships are tested. Not by betrayal. Not by some dramatic collapse. They get tested by a slow thinning that doesn't announce itself as a crisis. It looks like functioning. It looks like teamwork. It looks like life is getting full and the relationship is getting squeezed into whatever is left over.

And if you're a capable person, that kind of thinking can last a long time, because you're good at functioning through almost anything. The household stays stable. The calendar stays full. The responsibilities keep moving. You show up. You handle life.

But stability isn't the same as closeness.

At some point, you can feel the difference in your body. You're together, but you're not quite with each other. You talk, but it's mostly logistics. You share space, but it's parallel to it. You're still loyal, still committed, still doing the work of life, yet something in you starts to miss the emotional version of "us."

Why Strong People Often Miss The Moment To Reset

If you've spent years being dependable, you probably don't like drama. You don't want emotional chaos, and you don't want a relationship that feels like constant heavy conversations. You want peace. You want steadiness. You want something that feels mature, not fragile.

So when your connection starts to thin just a little, you do what strong people do. You minimize. You keep moving. You tell yourself it's just a busy season, just a temporary stretch, just life doing what life does.

And sometimes it is.

286

The problem is that strong people can tolerate more emotional distance than they should, not because they don't care, but because they've trained themselves to carry discomfort quietly. You've pushed through before. You've held a lot before. You've been the one who doesn't need too much, the one who stays composed, the one who keeps the environment steady. So instead of naming what you miss, you convince yourself it's not worth bringing up unless it's "bad enough."

That's how the reset gets postponed. Not out of laziness. Out of self-protection.

Because needing can feel risky if you've ever paid a price for it. You don't want to sound ungrateful. You don't want to be misunderstood. You don't want to start a conversation that becomes an argument about your tone. So you wait, hoping it resolves itself.

But love that keeps becoming asks for something different. Not intensity. Not pressure. Just honesty early, while things are still tender enough to adjust without damage. Sometimes it's as simple as saying, calmly, "I don't want us to slowly become roommates with history."

"I Miss Us" Is Not Weakness

If you've ever felt a quiet ache inside a stable relationship, you know how hard it can be to name it. Not because the words are complicated, but because the fear underneath them can be loud. You might worry that your partner will hear it as criticism. You might worry that you'll sound needy. You might worry that it will create tension instead of closeness.

So you hold it in and tell yourself you'll bring it up later, when you can say it perfectly, when you're less tender, when the timing feels safer.

But one of the most mature sentences in love is simple and clean: "I miss us."

That isn't an accusation. It's an investment. It says "This matters enough to address." It says "I'm not leaving. I'm leaning in." It says "I want more than cooperation. I want closeness."

When you can say it without heat, you create space for connection without defensiveness. And when your partner can hear it without shame, you create space for growth without ego. That's what becoming looks like in real life. Not constant intensity, just consistent willingness.

Love Gets Safer When It Stops Being An Identity Test

A lot of conflict turns destructive when love is carrying the burden of proving worth. When someone feels like they have to be perfect to be safe, disagreement feels like rejection. When someone's identity is tied to being right, feedback feels like an attack. When love becomes a validation system, even small disappointments can feel like a threat.

Wholeness changes that. It changes the meaning of tension.

Two people who are still trying to earn safety within the relationship tend to fight out of fear. Two people who are grounded in themselves can stay connected while working through hard things. They can be honest without becoming cruel. They can be tender without becoming avoidant. They can name the moment without turning it into a verdict.

Love becomes calmer when neither person is auditioning, defending, or trying to prove they're worthy of being chosen. That's when you stop arguing to win and start talking to build.

The Love That Keeps Becoming Has A Repair Culture

Long-term love isn't sustained by never missing each other. It's sustained by returning.

That's the real difference between couples who grow and couples who slowly harden. Not that one couple never has tension, but that one couple knows how to come back before distance becomes a new normal.

Repair culture means pride doesn't get the final word. It means you don't let sharpness sit in the room for days just because neither of you wants to be the first to soften. It means you come back after hard moments, not to rehash everything but to restore a sense of safety. It means apologies don't require begging. It means tone gets owned, not defended. It means reconnection isn't treated like a special event; it's treated like maintenance.

Repair doesn't erase hard moments. It keeps hard moments from becoming your identity.

Becoming Requires Rebalancing Strength

If you've lived in survival mode for a long time, you become reflexively strong. You know how to manage, handle, organize, solve, and stabilize. You know how to keep things moving even when you're tired. You know how to be composed even when you're carrying more than you've admitted.

But love that keeps becoming often asks for less armor and more presence.

That can feel vulnerable, not because you're fragile, but because you're used to being the one who holds it together. And holding it together can slowly become the thing that keeps you from being held.

Here's the shift: your strength doesn't need to disappear. It needs to be rebalanced. Strength becomes stability instead of defensiveness. Stability becomes the foundation that makes softness feel safe. Softness becomes the doorway to deeper intimacy because it gives your partner access to the real you, not just the functional version.

That's how love evolves without requiring you to become someone you're not.

Becoming Is Choosing The "We" Again

Love that keeps becoming includes honest resets and the willingness to notice when the connection is thinning and choose a return while the relationship is still soft enough to respond.

Sometimes that return is a conversation. Sometimes it's a softer tone. Sometimes it's laughter that doesn't get rushed. Sometimes it's asking a question you haven't asked in a while because you assumed you already knew the answer. Sometimes it's looking at each other and deciding again that you don't want to just run your life together. You want to live it together.

The couples who stay connected aren't the ones who never get tired. They're the couples who keep returning before distance becomes comfortable.

Closing Reflection

Love that keeps becoming doesn't rely on momentum. It relies on intention.

It's the kind of love that can handle growth without turning it into competition. It can handle stress without turning it into emotional distance. It can handle conflict without turning it into destruction. Perfect people don't build it. It's built by people who stay honest, stay humble, and keep choosing to come back.

In the next chapter, we'll return to the core truth holding all of this together: Two whole people make love complete not because they're flawless, but because they refuse self-abandonment and build intimacy with maturity.

The Practice: The Weekly Return Ritual

Schedule 15 minutes once a week on the same day, if you can, and ask each other these questions. No phones. No multitasking. Take turns and keep it simple.

- What was a moment this week when you felt closest to me?
- What was a moment this week when you felt distance from me, even if it was only a little?
- What is one thing you want next week that would help you feel more connected?

If you want to add one more question:

- How can I support you this week in a way you'll actually feel?

This conversation doesn't have to be emotional, but it needs to be consistent. Consistency is what keeps love becoming instead of thinning.

Journal Prompts

Answer what stands out. Skip what doesn't. Stay honest.

1. Where have I been simply functioning beside my partner more than emotionally connecting with them?
2. What does thinning look like in my relationship, and how do I usually respond to it?
3. What makes it hard for me to say "I miss us" without turning it into a bigger story?
4. What would a repair culture look like for us in this season?
5. What is one small weekly practice that would keep us emotionally close?
6. Where do I still use strength as armor instead of stability?

Wholeness Check-In

Becoming is harder when you're depleted. Before you interpret distance as a relationship problem, check your pillars.

- Mentally and emotionally: Am I present, or do I feel overloaded and short-tempered?
- Spiritually: Do I feel grounded, or am I operating from fear and control?
- Physically: Am I rested enough or am I running on fumes?
- Socially: Are outside demands draining my capacity for connection?

One small shift that would strengthen my love in wholeness:

____

____

____

____

Empowering Declaration

I build love with intention. I notice when our connection thins, and I choose to return. I practice repair without pride and honesty without harm and stay strong without armor. I choose a love that keeps becoming, and I keep becoming inside it.

Chapter 24
Two Wholes, One Complete Love

Now everything comes back to center. Not as a neat ending, and not as a perfect bow, but as a truth that settles into your body once you stop fighting it and start living it.

You don't become whole so you can never need anyone. You become whole so you can love without losing yourself. You become whole so love can feel lighter, safer, and more real. Whole people still need support. Whole people still want closeness. Whole people still get tired, triggered, and tender. The difference is that wholeness changes what love is responsible for.

Two halves can cling. Two wounds can collide. Two whole people can build.

Wholeness Is Not Strength On Repeat

A lot of people confuse wholeness with strength, especially if strength is what kept you afloat. Strength is powerful. It has helped you lead, provide, protect, endure, and keep moving through seasons in which you didn't even have space to grieve. But strength can also become a mask you wear for so long that you forget it's a mask. You can be capable and still feel unseen. You can be dependable and still feel alone. You can "handle it" and still be quietly abandoning yourself in the process.

Wholeness is not the belief that you can carry everything. Wholeness is the decision that you don't have to disappear to keep love stable. It's the difference between living like you're in a fortress and living like you're at home.

296

When Survival Becomes Your Personality

Survival is not only a season. Sometimes it becomes a lens. If you spent years stabilizing environments, your nervous system may still treat calm as suspicious. You may stay alert even when life is peaceful. You may keep scanning for the next problem because your body learned that safety was temporary. That isn't failure. That's adaptation.

But adaptation can outlive its usefulness, and when it does, it starts shaping love in ways you don't always notice. You begin confusing being needed with being loved. You begin treating support as weakness. You begin equating carrying more with commitment and interpreting closeness as exposure, so you stay responsible but not fully reachable.

Wholeness is when you notice those old rules and stop letting them run your relationships.

The Myth That Hurts Love The Most

A lot of people were taught some version of "Two halves make a whole." It sounds romantic. It sounds hopeful. It also puts pressure on love that love was never designed to carry.

When you enter love as a half, you expect love to complete you. You expect your partner to soothe what you haven't healed. You use the relationship as a measure of worth. You interpret normal conflict as a threat because the relationship is carrying too much weight. And that's how love becomes heavy, even when it's real.

Two whole people enter differently. Not flawless. Not finished. But responsible. They don't outsource identity. They don't turn their partner into a savior. They don't treat love like a test they have to pass to be chosen. They bring self-awareness to the relationship so love can become a place of shared growth rather than emotional survival.

What Two Whole People Do Differently

Two whole people still have issues. They still get triggered. They still miss each other sometimes. They still have hard seasons and awkward conversations, and moments when the tone gets sharp and they need to come back and clean it up.

But the posture is different.

They don't ask the relationship to carry their identity. They can receive love without turning it into proof. They can tell the truth without using it as a weapon. They can repair without pride needing to win first. They can set boundaries without guilt. And they understand something that matters more than people admit: An emotional culture must be shared.

A relationship can't stay healthy long term if one person is the stabilizer and the other is the passenger because that dynamic eventually produces resentment, even if both people are good. Two whole people choose shared ownership. Not because they're perfect at it, but because they're committed to building something that doesn't secretly cost one person their tenderness.

Mature Interdependence, Not Emotional Isolation

Wholeness doesn't mean you become emotionally independent in a cold way. It means you practice mature interdependence. You can need support and remain anchored. You can receive care and still keep your agency. You can be deeply connected without losing yourself. You

298

can be honest about being triggered without making the trigger your partner's responsibility to fix. You can ask for reassurance without turning reassurance into a demand.

That's what two wholes look like in real life. Not perfection. Stability. Peace.

Peace Is Not Boredom

This matters if you've ever felt uneasy in calm. Some people confuse peace with boredom because peace doesn't activate the nervous system the way chaos does. If unpredictability shaped your early understanding of love, steady love can feel unfamiliar. But unfamiliar doesn't mean wrong.

A calm relationship doesn't have to be shallow. It can be deep and steady at the same time. You don't have to chase intensity to feel alive. You can learn to trust peace.

The Real Goal: Love That Lets You Exhale

If you're in a relationship, I'm not asking you to judge whether your love is "good enough." It's giving you a clearer target. A love that honors wholeness feels like a place where honesty stays safe, tenderness isn't rare, boundaries protect peace, repair is consistent, and both people can keep becoming more whole without turning growth into distance. It doesn't feel like another arena in which you have to perform. It feels like a place you can breathe.

And if you're not in a relationship, this truth can still free you. You aren't waiting to be completed. You're becoming whole so you can recognize love that complements instead of consumes you.

Closing Reflection

Wholeness is not the absence of need. It's the absence of self-abandonment. You don't have to earn love by carrying more. You don't have to prove you're worthy by being exceptional. You don't have to stay braced in calm. You don't have to shrink to stay connected.

Two wholes make it complete because love stops being an identity rescue mission and becomes what it was always meant to be: a shared life, a steady partnership, a safe place to grow.

The Practice: The Return-To-Yourself Reset

When you feel yourself slipping into old survival patterns, don't try to fix your whole life in that moment, return to yourself. Name what's happening without drama, give your body a minute to soften, and choose one constructive response instead of the familiar reflexive reaction. Sometimes the most powerful shift is not a better argument but a calmer body and a truer expression of yourself.

Journal Prompts

Answer what stands out. Skip what doesn't. Stay honest.

1. Where do I still confuse being needed with being loved?
2. What part of me treats calm as suspicious, and what would help me trust peace?
3. Where do I overfunction to feel secure, and what would shared responsibility look like instead?
4. What does love feel like when I'm not proving myself, bracing, or performing?
5. What is one daily practice I can use to return to myself?

Wholeness Check-In

Notice what your nervous system does when life is quiet.

- Mentally and emotionally, do you stay anchored or start scanning for problems?
- Spiritually, do you feel grounded or default to control?
- Physically, does your body relax in safety or stay braced out of habit?
- Socially, do your relationships support your wholeness or reward your overfunctioning?

One small shift that would ground you:

____

____

____

____

____

Empowering Declaration

I am whole and I choose love that honors that. I release self-abandonment and overfunctioning. I welcome peace without interrogation. I practice mature interdependence with honesty and respect. Two wholes make it complete, and I'm living that truth now.

Part Three
Legacy

Legacy isn't only what you accomplish. It's what people experience when they're close to you. It's the emotional climate you create, the trust you build, and the patterns you interrupt so they don't keep traveling through generations.

This part is about the life you're living now, not the stories people will tell later. It's about alignment that holds up under pressure. It's about becoming someone who can be trusted, loved, and followed without fear.

We'll look at legacy in leadership, love, money, healing, home, and the everyday choices that quietly determine what gets passed down. At this point, wholeness stops being a concept you understand and becomes something your life proves.

Chapter 25
Legacy Starts with the Life You Live

For a long time, I thought legacy meant achievement. Titles. Impact. Recognition. The kind of story people tell about you when you aren't in the room.

That definition felt safe because it was measurable. You can point to a resume. You can show results. You can build a life that looks strong from the outside and feel like you're doing it right.

But the deeper I grew into wholeness, the more I realized legacy isn't primarily about what you accomplish. It's about what you create around you. Not only outcomes but atmosphere. Not only what people say but what they carry after being close to you.

If you've spent years being the capable one, this can land in a tender place because capability can become a hiding place. It can keep you productive while your inner life gets quieter and thinner. That's the quiet danger. Your life can look full and still feel emotionally undernourished.

Legacy doesn't begin later. It begins now, in the version of you who shows up today.

The Legacy Most People Never Name

We tend to associate legacy with big moments. The photos. The speeches. The milestones that get documented and celebrated.

But most legacy isn't loud. It's built in the moments that repeat. The tone you use when you're tired. The way you respond when you're disappointed. The way you listen when you don't agree.

The people closest to you will rarely remember the highlight reel. They will remember whether they felt safe bringing you the truth and whether your love came with pressure or with room to breathe. They will remember whether you were easy to reach or always somewhere else, even when you were physically present.

That's part of what makes this chapter personal, because you can be a good person and still leave people feeling tense around you. You can do so much for others and still teach them, without meaning to, that closeness requires carefulness. You can be loyal and still feel like you're slowly becoming unreachable.

You don't have to be perfect to build a legacy you respect. You do have to be honest about what your life is teaching right now.

The Atmosphere You Create Is Part Of Your Legacy

Legacy is the tone of your home. It's the integrity of your yes and your no. It's the quality of your attention. It's the way you come back after conflict. It's the steadiness you carry in hard conversations.

It's also the subtle impact your presence has on the room's nervous system. Do people soften when you walk in, or do they brace? Do they feel like they can tell you the truth, or do they edit themselves to avoid your reaction? That's not about blame. That's about awareness.

Because legacy is also what you normalize. When you normalize burnout, you teach people that rest is earned. When you normalize silence after hurt, you teach people that tension isn't safe to name. When you normalize emotional honesty, you teach people that connection can hold real life. When you normalize repair, you teach people that love doesn't disappear when things get uncomfortable.

This is one of the clearest truths of wholeness. What you practice becomes contagious. People learn what's possible around you.

When Achievement Becomes A Hiding Place

There was a season when I could execute anything. I could lead. I could organize. I could produce results. I could hold everyone and everything together. And from the outside, it looked like strength.

But inside, I started operating like I was armored.

Capability isn't the problem. The problem comes when capability becomes the only way you know how to be. That's when the private cost begins to add up. You stop noticing the tension in your shoulders because it's normal now. You stop noticing how restless your mind is because it's your default. You start feeling resentful when people assume you can carry more, but you keep saying yes anyway. You become the person everyone relies on, and quietly, you stop relying on anyone.

If you've lived in that space, you know what it's like to be admired and lonely at the same time. You're not lonely because you don't have people but because you're not fully with them. And you're not fully with yourself, either.

I remember a moment in which I should have felt peaceful but didn't. My calendar was taken care of, but my inner world was neglected. My life was full, but my soul felt thin. And what surprised me wasn't the exhaustion. It was the emptiness.

That's when the question shifted.

308

Not "What am I building?"

But "What am I becoming as I build it?"

That's the legacy question. Because legacy isn't what your hands produce if your heart is absent. Legacy is who you are, consistently, when your hands are full.

The Legacy Gap

Here's where most people feel the tension, even if they don't have language for it yet. You value family, but you never slow down enough to actually be present. You value integrity, but you keep making exceptions that cost you peace. You value love, but you avoid the conversations that would protect your relationships. You value faith and grounding, but you don't give your spirit time to breathe.

That distance between what you say matters and what your life actually demonstrates is what I call the legacy gap.

Most people don't create that gap on purpose. They create it through overload, distraction, unhealed patterns, and the constant pressure to be available, impressive, and fine. The legacy gap isn't a reason for shame. It's a reason for alignment. Alignment always starts the same way, with truth. Not with what looks good, what you wish were true, or what you can explain away. Truth is the starting line for wholeness, and it's the starting line for legacy.

What Alignment Actually Looks Like

You get aligned when your values, choices, and behavior match. It's when you stop performing and start living your life. It's when you become consistent in a way that feels honest, not rigid. It's when you don't have to keep negotiating with your peace.

Misalignment is exhausting. It's living with one foot in what you say you want and the other in what you're used to. It's saying yes while your spirit says no. It's smiling as your body tightens. It's staying silent as your integrity asks you to speak.

If you want to build a legacy, you will eventually have to disappoint the version of you that survives by pleasing everyone. You'll have to outgrow old rules. You'll have to stop bargaining with your peace.

Not because you're becoming selfish, but because you're becoming reliable. You're becoming someone whose life matches what they claim to value.

Legacy In Leadership, Love, And Ordinary Life

Legacy shows up differently depending on where you stand, but the root stays the same: consistency.

In leadership, legacy is what people learn about safety and truth by watching how you handle pressure. They may forget your exact words, but they won't forget whether you made it safe to be human while still holding the standard.

In love, legacy is the emotional pattern you create. Are hard conversations punished or welcomed? Is affection consistent or conditional? Do people have to earn your softness? The people closest to you will carry your relational patterns forward. That means your healing doesn't only shape your life. It shapes theirs.

In ordinary life, legacy is the relationship you have with your body and time. Do you treat yourself like a machine, or do you honor your humanity? Do you model rest and reflection as normal parts of a strong life or only as rewards you get after you collapse?

Legacy isn't just what you teach. It's what you permit. And if this feels like a lot, come closer to one simple truth. Legacy is what becomes normal in your presence.

The Quiet Legacy Of Everyday Choices

Most of your legacy will be built in moments so small they almost feel unimportant. These moments include the way you respond when you're tired. The way you listen when someone is emotional. The way you pause before you react. The way you return when you miss it.

If you're reading this and thinking, "I haven't always done that well," stay with me. Legacy isn't ruined by imperfection. It's shaped by your willingness to grow. The most powerful legacy isn't spotless performance. It's honest transformation.

People don't need you to be flawless. They need you to be real. They need you to be consistent. They need you to be safe enough to tell the truth to.

If you've been the strong one for a long time, this may be your invitation to show a different kind of strength. The kind that includes tenderness. The kind that includes repair. The kind that includes rest without guilt.

Closing Reflection

Legacy isn't a trophy you earn later. It's the atmosphere you create now.

You don't have to wait for life to get easier, quieter, or more perfect. You can build legacy in your real life, in your real responsibilities, in your real relationships. Wholeness doesn't ask you to become someone else. It invites you to become more honest, more present, and more aligned.

As you move into the next chapters, keep this in your pocket: the life you live is already teaching something. You get to decide what it teaches next.

The Practice

Choose one small habit that represents the person you're becoming. Keep it specific and repeatable. Not impressive. Repeatable.

My next small practice:
My cue:
My first step:

Journal Prompts

Answer what stands out. Skip what doesn't. Keep it honest.

1. When I picture legacy, what shows up first, and what does that reveal about what I value?
2. Where am I out of alignment right now, and what is the cost of staying there?
3. What is one daily pattern I want to be known for five years from now, and what would it take to begin it this week?
4. What would change if I measured success by peace and integrity, not only by performance?
5. Who is watching me more closely than I think, and what do I want them to feel when they think of me?

Wholeness Check-In

Reflect on how your pillars contribute to your legacy

- Where am I pushing past a limit instead of honoring it?
- Where do I need to repair, clarify, or communicate more directly?
- Where am I acting out of obligation that no longer fits my values?
- If someone learned how to live by watching me this week, what would they learn?

One small shift that would strengthen my legacy:

____

____

____

____

____

Empowering Declaration

I choose intention, not momentum. My legacy begins in the ways I show up today. I honor what I've carried, release what no longer fits, and build what lasts through aligned choices. I lead from wholeness, love from wholeness, and create a life that reflects what I truly value.

Chapter 26
The Inheritance of Wholeness

Some patterns get passed down through what was celebrated. Others get passed down through what was avoided. Either way, patterns have a way of becoming normal long before you ever realize you're living inside them. And once something becomes normal, it doesn't just shape your behavior. It shapes your expectations. It shapes what you tolerate. It quietly trains you on what to call love, what to call strength, what to call "just life."

You inherit ways of coping, communicating, and handling money, intimacy, conflict, stress, and success. You inherit what people did when they were upset, and you inherit what they refused to name. Sometimes you inherit tenderness. Sometimes you inherit toughness. You can inherit the unspoken rule that hard things don't get talked about until they explode or until they disappear into time.

And here's the part that matters: a lot of these patterns once made sense. They protected someone. They preserved something. They helped people survive. But survival tools don't always make good legacy tools.

What kept your family steady in one era can keep you stuck in another. And if you don't name the pattern, you'll keep reenacting it and calling it personality. You'll defend it as loyalty. You'll excuse it as maturity. All while something in you quietly knows that you don't want to live this way or pass down these patterns.

How Patterns Hide In Plain Sight

Patterns rarely announce themselves. They don't show up with warning lights. They show up as autopilot.

They sound like the tone that slips into your voice when you're tired or the silence you reach for because honesty feels too costly or the control that takes over the moment life starts feeling uncertain. They can show up as overfunctioning, when you carry too much, fix too fast, stay ten steps ahead, and hold the emotional climate because you can feel tension before anyone else even names it. If you've been praised for being the strong one, that pattern can feel like love. It can feel like leadership. It can feel like responsibility.

Patterns can also show up in the opposite direction, when you pull away. You avoid, delay, minimize, and disconnect because conflict has always felt like it costs too much. Somewhere along the way, you learned that saying what you really feel creates more problems than it solves, so you keep it tight. You keep it quiet. You keep it moving.

Those may look like opposite styles, but beneath both is the same nervous-system question: "How do I stay safe right now?"

Once you understand that, you can finally ask the question that changes everything: "Is this pattern keeping me safe, or is it keeping me small?"

The Moment You Realize This Isn't Just You

There's usually a moment when the old way stops feeling normal and starts feeling heavy.

For some people, it's the day they hear themselves speak in a tone they promised they'd never use. For others,

318

it's noticing how fast they shut down when something tender comes up. For many high-capacity people, it's realizing that stress doesn't just make them productive. It makes them tight. It makes them more efficient, more controlled, more serious. It turns them into a project manager of life.

On the outside, that can look like leadership. On the inside, it can feel like pressure. It can create distance in close relationships.

That's when you realize the pattern looks productive, but it's really protection.

Not because you don't love people, but because your nervous system learned something early and powerful: control equals security. So when life feels uncertain, you don't just respond. You tighten. You handle. You manage. You try to get ahead of the feeling before the feeling gets ahead of you.

At some point, you see it clearly. Your strength has become a shield.

That realization doesn't need to shame you. It can sober you in the best way by clarifying what's at stake. If stress keeps leading you, you won't only pass down a schedule or a standard. You'll pass down a way of living. You'll pass down the message that love means carrying. You'll pass down the belief that success requires self-erasure. You'll pass down a nervous system that never fully exhales.

Understanding Isn't The Same As Repeating

There's a difference between understanding why a pattern formed and excusing why it remains.

You can honor the version of you who needed that tool and still release it now. You can respect what helped you survive and still tell yourself the truth: "This tool can't run the whole house anymore."

Sometimes people stay loyal to patterns because they confuse familiarity with love. They think "If I change, I'm betraying my roots." But breaking a pattern isn't disrespecting your roots; it's strengthening them. It's saying "I love where I come from, and I'm choosing to grow beyond what hurt us."

That's not rebellion. That's maturity, one of the clearest forms of legacy.

Compassion Without Repeating The Cycle

This is where wholeness gets practical. If you're changing, you may have to change how you relate to people who still expect the old version of you. Not with drama. Not with speeches but with clarity.

Sometimes it means you stop volunteering for conversations that you know won't be safe. Sometimes it means refusing to rehash the same argument. Sometimes it means you set a boundary and don't overexplain it, because you're not trying to win the case, you're trying to keep your peace intact. Sometimes it looks like tolerating someone else's disappointment without rushing to rescue them from it.

When you break a pattern, you change the system, and systems push back.

That pushback doesn't mean you're doing it incorrectly. It usually means you're doing it for real. Your job isn't to convince everyone. Your job is to stay aligned with who you're becoming.

You can love people and still protect your peace. You can honor your family and still refuse what harms you. That isn't cold. That's adult love. That's legacy love.

Why Pattern Breaking Feels So Personal

Pattern breaking isn't just a mindset shift. It's a nervous system upgrade.

Even healthy change can feel unsafe at first, not because it's wrong, but because it's unfamiliar. If you grew up around shutdown, honest emotion may feel like too much. If you grew up around chaos, stability may feel suspicious. If you grew up around criticism, being seen may feel risky. If you grew up in a culture of scarcity, rest may feel irresponsible.

This is why people can know all the right things and still repeat the same cycles. Knowledge isn't the same as integration. Integration happens when you practice a new response while your body is still learning that it's safe.

So if you're reading this and wondering "Why is this taking me so long?" let that thought soften. This work is deep. And the fact that you can see it means you're already changing it.

What Actually Creates A New Inheritance

The pattern breaks when you pause long enough to notice what's happening inside you before you react. You notice the tightening. The urge to control. The impulse to withdraw. The need to prove your point. The reflex to shut down. You notice it not to judge yourself but to interrupt the script.

Then you make a conscious choice. Maybe not perfectly. And if you miss it, you repair, because repair is what keeps one moment from becoming the new normal. Generational patterns end when you practice a new pattern until your life starts exhibiting something different.

Closing Reflection

You don't break patterns by fighting yourself. You break them by telling the truth and trying a new approach until your nervous system learns that it's safe to be whole.

Your legacy isn't determined by what you inherited; it's shaped by what you choose next. And every time you pause instead of reacting, you create a new inheritance.

The Practice

When you feel the old script rising, don't rush to fix it or justify it. Pause long enough to come back into your body. Let your breath slow down. Let your shoulders drop. Let your nervous system catch up to the truth that you're safe enough to choose.

Name what's happening with one honest sentence. Nothing fancy. Just true.

Then choose one response. The kind of response you'd be proud to pass down. The kind that keeps you aligned with who you're becoming.

My next small practice:

Journal Prompts

Answer what stands out. Skip what doesn't. Stay honest.

1. What patterns did I grow up seeing around conflict, money, affection, and stress, and which ones show up most in my life now?
2. What's one pattern that protected me earlier in life, and what does it cost me now?
3. When I'm triggered, do I move toward control, avoidance, or shutdown, and what am I afraid will happen if I soften?
4. What is one pattern I don't want to pass along, and what is the smallest new behavior I can practice the next time the trigger shows up?
5. Who benefits when I break this pattern, and what becomes possible in my relationships as a result?

Wholeness Check-In

Look at you pillars through the lens of legacy.

- What familiar script am I about to run right now?
- What emotion am I trying to avoid or control?
- What would wholeness, not perfection, look like in this moment?
- What is one honest thing I can say that would shift the direction of this pattern?
- If I miss it, what repair will I make so this moment doesn't become our new normal?

One small shift that would strengthen my legacy:

____

____

____

____

____

Empowering Declaration

I break negative patterns with honesty and compassion. I notice what's familiar without letting it lead me. I take ownership of my responses, and I return to repair when I miss it. I release what no longer fits, and I practice a new way until it becomes my normal. I build legacy through wholeness, one choice at a time.

Chapter 27
Leaving an Inheritance of Trust

We live in a world that celebrates visibility, but legacy lives in trust. Trust is what makes people feel safe with you. It's what makes partnerships steady. It's what makes teams resilient and families feel like home.

You can build a beautiful life on paper and still feel like you're standing on shaky ground if trust is missing. You can also be living an imperfect, very real life that still feels deeply meaningful because trust is present.

Trust isn't a vibe. It's evidence. It's built in the way you show up when it's inconvenient. It grows through consistency, honesty, and repair. It weakens you through avoidance, defensiveness, and broken agreements that never get named.

If you want to think about legacy in one sentence, let it be this: The trust you build becomes permission others live by.

When people trust you, their shoulders drop. They stop performing. They tell the truth sooner. They bring the real thing into the room instead of the watered-down version they think you can handle. And if you've ever been around someone who felt truly safe, you know how rare that is.

Trust Is The Quiet Inheritance People Carry Forward

Most people hear the word "inheritance" and think of money, property, and what gets passed down in a will. But trust is its own inheritance. It becomes the emotional "money" people spend for the rest of their lives.

If you grew up around steady trust, you learned that love can be consistent. That conflict can be survivable. That honesty doesn't have to cost you belonging. You didn't have to guess the mood. You didn't have to monitor the room temperature to feel safe in the space.

If you grew up around shaky trust, you may have learned the opposite. You learned to watch and interpret. You learned to guess what was safe to say. You learned that people could feel close one day and unreachable the next, and that love could turn cold when things got uncomfortable.

This chapter isn't here to shame your past. It's here to give you choices. Because no matter what you experienced, you get to decide what you pass down.

Where Trust Actually Gets Built

Trust doesn't live in one category of life. It doesn't stay neatly in romance, parenting, or leadership. It has separate compartments. Trust is more integrated than that. It starts internally, then spreads outward.

It shows up in the way you treat yourself, especially when you're tired or stretched. It shows up in the way you treat people when the moment is tender. It shows up in the way you hold responsibility without using it as leverage. And it shows up in the quiet alignment between your private life and your public life, because people can feel the difference between someone who appears "solid" and someone who's actually grounded.

This is why self-trust matters more than most people realize. When you don't trust yourself, you start reaching for security in ways that create the opposite. You overexplain. You overpromise. You overextend. You try to stay ahead of disappointment by saying yes too fast, only to resent it later.

328

But when you trust yourself, your yes becomes clean. Your no becomes calm. Your presence becomes steady. And people can feel that steadiness without you needing to announce it.

The Real Show Of Strength Is How You Return

One of the most humbling lessons in growth is realizing that trust isn't built by never missing it. That's not real life. That's performance. Trust is built by how you return when you do.

There are moments when your tone lands more sharply than you intended, when you prioritize efficiency over connection, when you assume someone knows what you mean instead of taking a minute to say it well. In older versions of yourself, you might have justified it quickly. "I'm tired. I've got a lot going on. I didn't mean it like that."

But wholeness teaches something better than justification. It teaches repair.

Repair doesn't have to be dramatic. It just has to be honest. It sounds like coming back and saying, "I want to revisit that. My tone was off." Or "I made an assumption instead of checking in." Or "I was stressed, and I let that lead me. I'm sorry."

When you repair, you teach people something powerful without preaching it. You teach them that love doesn't disappear when things get uncomfortable. You teach them that conflict isn't the end. You teach them that relationships can hold both truth and safety.

If you didn't grow up around repair, practicing it now might feel vulnerable in ways that surprise you. That's okay. Vulnerability isn't danger. Most of the time, it's the doorway to trust.

Consistency Builds Trust More Than Intensity Ever Will

People try to build trust through intensity. Big gestures. Long talks. Emotional promises. One powerful moment that feels convincing…but then fades because nothing changes afterward.

Trust grows differently. Trust grows through follow-through. Through repeated evidence. Through the quiet, boring faithfulness of doing what you said you would do and telling the truth when you can't. Consistency is what the nervous system recognizes. It's what your partner relies on. It's what your children notice. It's what your colleagues respect.

If you want to leave an inheritance of trust, focus on the promises you can actually keep. Speak less. Do more. And when you do speak, mean it.

Repair That Rebuilds Trust Without Shame

A clean repair doesn't require you to grovel, and it doesn't require you to turn into stone, either. It's not self-punishment. It's leadership.

It's being willing to name what happened without dressing it up. It's being willing to acknowledge the impact without arguing. It's being willing to say what you'll do differently in a way that's specific enough to be real. And it's being willing to ask what the other person needs so safety can return.

That kind of repair does something beautiful. It protects dignity on both sides. It keeps you from spiraling into defensiveness and collapsing into shame. It teaches you that "We can come back."

330

Trust Becomes Easier When Expectations Stop Being A Guessing Game

One of the simplest ways to strengthen trust is to make the invisible visible.

A lot of stress in relationships comes from emotional guessing. "I thought you knew. I assumed you'd do it like I would. I didn't want to bring it up. I didn't want to make it a thing." And then resentment builds because everyone's living with unspoken expectations.

Trust strengthens when there's clarity about what you can count on. Not rigid rules, just shared understanding. Something like "Here's what I'll do. Here's what I need. And here's what we'll do when we miss it."

When people know what to expect, they relax. And if you've been carrying relationships on intuition and emotional guessing, clarity can feel like relief. Not controlling. Just stabilizing.

The Small Leaks That Quietly Weaken Trust

Most trust breakdowns aren't caused by one big betrayal. They're caused by small leaks that go unaddressed.

It's the habit of pretending things are fine when they're not. It's the instinct to protect the ego rather than the relationship. It's being warm one day and cold the next without explanation. It's saying yes to keep peace, then feeling resentful later. It's letting time do the job that only truth can do.

If any of that sounds familiar, don't spiral. This chapter isn't a verdict. It's an invitation. Name what you see. Choose one new behavior. Practice it until it's natural.

Because that's how trust becomes inheritance. Not through a big moment but through steady proof over time.

The Trust Promise

If you want to build trust intentionally, pick one promise to keep for the next two weeks. Keep it small enough to keep. That's the whole point. You're not trying to impress anyone. You're trying to create evidence.

Evidence calms anxiety. Evidence reduces second-guessing. Evidence builds steadiness.

At the end of two weeks, do a simple review. What changed in your stress level? What changed in your tone? What changed in your relationships? Then choose your next promise.

Here's one of the clearest signs trust is growing: people bring you the truth sooner. They stop waiting for the perfect moment. They stop walking on eggshells. They speak with more honesty and less fear.

That's not just trust. That's freedom.

Closing Reflection

Your legacy doesn't need to be loud to be lasting.

When you become someone who can be trusted, you give the people around you a gift they will carry forward. An inheritance of safety. Of honesty. Of steady love.

The truth that ties it all together is this: trust isn't only what you build with other people. It's also what you build inside yourself. Every honest boundary, every clean repair, every clear yes, and every courageous no strengthens your inner foundation. And that foundation becomes one of the safest gifts you can offer the people you love.

The Practice

Choose one small act you can do next that signals alignment.

My next small practice:

Journal Prompts

Answer what stands out. Skip what doesn't. Keep it honest.

1. What does trust mean to me? How do I know when I feel it, and how do I know when I don't?
2. When do people experience me as consistent? When do they experience me as unpredictable? What is happening inside me when I shift?
3. What is one area of my life in which I need to stop overpromising and start being more honest?
4. With whom do I need to rebuild trust, and what is one concrete step I can take this week that proves I'm serious?
5. If my legacy were summarized in one word, what do I want that word to be, and what does that require of me daily?

Wholeness Check-In

Reflect on your pillars through a lens of strengthening your legacy.

- When am I asking others to trust me while I'm not trusting myself?
- What is one commitment I've made that I need to honor or renegotiate?
- With whom do I need to have a repair conversation today, even if it feels uncomfortable?
- What repeated behavior would prove trust over the next thirty days?
- If someone described me as trustworthy, what would they point to?

One small shift that would strengthen my legacy:

____

____

____

____

____

Empowering Declaration

I build trust with consistency, honesty, and repair. I keep my word, and I tell the truth with care. I don't hide behind defensiveness or disappear into silence. When I miss it, I return with humility and make it right. I choose a legacy of safety, steadiness, and love that people can rely on.

Chapter 28
Passing the Torch

When people think about legacy, they often picture something big. A name on a building. A title that carries weight. A monetary inheritance. A public impact that can be measured.

But most legacy isn't built in public. It's built in relationship. It's the emotional imprint you leave on the people closest to you. It's the tone of your home. It's the way you respond when someone disappoints you. It's what your children, your partner, your team, and your friends learn about love and safety because of the way you live.

I've watched high performers chase legacy in the form of achievement while quietly losing the kind of legacy they wanted. They wanted their kids to feel secure. They wanted their relationship to feel steady. They wanted to be remembered as present, kind, and trustworthy. Unfortunately, they were so focused on what they could produce that they stopped noticing what they were passing down.

If you want a legacy of wholeness, it won't be built only through what you accomplish. It will be built through how you treat people when you're tired, pressured, and stretched. Especially then.

What You Model Becomes Someone Else's Normal

You teach people what to expect from relationships by how you show up in yours. You teach people how to treat you by what you tolerate. You teach people what love feels like by the ways you love them.

If you grew up in an environment where taking on too much responsibility was praised, you may have learned to earn your place by being useful. If you grew up around tension that never got repaired, you may have learned to keep moving and never talk about what hurt. If you grew up with a lot of silence, you may have learned to read the room instead of saying what you need.

Those patterns don't magically disappear when you become an adult. They show up in parenting. They show up in leadership. They show up in partnership. And if you don't interrupt them, they quietly become the culture you pass down.

That's why your legacy isn't only what you tell people. It's what you teach them through your nervous system. Through your consistency. Through your boundaries. Through your repair. Through your ability to stay grounded when things get messy.

So here's an honest question worth contemplating: What is becoming normal in your presence? Not because you say it out loud, but because you live it out loud.

Influence Doesn't Require Perfection

Some people hear "legacy" and immediately feel pressure. Then they hear "influence" and feel it even more, because now it sounds like you're responsible for everybody's outcome.

That's not what this is.

Influence is less about getting it right and more about being real. A legacy of wholeness is built when the people you influence learn that emotions are safe, truth is welcome, boundaries are normal, and repair belongs in love.

Perfection isn't required for that. Humility is.

The willingness to say "I missed that." The willingness to admit you overreacted. The willingness to come back and make

it right instead of trying to move on fast and pretend it
didn't matter.

Because here's what's true: your legacy isn't built by
never failing. It's built by what you do after you fail. Do
you excuse it? Do you justify it? Or do you own it and
repair it?

A child doesn't need a flawless model. A child needs a
safe one. A team doesn't need an untouchable leader. A
team needs a steady one. A mentee doesn't need a perfect
guide. A mentee needs an honest one.

Mentorship Is Legacy In Motion

Mentorship isn't always a formal program. Most of the
time, it's a way of paying attention.

It's noticing who is watching you and choosing to be
intentional about what they receive. It's realizing that your
consistency is teaching something. Your reactions are
teaching something. Your boundaries are teaching
something. Even the way you handle pressure teaches
something.

Mentorship happens when you share what you learned
the hard way so that someone else doesn't have to bleed for
it. It happens when you speak encouragement in a culture
that's quick to critique. It happens when you make room
for someone else's voice instead of filling every silence
with your own competence.

In a world that rewards self-promotion, mentorship
becomes a legacy act because it quietly says, "I don't need
to be the center of this. I can build with you. I can open
doors and let you walk through first."

And when your life is rooted in wholeness, your
mentorship doesn't come from ego. It comes from

overflow. You don't mentor to feel needed. You mentor because you remember how it felt to be unseen.

That's where legacy deepens. Not when you collect credit, but when you leave someone stronger, steadier, and more confident in their own voice.

The Part That Feels Tender: Releasing Control Without Withdrawing Care

If you're someone who carries responsibility well, passing the torch can feel emotional in a way people don't talk about.

When you've been the one building, protecting, solving, and holding the standard, it's natural to want the next person to do it your way. That doesn't always come from control. Sometimes it comes from love. From investment. From fear of watching something you value fall apart.

But legacy isn't preserved by a tight grip. Legacy survives when your values are clear enough to travel without your supervision.

That's the difference between influence and control. Control says, "I trust you, as long as you do it my way." Influence says, "I trust you with what matters, and I'll let you create the way you carry it."

This is one of the most mature moves a strong person can make. You stay clear about what matters, you stay honest about what you feel, and you allow yourself to be surprised. It might not look exactly like you would've done it, and that's the point. Legacy isn't about preserving your exact method. It's about passing forward your values in a way that leaves the next person free.

A Legacy Conversation That Keeps Dignity Intact

Sometimes the most powerful influence you'll have isn't in a speech. It's in a clear, intentional conversation.

It's when you can look at someone you're guiding and say, with warmth and clarity, "Here's what we protect. Here's what can evolve. I trust you to make it yours, and I'm here if you want counsel."

That kind of language does two things at once. It communicates standards without domination and support without hovering. It leaves the other person with dignity instead of pressure. And dignity is part of wholeness.

The Quiet Truth: Legacy Is Built In How You Come Back

If you want to make this chapter practical, keep it simple.

Legacy grows in the moments after tension, after disappointment, after misunderstanding, after a miss. When you come back with humility instead of ego, you teach people that relationships can hold truth without punishment.

That's the kind of influence people remember.

And it's the kind of influence that outlives your accomplishments, because it doesn't only shape what people do. It shapes what they believe is possible in love, in leadership, and in themselves.

Closing Reflection

Legacy doesn't require you to be loud. It requires you to be intentional. The people closest to you aren't watching for perfection. They're watching for presence. When you choose repair over pride, honesty over image, and boundaries over burnout, you build a legacy that can hold weight.

The Practice

Choose one relationship in which you want to strengthen trust and emotional safety. Not with a grand gesture. With a repeatable rhythm. Picture one moment you need to come back to, even if it's small. Then keep your repair clean. Name what happened without defending it. Own your part without collapsing. Acknowledge what you understand about their experience. Then name one specific way you want to show up differently moving forward.

My next small practice:

Journal Prompts

Answer what stands out. Skip what doesn't. Stay honest.

1. When I think about the people I influence most, how do I want them to feel when they think of me five years from now?
2. What pattern from my upbringing do I refuse to pass down, and what will I do differently this week?
3. Where do I confuse control with leadership or protection, and what is a healthier way to show up?
4. What honest repair conversation have I been avoiding, and what is the cost of avoiding it?
5. Who could benefit from my mentorship right now, and what is one specific way I can invest in them without overextending myself?

Wholeness Check-In

One small shift that would strengthen my love in wholeness:

- Self: How am I trying to influence others while neglecting my own emotional health?
- Relationships: Where do I need to repair, apologize, or clarify before I try to teach anyone else?
- Influence: Who is watching me right now, and what are they learning from my patterns?
- Legacy: What would shift if I treated my home, my friendships, and my team as my primary legacy work?

One small shift that would strengthen my legacy:

____

____

____

____

Empowering Declaration

I lead with presence, not pressure. I influence with integrity, not control. I pass forward what matters most through consistency, repair, and love that stays reachable. I release the need to hold the reins and choose to build a legacy that can travel through other people with trust, dignity, and freedom.

Chapter 29
Building Legacy Together

Some people carry a legacy like a solo mission. They believe they have to do it alone, prove it alone, build it alone. If that mindset feels familiar, it's usually not arrogance. It's survival. It's the quiet belief that asking for support is a sign of weakness, that dependence leads to disappointment, that the safest way to be secure is to be self-sufficient.

And if you've been the reliable one for a long time, you might not even notice how automatic that story has become. You don't call it isolation. You call it being responsible and being capable.

A legacy that lasts is rarely built alone. It's built with other people. It's built in partnership. It's built in community. It's built in rooms where trust is cultivated and people keep their word. And if you're building a legacy relationship, eventually the focus shifts from your goals to your impact. Not because you lose yourself, but because aligned strength can hold weight without crushing either of you.

In a healthy partnership, you don't compete for importance. You coordinate for impact. You don't keep score. You keep promises.

The Legacy Of A Partnership Is Its Culture

Every partnership has a culture, whether you name it or not. It has a tone. A default posture. A way of speaking when life is easy and a way of speaking when life gets tight. It has a pattern for how you resolve conflict, handle stress, and respond when someone misses the mark. That

348

culture becomes your legacy long before anyone sees your results.

Some partnerships create culture by default. Hard conversations get delayed until resentment becomes the language. Stress gets treated like permission to go cold or go sharp. Intensity gets confused with intimacy. Decisions get made under pressure, and then everyone acts like the pressure is gone even though the residue is still sitting in the room.

A legacy partnership doesn't leave culture to chance. It decides what matters. It practices what it says it values. It tells the truth early. It returns quickly. It treats trust as an asset that must be protected.

Because you can do incredible work publicly while privately living in constant tension. The work can look powerful. The culture can be fragile. And when the culture collapses, the legacy often collapses with it.

So before you ask "Are we productive?" ask something more honest: "What is the tone of our partnership when we're under pressure? What is the tone when we're disappointed? What is the tone when one of us needs rest?" Those answers will tell you what you're building.

From Strong Team To Safe Team

You and your partner can be a great team and still be emotionally distant. You can coordinate schedules, handle responsibilities, keep the house running, and still feel alone because safety is inadequate.

Many couples don't need a new level of romance. They need a safer way to handle hard moments. This safer approach includes fewer assumptions, more clarity, and a shared language for what happens when one person is tired, tender, triggered, or overloaded.

This is where wholeness matters, not as a concept but as a lived experience. Wholeness doesn't just make you more capable. It makes you more reachable and helps you stay connected even when your nervous system wants to shut down or take over.

The absence of conflict doesn't define a legacy partnership. The presence of repair defines it. It's what you do after the rupture that determines whether your relationship feels like a shelter or a pressure cooker.

Community Is A Legacy Multiplier

Legacy expands when you stop trying to do everything inside your own walls. Community becomes a multiplier. It brings accountability, shared wisdom, and a mirror that keeps you honest. It helps you stay connected to the truth when old patterns try to pull you back into isolation, perfectionism, or control.

A lot of high achievers embrace community in theory but not in practice. They have contacts. They have networks. They have people they can call for information or an opportunity. However, they don't have many people who can tell them the truth about their patterns without the relationship breaking.

Wholeness invites a different kind of community. Real community is made of people who can celebrate you without needing you to stay impressive and challenge you without turning it into shame.

If you've been the strong one, this may be the part that feels tender. Strong people often build a community that depends on their capacity. They are the helper. The advisor. The fixer. The one others call when things are falling apart.

350

That's beautiful. It's also exhausting if nobody is allowed to carry you as well.

Legacy-level community includes reciprocity. It includes relationships in which you can be honest, not just useful.

Service, Impact, And The Deeper Question

At some point, legacy becomes a deeper question. What are you here for? What are you building that matters beyond your comfort, beyond your ego, beyond your own story?

Calling often shows up as a steady pull toward contribution. For some people, that contribution is raising emotionally healthy children. For others, it's leading with integrity in a system that rewards shortcuts. For others, it's building something that restores dignity, strengthens relationships, and creates opportunity.

And the truth is, impact isn't only public. It's private, too. It's the way you show up for someone who can't repay you. It's the way you mentor. It's the way you use your voice when it would be easier to stay silent.

A legacy of wholeness asks what you want to multiply in the world. Not perfectly. Honestly. Are you multiplying fear or faith? Chaos or clarity? Control or connection. Image or integrity?

You don't have to answer that with a grand mission statement. Answer it with your next aligned step and then keep answering it with your actions.

The Two Legacies Every Couple Leaves

Every couple leaves an internal legacy and an external legacy. The internal legacy is what you build inside the partnership: trust, safety, friendship, alignment, and the ability to repair without losing respect. The external legacy is what flows out of it: how you show up in the world, how you parent or mentor, how you lead, how you serve, and how you love other people well because you're loved well at home.

Legacy shows up in patterns, not in big announcements.

- Do you return after rupture?
- Do you assume the best or reach for the worst?
- Do you keep respect intact when you're tired?
- Do you make room for each other's voices?
- Do you repair quickly enough that the distance doesn't get comfortable?

Those patterns become the story your relationship tells not just to other people but to your future selves.

Keeping The Relationship Up To Date

This isn't about perfection. It's about keeping your relationship current.

A lot of distance isn't caused by betrayal. An outdated connection causes it. You're both changing, life keeps moving, and the relationship keeps running on old assumptions. Meanwhile, the current version of each of you is quietly waiting to be seen again.

Legacy love stays awake. It doesn't wait until something breaks to check in. It notices the thin places early and treats them like something worth tending, not something to power through.

One of the simplest ways to do that is a short weekly check-in that feels like maintenance rather than a "serious talk." Just enough space to say what's real while it's still soft enough for you to adjust.

Intentional Agreements That Protect The "We"

Most couples already live by agreements. They're just unspoken. Who handles what. What counts as respect? What does support look like? What's acceptable when stress rises? What happens after conflict? What gets talked about outside the relationship?

When agreements stay unspoken, you end up renegotiating the relationship in every argument. That's why the same fight keeps returning in different outfits.

Legacy couples do something quieter and wiser. They name the agreements before pressure forces the conversation. They don't wait for a rupture to clarify what should've been protected all along. That doesn't make your relationship rigid. It makes it trustworthy.

Closing Reflection

Legacy isn't only about what you build. It's also about how you build it. When your partnership has a healthy culture, it becomes a shelter for your future. It becomes a place where love can grow and impact can expand without costing you your peace. You don't need a massive platform to leave a meaningful legacy. You need a life that's aligned and relationships that are trustworthy.

Build together. Speak honestly. Repair quickly. Keep your word. That is legacy.

The Practice

Schedule a short alignment meeting with your partner, a close friend, or a trusted collaborator. Thirty minutes is enough. Not to solve everything but to keep the culture current.

Go in with one goal: clarity without blame. Name what's working and let appreciation land. Name what feels off in a way that's factual and human, not heated. Then choose one specific adjustment for the next seven days that both of you can follow through on.

End with one commitment each, and then do the part that makes this legacy.

My next small practice:

Journal Prompts

Answer what stands out. Skip what doesn't. Stay honest.

1. What does partnership mean to me right now? Where am I aligned with it and where am I resisting it?
2. What culture am I creating in my closest relationships, and what would I change if I were watching from the outside?
3. Where do I need to replace assumptions with agreements, and what is one agreement I can clarify this week?
4. What kind of community do I need in this season, and what has kept me from building it?
5. What is one way I can contribute to something bigger than myself this month without burning out?

Wholeness Check-In

Explore your pillars through a lens of love and relationships.

- Self: Where am I carrying everything alone?
- Partnership: Where do we need a clearer agreement, a clearer plan, or a clearer boundary?
- Community: Where am I isolated, even around people?
- Legacy: What impact do I want my partnership and my community to have on others?

When you hit a rough patch, don't wait for it to "blow over." Come back on purpose. Ask what was heard, what was needed, what you want each other to understand, and what you'll do differently next time. Then end with a statement that protects your culture: "I'm still with you. We're on the same team."

One small shift I will take to create clearer boundaries.

____

____

____

____

Empowering Declaration

I build legacy with other people, not in isolation. I replace assumptions with agreements and distance with repair. I choose honesty early, honor always, and growth as a shared rhythm. I don't carry everything alone. I build with trust, with community, and with love that stays steady under pressure.

Chapter 30
The Wholeness Legacy Plan

Not every legacy will be loud. Some legacies will be quiet and powerful in a way nobody can screenshot. A woman who learns to rest without guilt. A man who learns to apologize without shame. A couple who learns to communicate without control. A family that breaks cycles and builds something steadier than what they inherited.

If you want a legacy you respect, you don't wait until life calms down. You decide what you're living for while life is still loud.

This is the part most people don't realize until later. Legacy doesn't show up one day fully formed. It forms as you're living. It forms in the way you respond when you're tired. In the way you speak when you're disappointed. In the way you handle pressure without turning it into a personality trait. It forms in what you practice so often that it becomes your default.

Don't Let Life Define It For You

It's easy to drift into legacy without intention. Not because you're careless, but because you're busy. You're responding to what's urgent, handling what's next, assuming the bigger picture will work itself out. Then one day, you look up and realize you've built a life that looks successful but doesn't feel true.

That's one of the quiet heartbreaks of high-capacity living. You can accomplish a lot and still feel misaligned. You can be admired and still feel like you're living slightly outside yourself.

Wholeness requires definition.

Not the rigid kind. The honest kind.

It's the decision to choose your values before the moment chooses them for you. Because when you don't decide what matters, your nervous system decides. Your schedule decides. Other people's needs decide. The loudest thing in the room decides.

And then you're not building a legacy. You're just surviving a life.

The Legacy Question That Changes Everything

If you want a simple way to make legacy feel real, stop thinking about it as a future speech and start thinking about it as a present pattern.

Who do I become when it costs me?

That question will tell you more about your legacy than your goals ever will.

It brings you back to the places where legacy is actually built. Your character, your relationships, and your contribution. Not in a neat three-part formula but in the way your life holds together across those areas. It's possible to have strong character and weak boundaries. It's possible to have good intentions and inconsistent repair. It's possible to contribute a lot while quietly losing yourself.

Wholeness invites alignment, the kind where your values and your choices start matching more often, and the kind where the gap between what you say matters and what you live begins to close.

360

Legacy Is Not Intensity, It's Consistency

Many people try to build a legacy through intensity. Big moments. Big promises. Big emotional declarations. The kind of week where you feel inspired and decide you're going to change everything all at once.

Then life happens, and the old rhythm returns.

Wholeness is different. Wholeness builds legacy through consistency.

Not because consistency is glamorous, but because it's trustworthy. Your nervous system trusts what repeats. Your children trust what repeats. Your partner trusts what repeats. The people around you may forget what you said in a powerful moment, but they will remember what was normal in your presence.

This is why "return" matters so much. Because nobody lives perfectly aligned every day. The legacy is not whether you miss it. The legacy is how you come back when you do.

When you have a hard week, do you spiral into self-criticism, or do you return to what keeps you whole? When there's conflict, do you disappear into the distance, or do you move toward repair? When you're overwhelmed, do you overcommit out of guilt, or do you tell the truth about your capacity? Legacy is the art of returning without shame.

Boundaries Are Not Distance, They're Love With Honesty

Many people have complicated feelings about boundaries because boundaries can sound like separation. Like pulling away or being "too much." But in a life centered around wholeness, boundaries keep love clean.

A boundary is the truth about what you can hold in this season. It protects what is sacred. It keeps resentment from quietly growing in the corners. It helps you stay honest without becoming harsh.

When boundaries are weak, you start leaking. You say yes, but your spirit says no. You keep showing up and quietly lose respect for yourself. You keep accommodating and then wonder why you feel so irritated. Not because you're mean, but because your life is asking for a clearer structure than your heart has been willing to name.

And when boundaries are rigid, intimacy shrinks. You become protected but not connected.

A legacy boundary isn't weak or rigid. It's clear and kind. It sounds like someone who respects themselves and respects the relationship enough to tell the truth.

Sometimes the hardest part is resisting the urge to overexplain. If you're used to keeping the peace, you may try to make your boundary palatable. You might add more justifications, so no one feels uncomfortable. But legacy boundaries aren't negotiated every time someone resists. They are reinforced with calm consistency, because you're not trying to win. You're trying to live aligned.

Repair Keeps Your Love From Rotting

Relationships don't get damaged by conflict itself. They get damaged by what never gets repaired.

Unrepaired moments become stories. The tone you never cleaned up becomes a bruise. The silence becomes a pattern. The avoidance becomes an emotional debt that eventually manifests as distance, resentment, or shutdown.

Repair is the way you prevent one moment from becoming the culture. It doesn't require you to be dramatic.

362

It requires you to be humble. It requires you to come back. It requires you to choose the relationship over your ego and choose connection over being right.

If you want a legacy of wholeness, repair cannot be occasional. It must be normal. Not constant heavy talks, just normal returns. That is legacy love. Not perfection. Return.

Contribution Without Self-Abandonment

This part matters because many people build their contribution at an unsustainable pace. They build impact while neglecting the very foundation that makes their impact worth it. They serve while burning out. They lead while being emotionally unreachable. They carry a mission while their body quietly protests.

Wholeness doesn't ask you to stop contributing. It asks you to stop paying for contributions with your health, your peace, and your relationships.

A legacy contribution rhythm is the way you give without disappearing. It's the way you serve with boundaries. It's the way you build at a pace your nervous system can sustain. That isn't selfish. It's stewardship.

Exhausted people can still be impressive, but they rarely feel safe to live with. And over time, the people closest to them don't remember the impact as much as the emotional cost.

How To Make Legacy Practical Without Turning It Into Pressure

If legacy has felt abstract for you, here's the simplest way to bring it back into your life. Choose one small practice you can keep when you're tired. Choose something that protects your wholeness, strengthens your relationships, and keeps your contribution honest. This will support building a life that feels true from the inside out.

When you get off track, which you will sometimes, don't turn that into a verdict about who you are. Turn it into returning. Legacy is built by the people who keep coming back.

Closing Reflection

You were never meant to build a life that looks good but feels empty. Wholeness gives you something better than applause. It gives you peace. It gives you integrity. It gives you a legacy you can live with.

Let this be the moment you stop waiting for the perfect version of you and start practicing the aligned version of you. Your legacy is already forming. Make it intentional. Make it whole.

The Practice

Write a one-paragraph legacy statement. Keep it simple. This isn't a bio. It's a compass.

Use this frame in your own voice:

I want to be known for:
I want my closest relationships to feel like:
I want my work and contribution to create:
I will protect my wholeness by:

Journal Prompts

Answer what stands out. Skip what doesn't. Stay honest.

1. What do I want people to say about how they felt around me, and what needs to change for that to be true?
2. What is one habit that pulls me out of alignment, and what is the smallest shift I can make this week?
3. What boundary would protect my health, my relationships, and my peace right now?
4. What does repair look like for me when I'm wrong, and what words do I need to practice so I can return without defensiveness?
5. What contribution feels aligned and sustainable, and what is one next step I can take in the next seven days?

Wholeness Check-In

Reflect on how your legacy plan is reflected through your pillars.

- Self: Where do I feel most out of alignment right now, and what is one small return I can make today?
- Relationships: What relationship needs repair, clarity, or deeper presence from me this week?
- Work and calling: What am I doing that drains me but doesn't build my legacy?
- Legacy: If I fast-forward ten years, what decision today would I thank myself for making?

One small step I will take to contribute to my legacy plan:

____

____

____

____

Empowering Declaration

I define my legacy with intention, not impulse. I choose consistency over intensity and return over shame. I protect what keeps me whole, I hold boundaries with clarity, and I repair with humility. I build a life that feels true from the inside out. My legacy is already taking shape, and I choose to shape it with aligned decisions, steady love, and a rhythm that endures.

Chapter 31
The Legacy of Leadership

Your leadership legacy is the energy you leave in a room. People will remember that longer than they'll remember your slide deck. They'll remember whether your presence made things clearer or heavier. They'll remember whether they felt safe to speak or pressured to perform. They'll remember whether you brought steadiness or tension that made everyone tighten up and watch their words.

If you want a legacy you respect, the question can't just be "Did I perform well today?"

A better question is sharper and more honest. "What did my presence make possible for other people today?"

When you walked into that meeting, did the room relax or brace? When you set a standard, did it create excellence or anxiety? When someone brought you something hard, did you meet it with dignity or dominance? When you corrected someone, did you leave the person stronger or smaller?

Those questions aren't meant to criticize you. They're meant to wake you up. Because leadership isn't just what you do. Leadership is what people become around you.

The Legacy You Don't Realize You're Building

Every leader gives permission, even the ones who never think of themselves that way. You give permission through what you repeat, praise, and choose to ignore. You grant permission on what you let slide because you're tired, busy, or trying to avoid conflict. You permit your tone, timing, and how you handle pressure.

370

If you say you value balance, but you celebrate burnout, you teach people that exhaustion earns belonging. If you say you value honesty but respond to feedback as if it's a threat, you teach people to hide the truth until it's too late. If you say you value growth, but you shame mistakes, you teach people to play small and protect their images.

That's what makes leadership legacy so sobering. You can be a good person with great intentions and still build a culture that trains people to brace.

Whole leaders don't need fear to get results. They don't need control to feel respected. They can create structure without crushing people. They can tell the truth without using dominance as a means of delivery. When leaders model regulation under pressure, they give everyone else permission to do the same.

Not permission in a motivational way, but in a nervous-system way. People stop performing and start thinking. They stop hiding and start naming risks earlier. They stop guessing and start doing honest work because it's safe to be human and accountable in the same environment.

Pressure Writes The Story

The moments that define your leadership are rarely planned. They're the interruptions. The missed deadline. The tension between teammates. The decision you have to make with incomplete information. The public mistake. The personal crisis that hits during a high-stakes week. The moment you feel your body tighten and your instincts start reaching for urgency, sharpness, control, or withdrawal. Those are the moments when legacy gets written.

Pressure doesn't build character. It reveals it. And if you don't regulate yourself, you'll lead from urgency. Urgency can look productive, but it usually creates chaos. People scramble. They stop thinking clearly. They start protecting themselves. They start reacting to you more than responding to the work.

Legacy leadership is the ability to pause long enough to choose. Not pause as avoidance. Pause as command. Pause as emotional leadership. The kind of pause that keeps you connected to your values when your nervous system wants to take over.

Sometimes legacy leadership is as simple as refusing to dramatize a hard moment. You name what happened cleanly. You name what it impacts. You name what happens next. You own what's yours without collapsing into shame or shifting into blame. You protect people while you solve problems. You move toward learning instead of humiliation.

That's the kind of leadership people remember. Not because it was flashy. Because it was safe.

Who Becomes Possible Around You

One of the most revealing questions a leader can ask is uncomfortable "If the people around me led exactly like I do, would I be proud of what multiplies?"

People reproduce what they experience. Some leaders multiply courage. People become more honest. More accountable. They take healthy risks because they know they won't be punished for being human. They bring problems early because they trust the response won't be humiliation.

Other leaders multiply fear. People become guarded. They manage appearances. They hide issues until they explode. They perform "fine" while quietly preparing an exit plan.

You don't have to be in a formal leadership role to shape people this way. If you're a parent, a mentor, a partner, a team lead, or a friend who holds influence, you've seen it. You know what it feels like to be around someone whose presence makes you exhale. You also know what it feels like to be around someone whose presence makes you shrink.

Your impact is never neutral. The question is what your impact trains people to become.

The Real Flex Is How You Return

One of the most humbling lessons of wholeness is realizing that trust isn't built by never missing it. Trust is built by how you return when you do.

There will be moments in which you're sharper than you intended. Moments in which you choose efficiency over connection. Moments in which you assume instead of asking. Moments in which stress leads and you follow.

In the past, it was easy to justify those moments. "I'm tired. I have a lot going on. That wasn't my intent."

But wholeness teaches something better than justification. It teaches repair. And repair doesn't weaken your authority. It strengthens your credibility because it tells people, "I'm not above this. I'm accountable inside it."

That's what turns leadership into legacy. Not perfection. Humility with follow-through.

Feedback Becomes Someone Else's Inner Voice

If you've ever replayed a leader's words in your head years later, you understand the weight of this. The way you correct, coach, and evaluate people becomes part of how they see themselves. It can become fuel or a bruise. And most leaders don't realize how often they are shaping someone's inner voice in real time.

Legacy feedback doesn't use humiliation as a tool. It doesn't confuse dominance with clarity. It stays specific. It stays timely. It protects dignity while naming the standard.

It's firm without being personal. It's honest without being cruel. It's clear on what needs to change and equally clear that the person is still respected as they change.

You don't need a perfect script. You need a posture that says, "I'm here to build you, not break you."

Culture Is What You Reward And What You Ignore

Culture isn't built simply by adding it to your values poster. It's built on what gets rewarded and what gets ignored.

If you reward speed more than quality, people learn to rush. If you reward burnout, people learn to sacrifice their bodies for approval. If you ignore disrespect because someone is "valuable," the team learns that dignity is optional when performance is high.

Whole leadership refuses to normalize dysfunction in exchange for outcomes. It sets boundaries for behavior. It protects psychological safety. It makes the truth safe even when that's inconvenient.

When you do that, people can do excellent work with their dignity intact.

374

Mentorship Multiplies What You Really Value

Mentorship is one of the clearest places where leadership becomes generational. Real mentorship is helping someone see what they can't yet see and giving them enough room to build confidence through ownership.

It's asking strong questions, sharing context, offering feedback, then stepping back enough for them to lead. It's being present without being possessive. It's being invested without needing to be needed.

That's legacy because the people you mentor will reproduce the emotional culture you gave them, not just the skills you taught.

Closing Reflection

The world already has enough leaders who can produce outcomes. We need leaders who can produce outcomes without crushing people in the process.

Your legacy isn't a highlight reel. It's a pattern. Make the pattern worth inheriting.

Leadership is never just what you accomplish. It's what you make safe for other people to become.

So come back to the question that keeps you honest. Are you leading from pressure or from presence?

Pressure can get results. Presence builds trust. Presence builds people. Presence builds culture that lasts.

The Practice

Use this when you feel urgency rising, before a hard conversation, or at the start of a day where you know you'll be under pressure.

Take one minute and slow your exhale long enough to tell your body "We are safe enough to think". Then choose one value you want your presence to communicate today. Something simple, like respect, clarity, courage, compassion, steadiness, or excellence.

Let your first sentence in the next important moment reflect that value. After the moment passes, take two minutes and ask yourself: "What did I do well? What will I do differently next time?"

Journal Prompts

Answer with truth.

1. What made that person feel safe or unsafe?
2. When I lead well, people experience _________. Write it in your own voice, no corporate language.
3. What do I do under stress that protects me but costs me connection? What would a healthier version of that look like?
4. Who is watching me more closely than I think, and what are they learning from my patterns?
5. What would change if my definition of success included nervous system safety, relational health, and integrity, not just outcomes?

Wholeness Check-In

View these questions through a lens of legacy in leadership.

- Where am I leading from fear instead of values right now?
- What am I avoiding because I don't want to be uncomfortable?
- What truth do I need to say more clearly this week?
- How do I need to repair with someone I mentor?
- What does my team need that I'm overlooking with busyness?

One small shift that would strengthen my legacy:

____

____

____

____

____

Empowering Declaration

I lead from presence, not pressure. I create clarity without control and accountability without humiliation. I practice repair with humility and follow-through with integrity. My leadership makes truth safe and people stronger. I leave rooms clearer than I found them. I build culture through consistency, dignity, and aligned standards that honor both excellence and humanity.

Chapter 32
Money, Power, and Wholeness

Here's an honest entry point. When you think about money, what emotion shows up first?

Money has a way of touching parts of you that other topics can't reach. For some people, money represents safety. For others, it represents freedom. For still others, it represents dignity, worth, or finally being able to breathe. And when money becomes a stand-in for worth, you can have more than enough but still feel like it isn't enough, because what you're chasing isn't a number. It's a relief. Control. Peace. That you won't be caught off guard again.

This is why money conversations get tense even in good relationships. It's rarely about the receipt. It's about what the receipt represents.

A whole relationship with money starts with one separation that sounds simple but changes everything when you live it. Your identity is not your income. Your value is not your net worth. Your security is not your bank-account balance. Money can support your life, but it cannot hold the job of proving you're worthy.

If that sentence feels too idealistic, I understand. Plenty of people have lived through seasons when money affected their safety. It affected their options. It affected what was possible. This isn't denial. This is maturity. Wholeness means you learn to build money as a tool without turning it into a god, and you learn to pursue ambition without letting fear become the engine.

If fear is first, you may be carrying scarcity from your past. If shame shows up, you may have internalized messages about deservingness. If urgency rises, you might be chasing money as proof that you're safe now. If numbness shows up, you may be avoiding responsibility because it feels too loaded. Whatever shows up, let it be information, not indictment. You're not broken. You're learning where your story lives.

When Money Stops Being "Just Money"

Money rarely stays just money, especially in partnerships. It becomes a mirror. It reflects your beliefs about safety, trust, power, and responsibility. It also exposes what you learned about conflict because it has a way of making people reveal their default patterns.

Some people respond to money stress by tightening and controlling. They get hyper-responsible. They track everything. They guard. They correct. They feel safer when they're in charge.

Other people respond by avoiding. They delay. They look away. They minimize. They tell themselves it'll be fine. Not because they don't care, but because the pressure feels overwhelming.

Those aren't personality quirks. Those are nervous system responses. And that matters because you can't heal what you keep calling "just how I am."

If you've ever felt your chest tighten during a money conversation, that's not you being dramatic. That's your nervous system recognizing that the stakes feel personal. Underneath the numbers are questions like "Aam I safe, am I free, can I trust you, can I trust myself, will I be trapped, will I be judged, will I be controlled, will I be left holding the consequences?"

Wholeness invites you to bring those questions into the light, gently and honestly, because a relationship can't build financial peace in the dark. Financial peace comes from clarity. From shared understanding. From truth that doesn't punish.

When Power Is Inherent And Integrity Is A Choice

Wholeness is also where money meets power. Power can be positional, relational, financial, intellectual, or social. If you influence people, you have power. If you earn more, you have a certain kind of power. If you manage the accounts, you have a certain kind of power. If you control access to information, you have a certain kind of power. You don't get to opt out of it just because you're a good person. The question isn't whether you have power. The question is how you use it.

Whole people tend to use power to protect, build, and create opportunities. Wounded people tend to use power to control, impress, or avoid feeling small. Sometimes the shift from stewardship to control happens quietly, especially when stress rises. You may not be trying to dominate. You may be trying to feel safe.

Wholeness doesn't shame you for wanting safety. It teaches you how to build safety without harming others.

If you've been harmed by power, you may overcorrect by avoiding it. You might say, "I don't care about money," when the truth is that money feels loaded to you. Or you might say, "I don't want to talk about it," when the truth is that you don't want to feel the fear underneath it. Avoidance makes sense as a protective measure, but it doesn't build legacy. It builds delay, and delay has a cost.

The goal is not to become money obsessed. The goal is to become clear.

The Legacy Most People Don't Realize They're Building

Financial legacy is one of those topics people often reduce to a will, an insurance policy, or money that gets handed down. Those things matter. They matter a lot. But a financial legacy is bigger than documents. It's the habits, beliefs, and emotional patterns around money that get passed down, often without anyone realizing it.

Children don't just inherit what you leave. They inherit what you normalize.

They inherit what money meant in the home. They inherit the tone you used when bills were due. They inherit whether money talk was calm or chaotic, whether it felt like teamwork or tension. They inherit whether generosity was joyful or performative, whether spending was reckless or shame filled, whether saving was wise or fear driven. They inherit whether you treated money as a tool or as a mood.

Even if you don't have children, your financial legacy still exists. You pass it into partnerships, friendships, and the people who watch the way you live. You pass it on to your future self because the habits you practice today become the atmosphere you live in later.

So yes, a legacy mindset includes provision. It includes building wealth. It includes stability and access. But it also includes emotional stewardship. It includes the kind of relationship you have with money as you build it.

Provision Without Pressure

Here's one of the most important truths about financial legacy. It isn't only about how much you accumulate. It's about whether your financial life creates peace or pressure.

There are people who have less money but more peace. Peace isn't only about your income. It's clarity. It's alignment. It's living within truth.

A whole financial legacy aims for provision without turning life into a pressure system. It aims for freedom without building freedom on the back of constant stress. It aims for generosity without self-abandonment.

This is where many high performers get tripped up. They pursue a financial legacy through achievement while quietly losing the legacy they actually wanted. They wanted their family to feel secure and their home to feel calm. They wanted to be remembered as present, kind, and trustworthy. But they were so focused on what they could produce that they stopped noticing what they were passing down emotionally.

Wholeness asks a tender question: if you fast-forward 10 years, will your people remember you as successful or as safe? And if you could choose both, would you know how to build both without sacrificing one?

You can. But it requires a new definition of success: one that includes nervous-system peace, relationship health, and integrity as part of wealth.

When Money Becomes A Measuring Stick

Money becomes dangerous in the soul when it becomes a measuring stick. When it becomes the way you prove you're enough. When it becomes the way you silence old fear. When it becomes the way you protect yourself from ever feeling small again.

That's when money stops being a tool and starts becoming an emotional regulator.

You may feel this when you notice how hard it is to slow down even after you reach a goal. You hit a number, and instead of relief, you feel a new sense of urgency. You reach stability, and instead of peace, you feel the need to secure more. You build a cushion, and instead of exhaling, you start scanning for the next threat.

That isn't greed. Often, it's unresolved vulnerability dressed up as ambition.

Wholeness doesn't tell you to stop building. It tells you to stop using building as a substitute for healing.

The Relationship Patterns Money Exposes

Money doesn't create problems out of thin air. It exposes patterns that were already there.

In some relationships, money reveals control. One person holds the information and makes the decisions, then calls it "being responsible," while the other feels like a dependent rather than a partner.

In other relationships, money reveals avoidance. One person carries all the planning and feels resentful, while the other person stays vague and feels judged.

Sometimes money reveals a subtle imbalance in emotional labor. One person is the financial adult and the emotional adult. They track, plan, anticipate, calm, and clean up. They don't only manage money. They manage the relationship's anxiety about money. That becomes exhausting.

Financial legacy isn't built when one person becomes the system. It's built when a couple becomes a system together, even if their roles are different.

The goal is not identical involvement. The goal is shared ownership and shared clarity, where nobody has to guess, nobody has to hide, and nobody has to carry the full weight alone.

The Financial Legacy You Want

Put plainly, most people want a financial legacy that includes three things: stability, freedom, and generosity.

Stability means your life is not fragile. Freedom means you have options. Generosity means your abundance is not trapped inside you. It moves outward.

But in order for a financial legacy to be whole, it also needs something many people skip: emotional cleanliness. The ability to talk about money without shame. This emotional cleanliness includes making decisions without fear, setting boundaries without guilt and building without becoming emotionally unavailable. This is where wealth becomes legacy, not just accumulation.

Legacy wealth looks like children who don't panic at the topic of money. It looks like partners who can have clear conversations without turning them into power struggles. It looks like a household in which the word "budget" isn't a punishment and the word "invest" isn't arrogance. It looks like a home in which money is handled with maturity, not secrecy. Secrecy doesn't create safety. It creates suspicion.

Building Wealth Without Losing Your Soul

A whole person sets financial goals and also sets boundaries for their soul.

That isn't corny. It's necessary. Money can easily become the place where you keep bargaining with yourself. Just one more push. Just one more year. Just one more deal. Just one more season of overwork. And then I'll rest. But rest never arrives because your nervous system has learned to equate it with risk.

If you want a legacy you respect, you have to build in a way that leaves you intact. You have to build in a way that doesn't require you to abandon your body, your marriage, your joy, or your integrity to prove that you can win.

This is where values become real. If your financial success comes at the expense of your health, it isn't success. It's trade. If it costs you your partnership, it isn't legacy; it's an achievement with a leak. If it costs you your peace, it isn't freedom; it's bondage with a nicer title. Wholeness says you don't need to bleed to be significant.

Money As A Trust Practice

Here's a powerful shift: money becomes easier when you treat it as a trust practice instead of a stage on which to perform.

Trust practice means you tell the truth early. You don't overpromise. You don't hide. You don't avoid. You don't pretend. You build agreements and you follow them. You make repairs when you miss it.

When money is a practice of trust, the nervous system settles because it's not guessing. It's not waiting for surprises. It's not bracing for blame. It's not trying to decode silence.

And when trust grows, money becomes less charged. Not because you have unlimited funds, but because the relationship can hold the truth without collapsing.

Your Family Inherits What You Normalize

This is where financial legacy becomes generational. Your children and loved ones will not only inherit your assets. They will inherit your relationship with money. They will inherit what you modeled about responsibility, restraint, generosity, and fear.

Your loved ones will learn whether debt is hidden or discussed. They will learn whether spending is used as a form of comfort. How you choose to move teaches them whether money is talked about with shame or with clarity and whether wealth is treated like a weapon or a resource. They will also learn whether you believed you had to sacrifice yourself to provide.

That last part matters more than many people realize. Some families inherit money and still inherit anxiety. They inherit homes and still inherit pressure. They inherit opportunity and still inherit the belief that love equals performance.

A whole financial legacy includes provision, but it also includes peace.

Closing Reflection

Money and power don't define you. They reveal you. When you lead with wholeness, resources become tools for impact, not chains or obligations for performance. You can pursue abundance without losing integrity. You can build wealth without sacrificing health, partnership, or peace. A whole financial life feels steady in its decisions, honest in its numbers, and respectful in its conversations. It feels clean. It feels aligned. It feels like money is finally serving your life instead of silently running it.

And if you're realizing you want that kind of legacy, you're not too late. You're awake.

The Practice

This week, choose one small action that brings your financial life into alignment without turning it into a whole project. Pick something that signals maturity, not perfection. Something repeatable. Something your future self will feel.

Maybe it's a calm conversation in which you name what money represents for you without blaming anyone. Maybe it's a simple routine of checking your accounts weekly so you're not avoiding reality. Maybe it's deciding on one boundary that protects your life from financial overreach, like not making big purchases when you're stressed, or not saying yes to commitments that put you in a state of quiet panic later.

Let it be small enough that you can do it even when you're tired, because that's what will make it legacy.

Journal Prompts

Take your time with these questions.

1. When I think about money, what emotion shows up first, and what story is that emotion protecting?
2. What did I learn about money growing up that I still live by, even if I've never said it out loud?
3. In my relationships, where does money create closeness and where does it create tension?
4. What does "financial peace" mean to me in this season, not in a fantasy life but in my real life?
5. If someone watched how I handle money for a month, what would they learn about what I believe I deserve?

Wholeness Check-In

If money has been triggering you, don't only check your spreadsheet. Check your inner world.

- Where am I using money to try to regulate fear instead of building stability with truth?
- Where am I avoiding clarity because it brings up shame?
- Where am I managing what should be shared financially and resenting it instead of building shared ownership?
- Where is my ambition healthy, and where is it quietly punishing me?
- What is one honest step I can take today to bring me back into alignment?

One small shift I will make:

____

____

____

____

Empowering Declaration

I separate my identity from my income. I hold power with humility and clarity. I tell the truth about money without shame, and I make decisions from alignment, not anxiety. My resources support peace, partnership, and purpose. I build wealth without sacrificing integrity, health, or love. Money serves me as I live my life, and my life reflects what matters most.

Chapter 33
The Legacy of Healing

You didn't choose what happened to you, but you do choose what you do with it.

That sentence can sound sharp until you hear what it's really saying. Responsibility is not blame. Responsibility is power. It's the moment you stop waiting for the past to permit you to be free.

A lot of people treat healing like something they must do in order to move on, but the deeper truth is that healing is not only about you feeling better. Healing is about what your life teaches when you're not trying to teach anything at all. It's about what becomes normal in your home. It's about what your nervous system models in hard moments. It's about what your relationships inherit, even when nobody talks about it. This is why healing becomes legacy.

Whether you realize it or not, you are always passing something forward. You pass forward the way you respond to tension. You pass forward the way you handle disappointment. You pass forward what you normalize when you're tired. You pass forward what you do when you feel exposed. That is what makes this chapter personal. It's not about getting everything right. It's about becoming intentional enough to stop calling survival "just who I am" and start calling it what it really is: an old strategy that worked for you in the past but costs too much now.

Healing Is Not An Identity, It's A Practice

One of the quiet traps people fall into is turning pain into a permanent name. It becomes the explanation for everything. It becomes the lens through which you see. It becomes the reason you stay guarded, even when love is present.

Wholeness never asks you to deny what happened. It asks you to stop letting what happened run the present.

That's where the real work begins, because so many of the patterns we repeat don't feel like pain. They feel like "maturity." They feel like "I'm just being practical." They feel like "I'm not about to let that happen again." They feel like wisdom. And sometimes they are wise, but sometimes they're protection wearing a better outfit.

You can be incredibly competent and still be emotionally unavailable. You can be loyal and still be guarded. You can be consistent and still be hard to reach. You can look stable and still be bracing inside.

The goal isn't to shame yourself for any of that. The goal is to notice it with honesty so you can choose something else.

The Way You Survived May Not Be The Way You Want To Live

Most survival patterns began as intelligent adaptations. Your system learned what it needed to learn to keep you safe. If you grew up around emotional unpredictability, you might have learned to read rooms like a second language. If you grew up around criticism, you might have learned to perform at a high level to reduce risk. If you grew up in a world of silence, you might have learned to keep your needs to yourself so you wouldn't be disappointed. If you grew up carrying too much too early, you might have learned that being the reliable one was the safest role.

None of that makes you broken. It makes you trained. But training can outlive its usefulness.

And when it does, it doesn't disappear on its own. It shows up in your relationships as a reflex. It shows up in your parenting as tone. It shows up in your leadership as pressure. It shows up in your love as control, distance, overfunctioning, or self-editing that slowly becomes the norm.

This is why legacy healing isn't just insight. It's an upgrade. It's your nervous system learning that you can be safe without bracing, and you can be loved without performing, and you can be honest without it turning into a war.

The Moment You Realize "This Isn't Just Me"

There's usually a moment when the old way stops feeling normal and starts feeling heavy. For some people, it's the day they hear themselves speak with a tone they promised they'd never use. For others, it's realizing they've become polite but not present. For many high-capacity people, it's recognizing that stress doesn't just make them productive, it makes them tight. It makes them faster, sharper, and more controlled. It turns them into a project manager of life. On the outside, it looks like leadership. On the inside, it feels like pressure. And at home, it can feel like emotional distance nobody intended.

That's when you start seeing what's actually happening. The pattern looks productive, but it's protective because somewhere along the way your system learned that control is safer than vulnerability, self-reliance is safer than needing and staying ahead is safer than slowing down. When you realize that, you don't have to spiral. You have to tell the truth. The truth gives you choices.

Understanding Is Not The Same As Repeating

There is a difference between understanding why a pattern formed and excusing why it remains. You can honor the version of you who needed that tool and still release it now. You can respect what helped you survive and still tell yourself, with kindness and clarity, "This tool can't run the whole house anymore."

Sometimes people stay loyal to patterns because they confuse familiarity with love. They think that if they change, they're betraying their roots. But breaking a pattern isn't disrespecting your roots. It's strengthening them. It's saying, "I love where I come from, and I'm choosing to grow beyond what hurt us." That's not rebellion. That's maturity. And maturity is one of the most powerful forms of legacy.

The Real Legacy Shift Is Internal

Here's the part that matters most. You don't break patterns by fighting yourself. You break patterns by learning to stay present when the old reflex rises.

Legacy is built in moments you used to rush past. It's built in the moment you feel your body tighten and you pause instead of pushing harder. It's built in the moment you feel the urge to control, but you choose clarity instead. It's built in the moment you want to shut down, but you stay reachable. It's built in the moment you want to defend your intention, but you choose to own your impact.

That's a different kind of strength. Not the strength of endurance. The strength of wholeness.

And yes, it will feel personal, because it is. Pattern breaking is not only an idea. It's a nervous-system upgrade.

398

Even healthy change can feel unsafe at first, not because it's wrong, but because it's unfamiliar.

So if you find yourself wondering, "Why is this taking me so long?" let that thought soften. This work is deep. And the fact that you can see it means you're already changing it.

What Actually Creates A New Inheritance

A new inheritance is created through repetition. It's created when you practice a different response often enough that it becomes your new normal. That's the real shift. Your life starts teaching something different because you start living something different.

You will still get triggered sometimes. You will still have days where you default. That does not cancel your growth. The legacy difference is what you do next.

You return.

You repair.

You choose again.

That's what turns healing into legacy.

Closing Reflection

You don't break patterns by becoming harsh with yourself. You break patterns by telling the truth and practicing a new way, again and again, until your nervous system learns that it's safe to be whole.

Your legacy isn't determined by what you inherited. It's shaped by what you choose next. And every time you pause instead of reacting, you create a new inheritance.

The Practice

When old patterns or behaviors show up, take a moment to pause and just be still. Name what's happening in one honest sentence. Then choose one whole response. The kind you'd be proud to pass down.

My next small practice:

Journal Prompts

Answer what stands out. Skip what doesn't. Keep it honest.

1. What patterns did I grow up seeing around conflict, money, affection, and stress, and which ones show up most in my life now?
2. What did these patterns protect me from earlier in life, and what are they costing me now?
3. When I'm triggered, do I move toward control, avoidance, or shutdown, and what am I afraid will happen if I soften?
4. What is one pattern I want to end with me, and what is the smallest new behavior I can practice the next time the trigger shows up?
5. Who benefits when I break this pattern, and what becomes possible in my relationships as a result?

Wholeness Check-In

Look at your pillars through a lens of patterns in your life.

- What familiar script am I about to run right now?
- What emotion am I trying to avoid or control?
- What would wholeness look like in this moment?
- What is one honest thing I can say that would shift the direction of this pattern?
- If I miss it, what repair will I make so this moment doesn't become our new normal?

One small shift that would strengthen my legacy:

____

____

____

____

Empowering Declaration

I break patterns with honesty and compassion. I notice what's familiar without letting it lead me. I take ownership of my responses, and I return to repair when I miss it. I release what no longer fits, and I practice a new way until it becomes my normal. I build legacy through wholeness, one choice at a time.

Chapter 34
The Wholeness Legacy:
A Life Well Loved

There's a kind of peace that doesn't come from having less to do. It comes from having less to prove.

People spend years chasing the version of life that looks like it should feel good. You build. You perform. You achieve. You carry. You stay responsible. You stay strong. You keep moving.

And then there's that moment. Sometimes it's quiet. Sometimes it surprises you. You look up and realize that your life can be full and still feel thin. That you can be surrounded by people and still feel alone. That you can be doing everything "right" and still feel something inside asking, "Is this who I want to be while I build all of this?"

That's not you being ungrateful. That's you being honest. That's wholeness waking up.

This chapter is not meant to give you a perfect ending. It's here to give you a deeper understanding. A lived one. The kind that doesn't just land in your head but settles into your body. Because legacy, when it's real, is never only what people say about you later. It's what your presence teaches right now.

The Legacy You Leave Isn't Only What You Do, It's Who People Become Around You

Think about the people closest to you. Your spouse. Your children. Your friends. Your team. The people who live in your atmosphere, not just your highlights. They're not only watching what you accomplish. They're absorbing what it feels like to be with you.

They're learning whether love is steady or unpredictable. Whether the truth is welcome or risky. Whether mistakes get handled with dignity or shame. Whether repair is normal or rare. Whether rest is respected or treated like laziness. Whether boundaries are honored or punished.

That's what makes this kind of legacy so tender. You can be a good person and still leave people bracing. Not because your heart is bad, but because your nervous system is tired. It's because you learned to lead with control instead of presence, and to protect yourself by staying sharp, busy, or emotionally unavailable.

Wholeness doesn't accuse you of that. Wholeness invites you to choose differently.

And the reason that matters is simple. People don't only carry what you said. They carry what you normalized.

A Wholeness Legacy Is What Happens When Your Inner Life And Outer Life Finally Match

For many strong people, the mismatch is subtle. You believe in peace, but your body stays on alert. You value connection, but you default to efficiency. You care deeply, but your tenderness is put off until everything is handled. You want intimacy, but you don't always know how to be reachable without feeling exposed.

That gap doesn't come from a lack of love. It comes from lived conditioning. It comes from being trained, over time, to survive.

406

And survival can be impressive. That's the tricky part. You can build an entire life on survival skills and still look like you're thriving.

But wholeness asks a different question. Not "Can I handle it?" but "Can I be here?" Not "Can I keep it together?" but "Can I stay connected?" Not "Can I do what needs to be done?" but "Can I do it without abandoning myself or the people I love?"

A wholeness legacy is when you stop living two separate lives, the strong public life and the private life that's depleted, and you begin living one integrated life that is honest all the way through.

That's what makes your presence feel different. That's what makes your love feel safer. That's what makes your leadership feel steadier. That's what makes your home feel like a place where people can exhale.

The Strongest People Don't Always Realize What Their Strength Costs The People Who Love Them

Here's a truth that can sting a little, but it's worth telling gently. Strength becomes a problem when it becomes your only identity in a relationship.

When you're always the capable one, people may start relating to you as if you don't need anything. They may start taking your steadiness for granted. They may assume you'll be fine because you're always fine. You also might unintentionally reinforce all of this because you've been trained to stay composed even when you're carrying too much.

Over time, you can create an unspoken dynamic in which you are essential but not fully known. Relied on but not fully considered. Admired but not fully held.

The hardest part is that no one may be doing anything "wrong." You could be in a relationship full of loyalty and still feel emotionally alone because loyalty isn't the same as emotional partnership.

Wholeness doesn't ask you to become less strong. It asks you to become more reachable.

The legacy you really want isn't "They handled everything." The legacy you really want is "They were safe to love. They were honest. They could repair. They knew how to be present. They made people feel steady."

Legacy Is Built By What You Do After You Miss It

If you want one thing to remember from this chapter, let it be this: Legacy is not built by never messing up. Legacy is built by what you do next.

The apology you make without being forced. The conversation you choose instead of the silence you want to hide behind. The return you make before pride hardens the room. The boundary you hold even when someone is disappointed. The softness you have even when you feel defensive.

That's where wholeness becomes real. Not in your intentions. In your returns.

Life will still be loud. You will still face pressure. You will still have moments when you snap, withdraw, overfunction, shut down, and avoid. That is part of being human. Wholeness isn't the elimination of those moments. It's the reduction of how long they last and the increase in how quickly you return.

This is what changes the emotional climate of a home. This is what changes the culture of a marriage. This is what changes the way your children learn to handle conflict.

This is what changes how your team experiences leadership. A whole person becomes a safe place to come back to.

A Wholeness Legacy Is Consistent, Not Loud

Some people think they need a big life to leave a big legacy. But the most powerful legacies are often quiet.

A parent who practices repair until their child stops fearing conflict. A spouse who learns to be honest without being harsh. A woman who stops performing strength and starts living in her body in peace. A man who learns to hold emotion without shame. A leader who creates excellence without anxiety.

Those are quiet legacies. And they are generational. What you practice becomes someone else's permission.

When you practice repair, you give people permission to be human. When you practice boundaries, you give people permission to respect themselves. When you practice truth with tenderness, you give people permission to be honest without fear. When you practice presence, you give people permission to stop performing and start relating. That is the legacy of wholeness. It travels.

Closing Reflection

Wholeness is not the absence of need. It's the absence of self-abandonment. It's the moment you stop using strength as armor and start using it as stability. It's the moment your love becomes safer because you become more present, more honest, and more willing to return.

Legacy isn't a trophy you earn later. It's the atmosphere you create now. The life you live is already teaching something. You get to decide what it teaches next.

The Practice

Choose one moment this week to practice a clean return. Not a dramatic moment. An ordinary one in which you typically rush, control, shut down, or overfunction.

Pause long enough to feel your body. Let your breath slow down. Let your shoulders drop.

Tell the truth in one simple sentence.

Then choose one action that protects your peace and protects the relationship.

My next small practice:

Journal Prompts

Answer what stands out. Skip what doesn't. Keep it honest.

1. What do the people closest to me experience most from me: steadiness, pressure, warmth, control, presence, distance? What do I want them to experience?
2. Where have I been praised for strength in a way that made it hard to be tender or reachable?
3. What does my home, my marriage, or my closest relationship "return to" under stress, and what do I want that default to become?
4. Where do I need to repair something I've been hoping time would fix?
5. If I could be remembered for one quality, what would it be, and what does it require of me daily?

Wholeness Check-In

Consider your pillars through the lens of legacy.

- Mentally and emotionally: Am I present enough to be kind, or am I overloaded and operating on edge?
- Spiritually: Am I grounded, or am I trying to control what I'm afraid to feel?
- Physically: What is my body asking for that I keep dismissing?
- Socially: Do my closest relationships support my wholeness, or do they reward my overfunctioning?

One small shift that would strengthen my legacy:

____

____

____

____

Empowering Declaration

I build legacy through consistency, not intensity. I choose truth early, clearly reinforce boundaries, and repair without pride. I return to myself and my values when life gets loud. My presence makes people feel safe, my love stays steady, and my life reflects what I value the most.

Chapter 35
The Home You Become

For a long time, the word legacy made me think of what would outlive me in visible ways. Accomplishments. Milestones. The kind of proof other people could point to and say, "She built something." That definition felt clean because it was measurable. You could track it. You could show it. You could stack it.

But as I grew into wholeness, legacy started to feel less like a trophy and more like an atmosphere. Not the kind you post about. The kind you live inside. The kind your family inhales without realizing it. The kind your closest people carry forward as their definition of normal.

Legacies aren't built in public. They're built in kitchens, car rides, and late-night conversations. They're built in the moments when your tone has power, your repairs matter, and your presence either makes people soften or brace.

If you've ever looked around at the life you've built and thought, "This is good…but I want it to feel safer," you're not being dramatic. You're noticing something many people ignore until distance becomes the only language left. Sometimes nothing is "wrong" in the obvious sense. The household is running. The commitments are being met. Everybody is showing up. And still, something inside you wants the people you love to experience you as reachable, not just reliable.

When Your Home Functions But Your Heart Feels Distant

Many of us were taught a version of love that looks like responsibility. It shows up. It pays bills. It holds things together. It keeps the wheels turning when life gets heavy. That kind of love deserves respect; in many families, it's the reason things don't fall apart.

But healing-focused love adds something that survival-based love can miss. Emotional oxygen. Space for feelings that don't fit the schedule. Room for truth that may feel awkward at first. A willingness to talk, not just manage.

If you grew up in an environment of unpredictability, it makes sense that you learned to build safety through control. You became disciplined. Dependable. The one people could count on. You learned how to stabilize the environment because you didn't want anyone else to carry what you carried.

That survival intelligence can build a beautiful life. It can also build an emotionally tense one if your nervous system never learns how to soften. You can create structure and still create pressure. You can create stability and still create distance. Not because you don't love people, but because you don't know how to stay emotionally open while you're staying responsible.

Wholeness invites you into a deeper kind of stability: one in which your home runs well and its inhabitants feel close to each other.

The Legacy Your Tone Leaves Behind

The home you create isn't only the physical space you live in. It's your emotional availability. It's the way your

416

voice lands when you're tired. It's what your presence communicates, even if you don't intend to send a message.

Your family absorbs more than your words. They absorb how your kindness responds when you feel pressured. They absorb whether disappointment turns into distance. They absorb whether your love stays steady when life gets messy, or whether it turns sharp and transactional when the day has been long.

And none of this requires shame. Shame makes people defensive. It makes people hide. Wholeness does something else. It makes you honest enough to notice your patterns without turning self-awareness into self-attack. Once you notice it, you can choose differently.

Wholeness doesn't ask you to abandon your standards. It asks you to bring your heart into them. It asks you to correct with care instead of control. It asks you to lead with firmness that still feels safe to the people living under your roof, sharing your space, sharing your life.

Repair As A Family Culture

One of the most powerful shifts you can make in a home is treating repair as normal. Not a special event. Not something reserved for the "big moments." Just a regular part of love.

Sometimes repair is as simple as circling back and saying, "That came out more sharply than I wanted." Sometimes it's "I'm feeling anxious and I don't want it to land on you." Sometimes it's an unguarded "Can we restart?" The power isn't in how impressive it sounds. The power is in what it teaches.

Repair teaches the people you love that conflict isn't the end of love. It teaches them that safety doesn't require silence. It teaches them that honesty can exist without humiliation.

When repair becomes normal, the air changes. People
bring the truth sooner. They stop walking on eggshells.
They stop trying to manage your mood. Your home gets
lighter, not because life is perfect, but because love has a
way back.

Presence Is Real Provision

Some people think provision is mostly material.
Stability. Opportunity. Structure. Experiences. Those things
matter, and they require real work.

But emotional presence shapes a family in different
ways. Presence is what lets people exhale. It's what tells
someone, "You don't have to perform to be loved here."
It's what makes a home feel like shelter, not just a well-run
operation.

Presence means you're reachable. Not just physically
in the room, but emotionally available there. It's the ability
to stay engaged instead of retreating behind competence.
It's the willingness to look up, make eye contact, and let
your attention land fully, even for a few minutes, even
when the day is demanding.

And if this is hard for you, you're not alone. Many
high-capacity people learned to lead first and feel later.
They learned to solve, produce, and stabilize before they
learned how to slow down and stay tender. This chapter
isn't asking you to become soft as a personality. It's
inviting you to become more present.

A Relationship Is A Shared Emotional Ecosystem

Marriage carries its own version of this truth. You can be a strong team and still feel emotionally distant. You can be loyal and still feel tired of the invisible weight of unspoken needs. You can handle everything and still feel like nobody is really holding you.

A healthier legacy in a relationship often comes down to small choices. The kind people overlook because they don't seem dramatic enough to count.

Choosing to talk instead of withdrawing. Choosing to ask instead of assuming. Choosing to rest together without guilt. Choosing to celebrate small joys without waiting for life to be easier.

Those choices don't look like a highlight reel, but they accumulate. They become safety. They become trust. They become an environment in which both people can breathe.

Two whole people not only create a complete partnership. They create a complete atmosphere.

What You Normalize Becomes Inheritance

This is the part that matters most. Legacy isn't only what you teach. It's what you normalize.

When you normalize repair, the people you love learn that conflict isn't the end of love. When you normalize rest, they learn that peace isn't something you earn after burnout. When you normalize truth with tenderness, they learn that they can be honest without being punished.

Your legacy will outlive your goals and accomplishments. It will outlive your career and hobbies. It becomes instinctive in the people closest to you.

And here is the freeing part: you don't have to build it through pressure. You can build it through presence. You can build it through wholeness lived at home.

Closing Reflection

Legacy is not limited to what you accomplish. It includes what you cultivate.

You can honor the version of you who learned to create stability through competence and still choose to become more emotionally reachable inside that stability. Your home can function and heal. Your standards can stay high, and your heart can stay soft. This isn't about becoming a different person. It's about becoming a more whole one so that the people you love can feel it.

The Practice

Choose one small act this week that shifts your home toward emotional presence. Not a grand gesture. Not a productivity goal. Just one real, repeatable moment that says "I'm here, and I want us close."

Maybe you begin one conversation with a simple, honest opener, the kind that doesn't demand anything but invites something real. Maybe you circle back after a tense moment and clean it up sooner than you normally would. Maybe you choose one meal during which your phone stays out of reach and your attention stays in the room. Maybe you catch yourself mid-tone and soften, not because you're wrong for being tired, but because you're choosing the atmosphere you want to build.

My next small practice:

Journal Prompts

Answer what stands out. Skip what doesn't.

1. What emotional atmosphere do I want my home to be remembered for, and what would it take to make that atmosphere more consistent?
2. When I'm stressed, what does my tone communicate, even if my intentions are loving?
3. When do the people closest to me experience me as most reachable, and when do they experience me as most guarded?
4. What do I tend to prioritize at home when life gets loud: efficiency, excellence, or emotional safety, and what does that cost?
5. What would change if repair became quick and normal in my home, not rare and heavy?
6. What do I normalize about rest, and how does that shape the people who live close to me?
7. What boundary would protect my energy without hardening my heart?
8. What is one small practice that would make my presence feel safer this week?

Wholeness Check-In

Reflect from a perspective of legacy.

- Mentally and emotionally: Do my thoughts about my family sound like partnership or pressure?
- Spiritually: Do I invite humility and grace into my home, or do I lead with control?
- Physically: How do my sleep, nourishment, and stress level show up in my tone?
- Socially: Do I have support outside my home so my family isn't carrying all of my emotional weight?

One small shift I will make this week:

____

____

____

____

Empowering Declaration

I am not only building a life. I am building an atmosphere. I make repair the default. I choose tenderness as strength. I choose emotional presence as part of my legacy. My home will not only function. It will heal. I will not abandon myself to create peace for others. I will model peace by becoming whole.

Chapter 36
The Legacy of Two Wholes

I've continued using one sentence throughout this book, not because it sounds pretty, but because it keeps telling the truth no matter what season you're in. People say two halves make a whole. But I believe two wholes make it complete.

That belief isn't a romantic idea to me. It's a hard-earned understanding. It's the difference between love that feels like rescue and love that feels like partnership. It's the difference between building a relationship that depends on need and building one that's rooted in alignment.

The first two parts of this book were about waking up, returning to yourself, breaking patterns, and learning healthier intimacy. Part Three is about what happens when that inner work becomes a lived environment. It becomes home. It becomes culture. It becomes the way you love, lead, and build a future without reenacting what you outgrew.

This chapter isn't meant to feel like an ending. It's meant to feel like a foundation. A quiet place to stand where you can finally say, "I'm not building from survival anymore."

The Hidden Risk Is The Old Story

Sometimes the greatest risk to a relationship isn't conflict. Sometimes it's the old story you bring into love without realizing it.

A story that whispers, "If someone loves me enough, I'll finally be safe." A story that insists, "If I build the right partnership, I'll finally be complete."

A story that hopes, "If I'm chosen deeply enough, the places in me that still ache will finally relax."

Those stories are understandable. They're human. They're also too heavy for love to carry.

When love is asked to prove your worth, it turns into pressure. When love is asked to regulate your unhealed places, it becomes exhausting. When love is asked to complete your identity, the relationship becomes an emotional contract that eventually collapses under the weight.

Wholeness is what frees love to be love. Not a rescue mission. Not an identity replacement. Not a bandage over wounds you're meant to tend with honesty and care.

Completion Love And Alignment Love

When two halves come together, there can be chemistry. There can also be a silent agreement that sounds romantic but becomes heavy over time. It can sound like complete me, regulate me, carry what I didn't heal, be the evidence of my worth.

That isn't love. That's survival trying to dress itself up as romance.

Alignment love sounds different. It says, "I choose you not because I'm unfinished, but because my wholeness recognizes your wholeness, and I see what we can build together."

Two whole people can love without disappearing. They can disagree without fear. They can grow without punishment. They can repair without humiliation. They can build a life that isn't a reenactment of old pain.

That doesn't mean they'll never struggle. It means the struggle has a healthier foundation. Conflict doesn't threaten identity. Discomfort doesn't require distance. Hard seasons don't erase emotional maturity. The relationship isn't about

saving either person from themselves. It's about supporting
two people who keep choosing to show up with integrity.

What Wholeness Requires From Each Person

Two wholes make it complete because neither person
is outsourcing their inner work. Each person is responsible
for their patterns, their grounding, their capacity for repair,
and their willingness to stay present. Wholeness isn't self-
sufficiency that refuses love. It's self-leadership that makes
love safer.

In real life, it looks like the moment you notice a
trigger rising, and you decide not to turn it into an
accusation. It looks like naming a need without turning it
into a demand. It looks like honoring a boundary without
punishing the other person for having feelings about it. It
looks like choosing repair before resentment has time to
take root.

And it looks like humility, the kind that doesn't
collapse or perform. The kind that tells the truth.
"I feel myself going into control."
"I'm getting defensive."
"I'm tempted to withdraw, but I don't want distance
between us."

Wholeness doesn't eliminate your human moments. It
gives you a healthier way to hold them.

Legacy Is Built In The Way You Keep Becoming

Longevity without emotional evolution can become
quiet exhaustion. Longevity with wholeness becomes a
legacy that heals more than just the two people inside it.

It heals children because they grow up watching repair
instead of silent coldness. It heals families by interrupting

428

scripts that say love must cost you your voice. It heals future generations by modeling partnership as emotional safety, not emotional debt.

Legacy isn't built by avoiding hard seasons. It's built by refusing to let hard seasons turn you into someone unrecognizable by your own peace.

This is life beyond survival. Life beyond performance. Life in which love is no longer asked to prove that you're safe.

Love is allowed to become what it was always meant to be: a partnership built by two whole people who keep choosing each other with maturity. A kind of love that doesn't just last; it grows.

If You Are Partnered

If you're married, partnered, rebuilding, or growing through the real work of long-term love, the highest form of commitment isn't just staying. It's growing.

It's the daily decision to protect your emotional safety. It's the willingness to practice repair before resentment accumulates. It's the courage to have the conversation instead of living in assumptions. It's the choice to build a shared rhythm that honors both people, not one person carrying the emotional load while the other avoids discomfort.

Two wholes create shared responsibility. Shared responsibility creates safer love. And safer love is what makes legacy possible.

If You Are Single

If you're single, you are not on standby for love. You are not in a waiting room where your real life begins only when someone chooses you.

Your life is already yours to build. Your healing is already yours to honor. Your wholeness is already yours to practice. That matters because the love you welcome later will be shaped by the love you stop abandoning now.

You will recognize alignment faster. You will require emotional safety sooner. You will be less tempted to romanticize inconsistency as chemistry.

Wholeness doesn't make you less open to love. It makes you more available for the right kind of love.

The Blueprint

Two wholes make it complete, not because they guarantee a perfect relationship, but because they create the conditions for a healthier one.

Wholeness creates space for truth with tenderness. It creates room for growth without punishment. It makes repair normal. It makes emotional responsibility shared.

Wholeness is not the finish line. It is the foundation. And from that foundation, love becomes less about being saved and more about being aligned. That is the legacy of two wholes.

Closing Reflection

If you remember nothing else, remember this. You don't have to keep living as if chaos is the price of significance. You don't have to keep proving your strength by carrying everything alone. You don't have to keep asking love to do the work that belongs to your healing.

You are allowed to build a life that feels both peaceful and powerful. If you are partnered, you can build a partnership that multiplies peace. If you are single, you can build a life that reflects your worth now, not later.

Wholeness is not a concept you visit when life finally slows down. It is a foundation you live from. And from that foundation, your legacy becomes real, steady, and yours.

The Practice

Choose one way you will practice alignment this week. Not perfection. Alignment. Start by noticing the pattern you default to when you feel unsafe. Maybe you move toward control. Maybe you withdraw. Maybe you perform and overfunction. Don't judge it. Just tell the truth about it because honesty is where new choices begin.

Then choose one small way to respond differently. One conversation in which you stay calm and clear instead of bracing. One repair you make sooner than your pride wants to. One boundary you hold without punishing your partner.

My next small practice:

Journal Prompts

Answer what stands out. Skip what doesn't.

1. Where do I feel the pull to be completed by love instead of complemented by it?
2. What old story about love still tries to define what I deserve or what I must tolerate?
3. What have I healed that my past self could barely imagine?
4. When I feel unsafe, do I move toward control, withdrawal, or performance? What would wholeness choose instead?
5. What would it look like to bring my needs into a relationship without turning them into demands?
6. If I'm partnered, what is one repair habit we can normalize this month? If I'm single, what is one standard I will honor without apology?
7. What does alignment look like for me in this season mentally, spiritually, physically, socially?
8. What kind of legacy do I want my love to leave behind in the people closest to me?

Wholeness Check-In

Reflect on the pillars from a lens of being whole in self, relationship and legacy.

- Mentally and emotionally: Are my thoughts rooted in self-leadership, or are they based in fear of being abandoned or unseen?
- Spiritually: Do I trust that I'm already worthy, or do I keep trying to earn love through performance?
- Physically: Am I caring for my body as a sacred space or using exhaustion as proof that I'm doing enough?
- Socially: Are my relationships aligned with who I'm becoming or with whom I learned to be to survive?

One small shift I will make:

____

____

____

____

Empowering Declaration

I am whole. I am becoming with intention. I do not outsource my identity to love. I bring wholeness into love and build partnerships that multiply peace, purpose, and emotional safety. My legacy will not be survival disguised as strength. My legacy will be alignment lived consistently.

Epilogue
Wholeness Is the Foundation

If you've made it here, take a breath and let your body catch up to what your mind already knows. Something in you is waking up. Not in a dramatic way. In a steady, undeniable way that feels like truth.

Wholeness doesn't mean you'll never struggle again. It means you stop abandoning yourself when life gets loud. It means you notice patterns sooner, tell the truth faster, and return to yourself with less shame and more tenderness.

You don't have to earn peace by carrying more. You don't have to prove your worth through exhaustion. You don't have to keep calling survival "just how you are," especially when something deeper in you has been asking for more than survival for a long time.

You can build love that feels safe. You can create a home in which repair is normal and honesty isn't punished. You can lead with strength that stays tender. You can live a life that matches what you value, even when it costs you to change, even when the old version of you wants to negotiate with the new one.

A Gentle Next Step

Keep it simple. Let one practice from this book become your companion for the next 30 days. Not as a performance. As a return.

Choose one truth you're ready to stop avoiding. Choose one boundary you're ready to hold without bargaining with yourself. Choose one repair you're ready to make sooner, not later. Then let that one choice be repeated until it feels normal, until your life begins to reflect it without your having to force it.

That's how wholeness becomes real. Not all at once. Over time. In the small, steady decisions that finally add up to a different way of living.

Closing Reflection

If this book has given you anything, let it be permission. Permission to stop performing strength. Permission to heal without rushing. Permission to love without erasing yourself. Permission to become someone whose presence feels like refuge, even for yourself.

You're not behind. You're not broken. You're becoming.

Becoming with intention is how a life stops being something you manage and starts being something you live. It's how love becomes safer. It's how legacy becomes personal. It's how wholeness becomes home.